Gospel in Industrial Society

Margaret Kane

GOSPEL IN INDUSTRIAL SOCIETY

SCM PRESS LTD

HN
39
.E5
K3
1980

334 02032 8

First published 1980
by SCM Press Ltd
58 Bloomsbury Street, London WC1

Photoset by Input Typesetting Ltd, London
and printed in Great Britain by
Richard Clay (The Chaucer Press) Ltd,
Bungay, Suffolk

Contents

I   I Believe . . . How can I Believe?

'I believe; help my unbelief' (*Mark 9.24*)

1 Upstairs, downstairs

'What goes on up there?' said Rosie, pointing to the ceiling of the club room. As the club was held in the church basement, she was in fact pointing up to the church. Her question was aimed at me, and I was unable to answer it. What could I say that could make sense to Rosie and the other club members?

At the time I was working in London as a display artist, and attending this church that was not far from my digs in the Kings Cross area. In the evening I helped with the girls' club. The girls who had left school were working in dead-end jobs in small firms and shops near by. One day a girl confided in me her sense of despair. Her mother had just given birth to twins, and the girl wondered what she herself had to look forward to now that she had reached the age of sixteen. None of the girls attended church. I do not think they had even been inside it. It seemed that there was a total separation between Christian faith as it was understood by those who worshipped in the upstairs church and life as it was experienced by the girls in the downstairs club.

Yet Christian faith is about the offer of life, and that is what these girls wanted. Given a chance, they would have opted for life, but the upstairs church did not present them with a viable option. And when it came to the point – when the question 'What is it all about?' was directed at me – I was unable to say anything.

My inability to make any sort of response was one of the causes that set me on to a search for some way of helping people to discover a faith that bites on the actual circumstances of their lives. That search is still continuing and is far from finished.

As far as the girls were concerned, what went on in the church was not a matter of more than passing interest. The vital question for them was what they could make of their lives. Once they left school they were thrust into a life of work, marriage and babies, which seemed to be totally determined by their restricted and depressed environment. Some of their brothers had tried to break through these limits and were now resident in a probation hostel which was the boys' equivalent of the girls' club. The tenement buildings in which their families lived sprouted washing from the windows and grubby infants and bedroom-slippered women from the doors. In the evenings tired men returned home from the railways, breweries, road works and public utilities – only to come out again to seek peace and quiet in the local pubs. Apart from occasional outbursts of anger and frustration the parents seemed to have stopped fighting against their lot, but the girls, for a few years, still felt that there should be more to life.

The question about the church was, however, important to me and to my friends who had joined me in helping in the club. I too had asked the question 'How can life be fulfilling?' There had been choices open to me, and conflicting desires and aspirations had made it difficult for me to find the answer. By sharing in the life of this church I was beginning to find a sense of meaning and direction in life. I had begun to realize that instead of being grasped, life must be given and received, and that it is God who gives us the fulfilment of our humanity. I felt that there must be a connection between the basement club and the upstairs church, for I now saw that the search for humanity and the search for God are one and the same.

Rosie's question had made me aware of the inadequacy of my faith. Though I felt that I had clues that gave direction to my life, I still had nothing that could help these girls in their much tougher situation. Though I believed it was God who was giving me my humanity, this was happening partly through my association with the girls. Something was happening between us that could not take place in isolation. *We* were receiving *our* humanity.

Nor did it stop at what was happening between us. The girls' whole environment was affecting the possibility of their humanity. A lot more people were and still are involved – their families, those who plan how and where people shall live, those who allow things to stay the way they are and those who might be able to make changes. It appears that none of us can receive our humanity without the others.

At this point the question for me was: how is it possible for people in today's typical situations to believe that God is involved in their lives? Is it possible for them to believe that in and through all that threatens their humanity, God is offering them the fulfilment of their humanity? In the end, is Christian faith a possibility for any but the privileged few? My search was and continues to be for answers to these questions.

In this book I describe the positive clues I have followed in my search. These have not only led to some answers, but have exposed the question itself as being an even bigger problem than I had realized.

It concerns nothing less than the whole nature of the Christian gospel and of mission in today's world. What does it mean to live as a Christian today? What may we hope and work for? How can we speak of God with any meaning in our technological society?

Answers to these questions cannot be found in the study. New understandings must come from reflecting with others on experience of life and how this may be seen in the light of faith in God. The fact that it is through involvement in life that I have been able to learn new things determines the shape of this book. Because the book is concerned with finding faith and living in faith, it is a theological book. But I am not a theologian in the usual sense of the term, for I am not employed full-time in theological teaching and research in a university or college. My work starts from situations of day-to-day life and from the mission of the church in the world. I work with people, trying with them to make sense of life and to find God in it. This demands theological skill and knowledge, more than I or any one person can muster. It is because all that I do is concerned with the truth about God that I claim to be a theologian. I speak with first-hand experience of the struggle to find faith in life, but in my use of biblical and historical material and in many other ways I am dependent on the work of academic theologians. I do not apologize for my lack of much that might be expected of a theologian, for I believe that the particular theological role I am seeking to fulfil in opening up possibilities of faith for those who are outside the influence of academic theological debate is crucial. I am simply concerned here to point out that what is written in this book differs from what might have been written by an academic theologian, for the book comes out of the particular theological processes in which I am involved.

As I shall be speaking of things with which I have personally been concerned, I must mention certain changes that have taken place in the outward circumstances of my life. I experienced a good deal of tension between the claims of my work as a display artist and the efforts I was putting into the girls' club. In my desire to get to grips with the question with which I was concerned, I applied for several jobs as a youth leader, but was turned down in each case for lack of training. In the end I accepted the fact that I needed training and went for two years to a theological college. What I relate in the rest of this book comes out of my experience in various posts as a full-time church worker. I committed myself to those who are searching for their humanity and I committed myself to the church with all its inadequacies as having a vital role. So I myself am part of the church I often criticize.

In this first part of the book I give examples of situations that highlight these questions and the specific beliefs I bring to them. Because I myself am involved, it is my personal understandings of Christian

faith that I describe, for it is my belief and unbelief that determine the
way I look at life and what I make of it. What I find is that, as I enter
more deeply into life, my faith is challenged by the fact that in many
of today's situations people's humanity is being threatened. This forces
me to say 'I believe . . . but, if life is like this, how can I believe?'

In Chapter II I ask the question 'Can Christian faith stand up to the
realities of life?' I am convinced that we can only answer this question
if we look at life as it is in some detail. Though I only look at one
particular part of life, the conclusions will be similar wherever you
happen to be. I have taken, as an example, that part of the world that
I know best – North East England – and I describe four main aspects
of life in this region. Rather than finding an answer to my question, I
discover that between Christian faith as I understand it and life as
many people are experiencing it, there is increasing tension.

In Chapter III I reflect on this tension and, as I look more deeply
into the meaning of Christian faith, I realize that in the crucifixion of
Jesus and all that led up to it, tension is both necessary and creative.

In the light of this discovery, in Chapter IV, I look at life in North
East England and identify signs of hope. To distinguish genuine signs
of hope from false expectations one needs some clues. The resurrection
of Jesus provides that clue and leads us to look for signs that point us
to the reality of God's grace in life as his invitation to men and women
to enter into a relationship with him in the community of faith. This
leads me to ask two further questions. How can the church encourage
and support those things in life which represent real signs of hope?
How can individuals recognize in these things the invitation of God?
There is no short cut to answering these questions, and any attempt
to take short cuts makes it not easier but harder for people to accept
the signs as signs of hope.

In Chapter V, while recognizing the need for a sensitivity to the
mystery of people and to the mystery of God, I say why it is that we
must speak about God.

2 *Life is an invitation*

It is my personal belief rather than a traditional statement of Christian
faith that I present in this chapter. Though I could not have arrived at
this faith apart from the Christian community, it is only as I have made
it my own that it has any power in my life. When I look at my life and
ask, 'Is it the creeds that give shape to it?', I have to say honestly, 'No'.
The faith I live by and which makes me what I am is not simply the
result of things I have been taught about Christian faith. It comes to
me from what, in that faith, has struck up against something in my
life.

Christians often give the impression that in their belief they have no unanswered questions and nothing further to explore. But I know that my present faith did not come to me ready-made, that it is the result of a long process that is still going on. What I want to do is to share with others, who may be at different points in the search, the faith I actually live by.

In various ways life brings pressures to bear upon us all. For the most part we take life for granted without being aware of the way in which our values and outlook are being formed by people and environment. It is our responses that make us into the kind of people we are, while we ourselves make some impression on life, though seldom in the form we might intend.

Some things force each of us to take notice and lead us to question and ask whether life is hostile or benign. In this way we enter into a kind of dialogue in which life addresses us and we respond in attitude and action rather than in words. It is in these responses that we either realize or fail to realize our true humanity, and we either contribute or fail to contribute to the humanity of our world.

I have come to believe that this dialogue with life is a dialogue with God. It is God who comes to us in the things that bring joy and in the things that shatter us. He comes to us in people, in events and in the awakenings of our hearts. In all this he is offering us the fulfilment of our humanity. The acceptance of what he offers leads to new discoveries about what it means to be human, while refusal leads to a closing down of possibilities. Our humanity can only be fulfilled if we accept it from God.

The question that faced me now was whether I could continue to hold this belief when I saw the way other people's humanity was being crushed through no fault of their own. It was not only my contact with the girls' club that made me ask this question. A short time before my involvement with the club, when I was looking for a job myself, I was overwhelmed by the fact that there were several million other people who wanted jobs and were unlikely to get them. What I heard about the depressed areas seemed so unbelievable to me that, instead of going home one week-end, I took a train to the mining and steel town of Dowlais in South Wales where nine out of ten men were unemployed. These men were not in a position to make choices, for all the choices seemed to have been made for them elsewhere. For them it was not a matter of acceptance or refusal, but simply of suffering what was happening. When people's humanity is being reduced in this way, how could I go on believing that in it God is offering them their humanity?

It was my own experience that had brought me to my present belief. Far more people than we think believe that in what they would describe as religious experiences they have been confronted by some power outside themselves.[1] There had been several occasions in my life when

I had experiences in which it seemed that God was urging me in a direction that I did not want to take. I had resisted the idea that I should give up my own dreams about what I should make of my life, and it was only when my own hopes were disappointed that I was ready to see that God's way might after all be best. The acceptance of God's pressure on me was now opening my life out in new ways. The question I now had to answer was, could what seemed true for me be true for everyone? In order to answer this question I had to examine experience wider than my own and this pushed me back to look again at what I receive from the Christian community in the Judaeo-Christian tradition. What is immediately striking about the Old Testament is that it is not concerned with how individuals find their humanity, but with how a nation finds its common humanity and how in this process each group and each individual plays its specific part.

It was Israel who first came to understand that God was involved in her life. It was as the Jews struggled with their situations, in the same way that we struggle with ours, that they came to the conviction that, in the events of their lives, God was coming to them offering them their full humanity. Life was as confusing for them as it is for us, and they too had to find their way step by step and with many set-backs. There were many times when they rejected God's offer, but they recognized that in all their unfaithfulness, God remains faithful, and that he does not leave man alone to cope with the consequences of his choices. It was the experience of God's creative work in her history that made it possible for Israel to believe that the same God is the creative energy at work in all things.

God's work of creation continues. We know that the world is not in a complete and final state; contours and climates are continually changing, and we now know something of man's own power to affect the process. The creation of man is the climax of creation. Adam represents not an individual but mankind, and into mankind God breathes his own life. The creation of man is still going on, and man's full humanity cannot be achieved in one individual, group or nation, but must be realized in mankind as a whole.

To think of God as Creator might give the wrong impression if we did not recognize that we meet the same God in Jesus Christ. The description of God as Trinity has not been thought up in order to confuse us, but to help us understand our actual experience of God. It points to God as the source and goal of all life, as coming to us in the person of Jesus Christ and in the Spirit as ever-present resource for living. It is this that makes it possible to interpret the whole of life in terms of personal encounter with God. Jesus confronted Israel with the question of her identity. The question of who individuals believed they were in relation to other people, as well as in relation to God, lay behind Jesus' controversy with those in authority as well as in his ministry to the outcasts. Against the background of Israel's tradition, in which the whole world and the whole of history is within God's care, it is possible to see in Jesus not an invitation to a privileged few but an open offer of humanity to all mankind.

In the light of this tradition, the question of choice and refusal can no longer be considered simply in individual terms, but becomes a question that must be seen in terms of relationships. The humanity that I seek is not simply *my* humanity but *our* humanity, and *we* have to discover it together.

My belief in God as Creator of the world and of mankind gives me certain expectations about life. If this is God's world, I must be basically optimistic about it. This leads me to look first for what is good in our technological society. There is so much that is wrong with our world that many people miss the positive side. I find much that is hopeful in the inventiveness that makes it possible for man to be freed from deprivation and drudgery. I believe God is in some way involved in the development of technology, and I reject any idea that we should dream of returning to a pre-industrial society.

On the other hand, I am not blind to all that makes technology a threat rather than a promise to human life. Why should the men of Dowlais only have work when a war is imminent? Why should the working of our economy condemn people to live in the conditions they do in the inner cities? It is not they who choose to live this way – but I believe it is not through God, but through the choices of men that things are like this. I do not believe that God has some ready-made plan for the world into which we have to fit. Men have real creativity and causality, and this can produce real threats to humanity. The fact that some men are rich while other men starve, some men have power while others are powerless, conflicts with my belief that it is to mankind as a whole that God has given responsibility for the world. I therefore seek a fairer distribution of resources and a wider distribution of power, so that all men can realize their dignity and worth in sharing corporate responsibility. We receive our humanity not only by individual choices but by those choices we make together.

I do not want to suggest that we are presented with simple choices, or that men will always deliberately choose what is destructive. We get caught up in situations that are complex, where issues are not black and white. We lack information and insight, and whatever choice is made is a matter of judgment and risk. There may be no choice at all save that of accepting whatever comes to us. It is only a fool who does not experience doubt and fear, and faith is needed if we are to have the courage not to shrink back, but to face the realities of life, and to say 'yes' to them, and so say 'yes' to God.

3 *Invitation to be human*

Life is an invitation to be human. It is above all in personal relationship
that we discover our humanity. Most people would say that they are
primarily concerned with persons, and it is generally assumed that
that is what we should be concerned with. There is, however, a pro-
fundity about what it means to be a person which defies definition.

> What does it mean to me to be me and what could I wish it to
> mean? You must reflect on what you regard as your own best and
> most worthwhile relations with others. You must further consider
> what you know or believe to be your own best wishes and hopes
> for those particular persons you care for most. If you will attend to
> yourself in relation to these other individuals who matter to you
> and to others who matter to you in relation to yourself, then you
> will have some idea of what is involved in being a person.[2]

As I examine my own experience, I realize that in my deepest relationships it is being accepted and valued as I am, with all my pecu-
liarities, that releases me to be open to wider relationships and to the
wider environment. It is this that enables me to discover new possibilities in being and becoming myself. These wider relationships are in
varying degrees of depth, but there is all the difference between being
treated as a person or not as a person. It is not easy to put into words
a difference of which we are nevertheless directly aware in experience.
Many people, for instance, complain that at work they are treated like
'cogs' in a machine. They sense that no value is attached to their
experience or to the social contribution they make to what is basically
an enterprise in human co-operation.

I am not suggesting that all relationships should be on a deeply
personal level. That would be absurd. I am simply pointing to the fact
that there are many things in life which deny, distort and frustrate
humanness. Not only are the priorities and values embodied in industrial society inhibiting in certain ways to personal growth, but individuals and groups treat each other as threats to be overcome rather than
as partners, and each of us at times uses other people for our own
ends, regardless of their own claim to consideration.

Destructiveness does not only threaten us from outside but from
inside. Many people find it extremely difficult to enter into personal
relationships of any depth, and many relationships that do exist have
a destructiveness built into them. There are, moreover, interpretations
of persons as 'nothing but' naked apes or beings who are totally
determined by their environment, and there are people who have a
low view of man which is not based on any worked-out theory. For
seven years I worked in a mining town and found in it a warmth of
humanity that is hard to surpass, but some doctors, who were glad to
make their living out of the miners, refused to join in any of the local

events, and looked upon their patients as less than human. It is this kind of wholesale cynicism about human beings that inhibits the possibilities of people.

At this point I do not want to pursue the negative factors, but the positive fact that in and through our personal relationships we can know what it is to have a personal relationship with God.

> The heart of all talk about personality is the reality of a certain quality of relatedness, of being encountered and drawn out by the grace and claim of the 'Thou' . . . And the need to speak of 'God' derives from the awareness that in and through and under every finite 'Thou' comes, if we are open to it, the grace and claim of an eternal, unconditional 'Thou' who cannot finally be evaded by being turned into an 'It'. This was the reality which the language of 'the personality of God' was trying to represent.[3]

Our relationship with God, this personal dialogue with life, is focussed in the person of Jesus Christ. I have come to this central point of faith by a somewhat circuitous route, for if we are to understand the person of Jesus Christ we must open up our understanding of both God and man. I have, for instance, already pointed to the fact that we may best understand the reality of God by thinking of him as Trinity, and I have suggested that there is mystery in persons. If the humanness of man is to be found in the quality of his relationships, the basic relationship which determines all his other relationships is his relationship with God. Jesus expressed man's true relationship with God in his continual seeking to know and obey the will of God in his own life. Jesus expressed God's relationship with man in his total commitment to man to the extent of dying for him, in the belief that man can become what he is meant to be, and in his refusal to be content with less than the best for man or from man. Jesus neither despises man nor does he idealize him. He knows what is in man, and is not surprised, though he is deeply grieved, by the self-seeking, treachery and cowardice he meets. He commits himself to man as he is:

> Out of love for man God becomes man. He does not seek out the most perfect man in order to unite Himself with him, but He takes human character upon Himself as it is. Jesus Christ is not the transfiguration of sublime humanity. He is the 'yes' which God addresses to the real man. Not the dispassionate 'yes' of the judge, but the merciful 'yes' of Him who was compassion.[4]

God's concern is with all men. It is the least acceptable people whom Jesus seeks out, for they are the ones whom others completely overlook. But this does not mean that he does not also care for the rich and the 'successful'. Jesus believes not in man as he is but in man as he can be. He 'expects a different, a new man: a radically changed

awareness, a fundamentally different attitude, a completely new orientation in thought and action.'[5]

What is required is summed up in love of God and love of neighbour.
Jesus came to make God's will prevail, and God's will aims at man's
well-being. These two commands cannot be separated, and it is no
longer possible to play off God and man against each other. Though
love of God and love of man are not the same thing, neither command
can be fully met without the other:

> The *common denominator* of love of God and love of neighbour there-
> fore is the *abandonment of selfishness* and the *will to self-sacrifice*. Only
> when I no longer live for myself can I be quite open for God and
> unreservedly open for my fellow man whom God accepts just as he
> accepts me. Loving my fellow man does not complete my task of
> loving God. I remain directly responsible to God and none of my
> fellow men can take this responsibility away from me. God however
> encounters me, not exclusively, but – since I am myself human –
> primarily in my fellow man and expects my self-surrender at that
> point.[6]

God's acceptance of us makes it possible for us to accept others. A
person who is used to being rejected finds it hard to enter into trusting
relationships with others. The injuries of the past remain painfully
present, so that slights are imagined where they are not in fact
intended. We have already recognized in our experience of human
relationships that to be loved and believed in liberates us from the
limits and hurts of the past for an open future. An illustration of this
truth comes from the mining community I have just mentioned. My
task was to build up a Christian community in a new area, and in such
a group I felt that people should know that they were accepted and
that they should accept each other. Those who complain about the
pettiness of church quarrels forget that the high expectations people
have of Christian communities are only matched by their bitterness
when these expectations are disappointed. There were many times
when tempers flared up over what might appear to be trivial incidents
– a hesitation in accepting someone's offer of help or a reference to
some child's academic success which was taken as a slight on one who
had not been successful. But these things are not trivial, for they are
the measure of the hurts that have been inflicted and are waiting to be
healed.

In Jesus' life we do not simply see the life of one man, but the life
of man. What we see in him is true of life in any time and place. In
those who crucified him we should not see men who were especially
wicked, but people like ourselves who acted from similar motives to
our own.

Jesus was the true man in that he expressed in his life what man's
life is meant to be – a life lived in unbroken relationship with the

Father and in selfless love for others. Those who rejected him and contributed to his crucifixion rejected their own humanity. Human beings have an immense capacity for not facing reality. There is a kind of optimism that prevents us from growing up. The cross is central because it makes any easy optimism about ourselves and about man in general impossible. At the cross God's self-giving for man is met by man's refusal to accept his own humanity. It is in this sense that Jesus Christ is our judge. But the cross also presents us with our hope, for it sums up the fact that Jesus Christ in his human life – and on behalf of mankind – subjected himself to everything in life that negates humanity and that nothing was able to separate him from his unity with God. The resurrection is a sign of hope, for it shows Jesus Christ as victorious over all the things that destroy life and shows him as the one through whom new life is given.

As I look at life in North East England where I am now working, I see among those who have authority a good deal of cynicism about people. They may start out with high ideals, but they find that it is easier to keep things in their own hands than to involve others. Educationalists indoctrinate instead of educating; industrialists claim that workers are neither capable nor willing to participate in the decisions of industry; politicians give up ideas of involving others when people do not respond in the way they had hoped, so they settle not for participation but for manipulation.

Unless people are convinced about the possibilities in their fellow human beings this is understandable, but it does not lead us into the kind of future that will bring a new world. Of course trusting people is a risk – for people do not respond in the ways we should like, and often they do not seem to respond at all. But what God in Christ risked for people leads me to believe that we should stake all we have on the possibilities of people.

4 *Invitation to share in purpose*

We are invited to share in purpose. This is good news for those who feel that the world lacks purpose, and who feel that they themselves have nothing to give point to their lives.

Our society is in fact organized in pursuit of a quite definite purpose – economic growth through the development of technology. Our world is characterized by man's increasing control over nature, and this extends to a control over human beings, in for instance medicine, databanks of information on individuals and brain-washing techniques. The expectation is that growth measured in material terms will continue. Where difficulties arise, as for instance with the possible exhaustion of raw materials, it is assumed that 'science will come up with something'. This outlook is spread across the world, for technology has for the first time made our world into one world. Work and the money we get for it gears us into this system, so that for many people any sense of purpose they have is found in their work – a fact that underlines the sense of meaningless felt by those who are unemployed.

This is a man-made world and man is at the centre of it, but it is not therefore a more human world. For many people work can be as meaningless as unemployment; rising expectations throughout the world lead to conflict between the 'haves' and the 'have nots'; efforts that might have gone into the production of things for the enhancement of life go into the production of armaments for the destruction of life. There is a fear that man may not after all be in control, but that he may be locked into the programmes and systems which he himself has devised. Those who are thought to have power, know how limited their power is and fear lest everything should fall apart. Things do not hang together, and the solution of one problem frequently gives rise to new problems elsewhere.

Some people dream of and work for a more human world. They realize the necessity of starting from the present technological realities, and look for help in analysing the processes of our present society and constructing viable alternatives. Many such people have found a useful tool in Marxism. It is one of the few tools available, and Marxist categories have permeated our thinking more than we realize. It offers an analysis of industrial society; it gives a purpose to history; it provides a spur to action. Some Christians, too, feel an affinity with Marxism. They agree with its belief in a historical goal for the world, its concern for justice and the role it sees for man. But in practice, and precisely because it makes man the centre and the measure of all things, Marxism fails to produce a new world or a new humanity. In fact it comes up against the same problem, for in Marxism too the humanity of man is inhibited by the very things that should release him for fuller life.

The understandings of religion that once gave a sense of cohesion and purpose to life will no longer serve, for they have nothing to say about science and industry, and, in the newly industrialized countries, the traditional beliefs of the older people are discarded by the younger generation.

The Christian churches have also failed in that they have not helped people to find in Christianity an interpretation of life within which they can come to terms with a technological world. This failure was forcibly brought home to me when I was working as a chaplain in the Sheffield Industrial Mission. I was visiting one of the many small jobbing mills in the area. The head rollers were elderly men who worked with teams of young lads and recent Arab and Pakistani immigrants. In general the mill suggested that pay and conditions were below the standard in the area. When I spoke to one of the rollers, he said, 'I don't know why you come here. I'm retiring soon and I'll think about being a Christian then. You can't be a Christian in this place and among this lot.' Christian faith to him was only relevant to individual and personal life, and had nothing to say to men who had to cope with the forces and pressures of industry.

There were many things in the mill which threatened the humanity of those who worked there. Most of the men seemed to accept these things as inevitable, but in fact they resulted from human purposes. It was not fate but men who decided to use science and technology for the production of material wealth without regard for the people involved. It is no good blaming science for the dehumanizing effects of technological society. Science does not of itself close down, but opens up, the possibilities of man's life. It is our attitude to science, what we expect of it and the way we use it, that threatens our humanity. If men are to change things, they must tackle the social as well as the individual forces that are at work, and they need a framework of ideas large enough to include all the factors affecting their situation.

Christianity which stands for God's offer of humanity and the humanizing of life does in fact provide such a framework. It is quite wrong to think it is concerned only with a narrow section of life. It is about fullness of life; not when you retire, but now. The opening up of possibility is what Jesus offers. He offers in place of our limited self-concern a different centre and a purpose that will draw out our full potential. He invites us into a relationship with God who saves 'men from being trapped in the anti-human features of materiality and history'.[7] Through him it is possible to believe that there is a potential in history that God wills to realize, and a future in which man will receive his full humanity. In Jesus' feeding, healing and forgiving a radical change began. These actions may be accepted as a sign that hunger, pain and conflict will be completely done away with in the future. By beginning this process in a human life, in total involvement in history and in the circumstances of the material world, Jesus brought man, history and nature into a single purpose. That purpose is the purpose of God, and it is brought about by the action of God who calls us to accept and share in this purpose as our own.

The carrying out of this purpose requires two kinds of change: a change in the material ordering of the world, and a change in men's values and expectations. It should be obvious that many of the goals our society is pursuing are not leading to fullness of life. The truth is that we have not received our humanity, because we do not know what it means to be human. The values Jesus lived by and holds out to us are those that belong to humanity, and they are the reverse of many of the values of our world. One example of this is the disregard for human life which is still a feature of many industrial practices. By

way of illustration I quote from the report of a young clergyman who
worked in a factory for several months:

> Amongst the issues that came to my attention . . . which merits
> special consideration is that of safety at work . . . I was appalled by
> the lack of attention to this. Safety was seen almost entirely as the
> individual's responsibility, in fact, avoiding dangers caused by oth-
> ers . . . For example, I was asked to lift one end of several hundred
> pounds of metal. Worst of all, I was asked to stand holding the end
> of a metal rack weighing at least one ton, when the rack was
> balancing precariously on the tail-plate of a lorry. The foreman
> refused to have it tied on, saying there was no need. The lorry was
> then driven the half-mile to the other factory at over 20 mph on the
> bumpy road. I believe that if I had not tied it on after the foreman
> had left, it would have toppled on to the road – probably taking us
> with it.

This is not an isolated example, for I was present at a meeting when
the report was discussed and a trade union official said that this kind
of thing was happening all the time, especially in some of the smaller
firms.

A second example comes from my own experience of working for a
few weeks in a factory producing calculators. The work-force was made
up mainly of women, many of whom had families to support. At the
time I joined the factory, production was being changed from group
work to continuous production lines. It seemed that any contribution
that individuals might have made from their own particular experience
and skills was deliberately being eliminated. Typical remarks in the
factory were: 'Don't do anything on your own initiative. It's bound to
be wrong', and, 'Why do they have to treat us like cabbages?' The
market for calculators is a highly competitive one and individual managers can scarcely be blamed for these actions, but this is an indication
of the kind of inhuman values that are supporting our society.

Changes of value cannot be introduced by violent revolution, or by
strengthening the forces of law and order. Christianity gives a third
option, to work for two revolutions simultaneously: a revolution of
values and a revolution in structures to embody those values. Jesus'
attitude to society must be seen in relation to his own time, but it still
holds good that justice, righteousness and peace are essential to any
society that would approximate to the kingdom. Changes in social and
political structures are necessary, but new forms will not in themselves
create those qualities.

Belief in the purpose of God for humanity has practical implications.
The belief that the future is in the hands of God, and that it will be a
new and different future, should give more rather than less incentive
to work to establish the qualities of that future in the present. Future
and present cannot be separated. The seeds of the future are already

present. These may be positive or negative, auguring more or less humanity for the coming generations. We know in broad terms what the criteria of God's kingdom are. We must identify the presence of those qualities about us and do what we can to strengthen them.

We must be all the more concerned with social and political structures, for they are essential to God's purposes for humanity. These structures should be shaped so that they enable men and women to realize their full stature. But all political structures are imperfect and provisional. They can be destroyed and they can be superseded. We must not therefore hang on to power at any cost, nor give ultimate value to any particular political form. If our political structure is destroyed, we shall not be destroyed with it, nor shall we be destroyed by losing our place in that structure. The work we have done will not be destroyed insofar as we have stood for truly human values. Those values will continue, though it may be in other forms and by other means.

Rather than looking back to the past, we shall look forward with hope. It is not easy to face the break-up of our world in the rapid changes of society. But a trust that God is already creating a more human future and calling us to work with him can give us courage so that we are not overcome by fear, and do not look for security by holding on to the past.

Although God's invitation is an open invitation to all mankind, it has no resemblance to the mass processes of technological society, in which individuality is seen as a problem and people are expected to be interchangeable and therefore individually dispensable. Within God's all-embracing call, he extends a personal invitation to each individual to find meaning and integrity in his or her own life by accepting their own unique vocation within the total purpose. For the individual who responds there is the promise that his capacities will be stretched, his experience used, and that he will become not less but more himself. The nature of our individual call depends on where *we* – that is mankind – are in relation to God's overall purpose.

It is no good preaching about individual vocation if at the same time we allow the system to deny people the possibility of responding. That the two revolutions – in the structures and in values – belong together is illustrated by the case of Carole. It is over a year since Carole left school and she still has no job. I happened to visit her home on some other matter. Carole's mother called her in and did all the talking while Carole stood mutely by her. I heard the story of Carole's regular visits to the careers adviser, her application for jobs and the fact that she fancied nursing or looking after children. Her mother went on to express her anxiety lest unemployment should lead to a wrong attitude to life, a casual pregnancy or an appearance in the courts.

But what is Carole's attitude to life to be, and how can she respond to what is happening to her? The possibilities of humanity for each of us depends on the humanity of others and on the humanity or lack of humanity in our society. Carole's vocation relates to the vocation of all of us to change that society – but as things are she can only endure and suffer the situation society has put her in.

The note of urgency is unmistakable in all that Jesus said about the coming kingdom of God. God's purpose presses upon us and there can be no question of complacency. There are things that can only be done in the present, opportunities that will not come again and a call to act decisively now.

5 *What we are up against*

I have stressed what is good in life, for it is against this background that we can recognize just how destructive evil is. There are powerful forces in life which alienate and divide men from each other and destroy their humanity. The strength of these forces came home to me when in 1969 I was staying for a few days in Chicago. I happened to arrive about the time of the first anniversary of the assassination of the black leader, Martin Luther King. There were rumours of new race riots breaking out in the city, and the people I met were on edge in case things flared up again. I began to share their feelings as a black youth made a jab at my handbag as I passed him in the street. A day or two later I returned to the student hostel where I was staying and went into the sitting room. Ten black men were in conversation in the room and one of them who was a resident of the hostel greeted me. As soon as I spoke the others moved away and I heard one say to his companion, 'I'd recognize the voice of the oppressor anywhere'. They were all Biafrans, and it came home to me then that the war that was going on at that time in their part of Africa, which I had thought of as *their* war, was also *my* war; and the race problem which I had thought of as a peculiarly American problem was also my problem. These students who had never met me before, saw me as a representative of a country which they felt had oppressed and humiliated their country, and they hated me.

It was not personal differences that divided us, but the attitudes, actions and events which over generations had been built into the relationships of our two countries, and between black and white people throughout the world. In this incident I got a glimpse of an evil that is far more destructive than anything for which an individual can be held responsible. It is an evil that has become part and parcel of the structures of our world.

I have used a glaring and obvious example of divisive and destructive forces that are present in society. Evil, however, should not be measured by its obviousness nor by the amount of violence it produces, but by its capacity to alienate people from each other and from their true humanity. We should not think that, because Britain is still a comparatively non-violent society, there is nothing to be concerned about. Anyone who thinks that British society is not divided should visit the streets of decaying houses still to be found in the centre of our towns. In one such street in Stockton I met Indian and Pakistani immigrants, divorced men and women with teenage families, people who had never had regular work and young married people living in the only first home they could afford. These are people at the bottom levels of a divided society. Groups alienated from the rest of society can be found among young unemployed people, especially West Indian youths. Or, in case these seem to be minority groups, listen to the poem of a shipyard worker:

> There's just one thing keeps me going
>> As I fight to keep my health.
> Its the thought that I might make it
>> In my quest for worldly wealth.
> Just to check my football coupon
>> And to find a winning line.
> That will be my day,
>> But till then I'll stay
> Beneath the minus sign.[8]

Technology has brought many benefits, and in this sense it is life-enhancing, but Marx was right when he said that it divided men, and that in doing this it was destructive of their humanity. Many people think that Britain is rapidly changing in the direction of social equality and classlessness, but we should not delude ourselves with the comfortable notion that prosperity and technology have done away with fundamental cleavages in society. It is true that our society has been remarkable for its relatively high degree of consensus and stability, but throughout this century and not least in recent industrial disputes, class conflict, as such, has been highly visible.

These conflicts are not simply about money but about power, security and a host of other things. They stem from the different relationships that groups have with the economic system, the different ways they view society and the different expectations they have of it. Though there is a certain amount of class mobility both up and down, this is mainly within the middle groupings, and has little effect at the bottom or the top of the pyramid. I shall return later to the fact that these long-standing class divisions have a crucial effect on the relationships of the church with the different groupings. But now I want to develop in a specific example the general theme of the destructiveness that is at work in our society.

A small engineering firm on Tyneside employing about three

hundred workers was bought up in the early 1970s by a larger national combine. For a couple of years all went well and work and profits increased. Then suddenly the parent company went bankrupt. Notices of redundancy were given to the work-force, but these were later rescinded as the National Enterprise Board came to the rescue of the parent company. Some changes were made and work was resumed. The workers then thought that their future was secure and put in for an increase in wages. This led to a protracted strike. Then the company closed the works down and this time there was no reprieve.

An analysis of why things worked out as they did would have to take account of the flooding of the market for the firm's product, bad labour relations, and the primacy of financial considerations on both sides. Powerful forces were at work in changing technology, pressures for survival in a competitive industrial system, and group attitudes formed over generations of industrial conflict. The remoteness of those who made the decisions from those whose lives were affected by the decisions contributed to both workers' and managers' feeling that they were up against an impersonal fate. People felt that 'the system' had taken over and they could do nothing. The responses that were made were often on the basis of expectations that had lost touch with reality, or of short-term policies which were no more than a reaction to outside pressures. I am not suggesting that no positive responses were made to the situation, but I want to underline the real power of the destructive forces that are at work in this kind of situation, how much they have been constituted by the past, how they appear to the people concerned as impersonal forces against which they are impotent, and that these forces add up to more than can be attributed to individual malice or 'cussedness'.

But there is a second point to be made. These forces only have the power they have because people in the first place give them that power. The sociologist Peter Berger says that we must at all costs hold on to the fact that although society may be said to make man, it is man who makes his own society. Man, simply by reason of the particular values he holds creates his society. The society he makes then gains a reality of its own and 'answers back', so that man is constrained by what he has made. He cannot simply wish it away, but just as in the first place he made this society by co-operative effort, so he can change it – by co-operative effort. In the end it is not fate but man who is responsible for his world.[9]

The German theologian Jürgen Moltmann picks up the same theme. He points out that a number of different factors work together as an interlocking system of 'vicious circles of death'. These include economic, political, cultural, industrial and psychological factors whose combined force produce a sense of impotence and meaninglessness. One feature of these forces is that their pressure falls most heavily upon certain groups. The same people are without jobs, live in the worst housing, have minimal education, feel politically powerless and inarticulate and have a sense of personal inadequacy impressed upon them by the rest of society. Though it is their deprivation that is most obvious, everyone is in fact deprived by this. That violence is the likely outcome of this sort of situation is today becoming apparent. Moltmann goes on to make the point that as the dehumanizing systems are interlocking, it is no use tackling any one factor in isolation:

> It is necessary to speak of 'liberations' in the plural and to advance the processes of liberation in several dimensions of oppression at the same time. One cannot liberate a particular area by setting up dictatorships elsewhere.[10]

There is weighty evidence that warns against any easy optimism in relation to these forces. A writer meditating on the death of millions of Jews in Nazi concentration camps in the 1940s points to the way in which a number of factors in German society – economic breakdown, political ineptness, the need for a scapegoat and Christian anti-semitic theology among others – contributed to the creation of Nazism as a kind of religion. He suggests that this was a primitive reaction to the failure of a scientific and rational civilization:

> The animality of our nature does not constitute our problem, which is one of men caught up in a scientific civilization. . . . Yet there is a primitiveness in the scientific context which characterizes our humanity. It is known by its fervour and infective solidarity. The group's enthusiasm stamps out effective individualism. It recalls the intoxicating technique of mantic and hysteria.[11]

The murder of the Jews was not simply due to individual wickedness, but to a corporate evil in society by which individuals were infected. The exact apportionment of responsibility was impossible.

What I have seen and experienced in life leads me to concur with this writer's conclusions about the impossibility of man on his own confronting these destructive forces:

> The lasting significance of Auschwitz for humanity lies in its disclosure of the human condition as something incomprehensible and insoluble in merely human terms.[12]

All the same, I do not believe that we can leave the matter there. There are things that can be done about it all. First of all, we should recognize the reality of the forces which are shaping us so powerfully: 'technology, the economic organization of the country, the industrial organization, the class into which a person is born.'[13] These forces have a powerful influence on how people experience and understand life. It is important, too, that anyone who is concerned with the effectiveness of Christian mission should recognize how much these forces have also shaped people's relationships with the Church:

> Different social groups have had quite distinct and different histor- ical relationships to the churches, and the various denominational expressions have been strongly coloured by social and political aspirations of particular groups. . . . The great bulk of the 'working class', and its antecedents back to the eighteenth century, have been, as adults, and for all effective purposes, estranged from the churches of all denominations.[14]

There is so much evidence to support the truth of this statement that it is amazing that anyone can continue to argue against it: the empti- ness of the churches in the down-town areas, the absence of working men from church congregations, the fact that there are few members of any church on the factory floor and that those who are there tend to belong to world-denying sects. Even more telling are the stories working men tell of their experiences in relation to the churches, where many have discovered that the things that matter most to them have no place in the churches' concerns.

In emphasizing this gap between the churches and the working class I do not want to add to the destructiveness of the situation. I believe there is salvation in the face of evil; but the fact is that the preachers of salvation have failed to engage with the people who suffer most. This failure will not be overcome until the church faces the fact that cultural, institutional and political forces dominate people's lives, and that in these forces there is evil to be tackled.

6 *You are accepted*

To recognize the forces that are at work in life does not mean that we should abdicate all responsibility for our own behaviour.

A group of managers from different firms discussed the things they felt were wrong in their day-to-day lives. The things they identified were: suppression of other people's ideas, failing to take account of others, using one's subordinates as means for one's own advancement while keeping them down, fear of making changes or questioning group assumptions, guarding sectional interests, turning a blind eye to questionable practices, passing the buck and refusing to take respon- sibility. In this conversation it was not clear how far any of these men felt that they were personally responsible for what was wrong. Sin as distinct from evil in general is about personal responsibility. If we are concerned about the ills of the world, individual sin has to be dealt with.

Self-justification is a common human propensity. We make a picture of ourselves as we would like to be and as we would like to appear before others. The things that are wrong are always someone else's fault. Rather than face our own fallibility and flaws we create a mask to shield us from the truth about ourselves. All this is evidence of our basic insecurity, suppressed dissatisfaction and inability to accept ourselves or to think that anyone else could accept us as we are.

It does not help when people preach about sin and try to convince us that we are worse than we are. This tends to make us even more concerned with ourselves. We may even accept their evaluation of us – and go one better by boasting about our sins: 'Well, you see I am that kind of person', 'I never could resist . . .' and so on. Our concern with ourselves is unchanged.

We need two things: we need to be told not how bad we are but how basically good we are, and we need to be released from our self-concern. It is not efforts at reformation, but love that can achieve these things.

Forgiveness is being accepted as we are – unconditionally. Being accepted and valued by someone else enables us to look at ourselves with honesty. The main thing that is wrong does not lie in specific things we have done but in our self-absorption. The discovery that we are loved reverses this. We are drawn out of ourselves by the love of another, and, though the first overwhelming effect of this love may not last, at least while it does last our centre of concern is moved from ourselves to the one who loves us. In this new perspective in which we see ourselves as being loved and accepted without condemnation it is possible to face the specific things that are wrong, and be released from their grip. This is the graciousness that comes from outside ourselves and does for us what we cannot do for ourselves.

Forgiveness is at the heart of the gospel. Jesus opened people's eyes to see themselves as accepted by God so that they were able to confess their sins and begin to live out of a new centre. If, however, people are only changed by love, they are not changed overnight. A lot of things have to be worked through, and this is a painful process. Everyone who knows what it is to love knows this, and so does anyone whose work involves them with people and personal relationships. The social worker knows the agony of bearing the failures of others as well as the joy of success, and more than one shop steward, finding himself caught between the expectations of his members and the possibilities of the situation, has said 'I am being crucified'. To accept people as they are, and to accept our solidarity with mankind, is to take upon ourselves the common burden of what is wrong – sin.

The opposite of acceptance is rejection. We know something of what it is to be rejected, and if we use our imagination we can know that we have a part in making other people feel rejected. Our own humanity is just as much at stake in our rejection of others as in their rejection of us. Jesus' crucifixion is the most complete picture there is of rejected love. It was the outcome of people's rejection of his expression of true humanity and his offer to them of their humanity. It should shock us into seeing what we do to other people and to ourselves.

Sin is the rejection of God's loving acceptance of us and a refusal to become part of his purpose of creating a human world. Our sin is not simply the petty meannesses of which we may be aware, it is the fear that has held us back from being ourselves so that we have not made available our unique life for loving God and loving our neighbour.

In order to draw out what this means I want to return now to the group of managers with whom I started this section. They rightly saw that what was wrong in their situation was primarily a matter of personal relationships. In their recognition of the reality of structural and role difficulties there was a danger that they would absolve themselves from any blame or responsibility in the matter. This was a danger, because if they believed that they were at the mercy of impersonal forces, then there was nothing they could do. If, however, they took some responsibility for what was wrong, it meant that they also had some power to put things right. The points I want to underline here are, first, that sin is primarily a matter of personal relationships; secondly, that a recognition of one's own sin is hopeful for it implies a belief that something can be done about putting things right; and thirdly, that by ourselves we cannot do what needs to be done, but we are dependent upon a graciousness that comes to us.

To understand sin in this way,

> sets us free to assert the primacy of personal relationships over historical structures, whether economic, social or political, and thus to do justice to the claim that it is love and not the dynamics of either history or nature which is the fundamental energy of the universe. To understand man as sinner is to make his personal dynamics and personal relationships the basic and defining features of him without in any way denying the distortions, difficulties, partialities and problems of these dynamics and relationships. 'Wrongness' at these inter-human relationships is not to be sidetracked to non-human causes such as structural ones, whatever part such structural distortions and oppressions can legitimately be shown to have played and be playing. It is vital not to 'side-track' 'wrongness' away in such a fashion because this also mislocates what is 'right' about man, namely, his capacity for personal relationships. . . . To retain any grounds for claiming absolute value for man as personal one must, in some sense, recognize man as sinner, i.e. with the roots of his 'wrongness' in himself – but without that fact thereby defining him as essentially wrong or absurd.[15]

The managers had to recognize that they were part of their situation. They could not be neutral; either they were contributing in some way to the humanity of their firms or they were part of the dehumanizing process. It is this solidarity with others and a shared responsibility for our situations that we all have to recognize.

In my approach to life, this understanding of sin in terms of rejection and acceptance within personal relationships leads me to be concerned with the people who are rejected. I seek to be involved in those parts of life where man's inhumanity to man is most acute. Experience proves that living by love and acceptance is not easy. It means bearing burdens, suffering with others and being rejected oneself. Under this pressure it is not possible to maintain the spirit of love and acceptance on one's own. I therefore seek both for myself and for others the resources that are to be found in Jesus Christ.

7 Participation in Christ

By this means, a kind of virtuous materialism may ultimately be established in the world, which would not corrupt, but enervate the soul, and noiselessly unbend its springs of action.[16]

All of us in one way or another are alienated from our true humanity. We experience this differently and may not be conscious of alienation except by a vague sense of the flatness of life, and a feeling that we may be 'missing out'. Novelists, poets, dramatists and artists express our common alienation in terms of disconnectedness. Things do not hang together, life is absurd. People do not talk *to* but *past* each other. There are plenty of people about, but each one feels cut off and lonely. Life itself is alienating, and what is most human about us is crushed by the mechanical forces of technological culture. We are out of touch with the sources of life in ourselves and in the world about us.

Answers are sought but not found – in revolt against the economic and political system, in commitment to some cause, in sinking the self in group or collective experience, in work, or in whatever anodyne is available.

If, however, life is experienced as alienating, the gospel offers reconciliation. The gospel puts man in touch with the deepest level of his own being and with the source of life: God. Healing cannot be achieved by our own efforts. It comes about by God's action as we accept his call to receive our humanity in the reconciling of all things in Jesus Christ. The church is a vital part of my Christian belief because it is only through the church that I know of this gospel; and it is only in the life of the church that I find a way of entering into what it offers: life in Christ. What I look for in the church and what I believe many other people look for in it, is a means of getting in touch with the springs of life in oneself and in the world. A problem arises when, as often happens, we fail to find what we look for in the church. When I was working as an industrial chaplain I returned one evening from visiting in the works to find a note pinned on my door:

Came to see you – found you out
Went to church – found it locked
Have gone to pub – it is open.

The man who left the note would not think of attending a church service, but he had looked to the church for something: perhaps an opportunity to be alone to face his own longing for something deeper than he was finding in his work in the forge and his home on the housing estate. The locked church was to him just one more sign that the church was unable or unwilling to open up this dimension of life for him.

The church, its buildings, its practices and its members often stand as a counter-sign, appearing not to be for but against life. This image is projected in its rigid baptism policies, its concern with its own affairs, its judgmental attitude to outsiders, beliefs that are offered as an indigestible package, conventionality that simply mirrors the flatness of the rest of life and a general closing down against life:

> The great objection brought against Christianity in our time, and the real source of the distrust which insulates entire blocks of humanity from the influence of the church, has nothing to do with historical or theological difficulties. It is the suspicion that our religion makes it followers *inhuman*.[17]

At the same time, and in spite of this failure, the church is a constant reminder that there is a depth in life to be plumbed and a way of life to be explored. Christianity is still part of the life of this country, and everyone has in one way or another come up against it either as sign or counter-sign. This persistent factor in our common life only survives because there is a church, and however ineffective the church may be, it is from the church that we gain whatever knowledge we have of Jesus Christ and of the gospel.

I am thankful for my own upbringing, with church every Sunday and prayers every night. For much of the time I simply took this for granted, but it was this background that made it possible for me, when things in my own life touched depths of joy, misery or plain bewilderment, to turn to God. At those times I looked and expected to find help in the church. When in fact I was disappointed in this expectation, I did not give up (after all where else could I look?), but I continued to look to the church until I found in it what I was groping after, a way in which my life could be brought into touch with the source of life in God.

As we discover new depths in ourselves and as we become more aware of the vastness of the world, we are inclined to ask: 'Is the Christ of the churches capable of embracing and forming the centre of this expanding universe?' It is not enough to be told to 'follow Jesus', as if it were possible or desirable to return to the world of the first century.

To be in touch with all the energy that is welling up in ourselves and in our world demands that we should be in touch with God – in all the scope that is suggested by thinking of God as Trinity.

The significance of being 'in Christ', and this is what the gospel offers, is that in him we are related to the whole creation and to all mankind. The resurrection shows Jesus as taken up into the life of God and points to the beginning of the reconciliation of all things. What was done in the historical life of Jesus has led to a movement of all creation towards God as the whole world, and all men are touched by God's Spirit in a new way. All that was alienated is now in Christ being reunited with its own being, with everything else and with the source of life:

> For he (God) has made known to us in all wisdom and insight the mystery of his will, according to his purpose which he set forth in Christ as a plan for the fullness of time, to unite all things in him, things in heaven and things on earth (Ephesians 1.9f.).

Far from being a battening down, this is an opening up of life.

Jesus Christ is our way into God. All this talk of reconciliation and participation is vague and inaccessible until in the historical life of Jesus man is approached in a concrete and personal way. For us in our world today Jesus Christ makes himself present through the church. Jesus Christ is not to be identified with the church, nor is he present only in the church, but he comes to us in specific ways through the church: in the word of the gospel, in the sacraments and in the Christian community itself. It is in and through the church that we find the meaning of our lives within the purposes of God, we find forgiveness and healing for all that is alienating in us, and we find a way of participating with others in Christ's life and reconciling work.

Sharing in the life of Christ involves a twofold journey: a journey outward to find Christ in those who are most in need ('As you did it to one of the least of these my brethren, you did it to me') and a journey inward to find renewal and life in God himself. The two journeys belong together, and both are necessary. Without the inward journey the service of others twists back into a new self-justification. Without the outward journey our self-concern simply takes new forms.[18]

The church is meant to be the community within which these two journeys take place for the individual, and for the church itself. It is this that I look for in the church. I look for ways in which the church is going outwards to permeate and transform the whole of society. It is often assumed that this is happening through the presence of individual Christians in life. But, in fact, though Christians are well represented in certain areas of life, there are other areas where there is practically no Christian presence. If this is to be remedied, there must be a deliberate strategy on the part of the church to enter those areas. Among the churches I find a variety of responses to the call to go outward. In some places, rather than engaging the world, churches are withdrawing into themselves as they feel their own lives threatened by secularization. In other places, churches want to enter more fully into life but, due to the pressure of traditional expectations or lack of understanding or skill, they find it difficult to do so. In those places where there is effective engagement and attempts to interpret what is happening in the world in terms of the gospel, this is being done without much comprehension or backing from the churches in general.

I look for ways in which the church is identifying with Christ in the poor and the deprived. I find clergy who are committed to living and working among people in the inner city areas in spite of pressure on the churches to withdraw from these areas in favour of those that are more 'responsive'. But I find even in the newer initiatives of the churches which, like community development, especially aim to reach the deprived, a tendency to attract the more articulate and upward spiralling members, to become 'respectable' and to leave the really needy behind.[19]

Involvement is not an end in itself. The church goes outwards to give people hope in the gospel and to point to and interpret the signs of God's kingdom in the world. This can only be done by a Christian community that is in touch with the resources of the gospel. This demands an inward journey.

In the churches' inward journey a context is provided in which people can enter into the reality of God in worship and prayer, struggle together to find God's word for them in the confrontation of the gospel and contemporary life, and experience relationships and mutual acceptance within a community of faith. These are the things that I look for and, although there are signs of hope, I find again and again that the worship of the church is failing to touch people at the deepest level of their being; that attempts to articulate the gospel have little connection with people's actual experience of life; and that in many cases Christians are as insensitive and divided as any other group of people. Many congregations are so busy with all sorts of other things that they do not have time to engage effectively in the outward or the inward journey. I am left with the feeling that, just as in everyday life people do not talk *to* but *past* each other, so the church is failing to connect with life as it is experienced by the majority of people. The result is that people simply do not see the church as a possible source of life.

This brings me back to the point I started from: to Rosie and the girls in the basement club, and to my concern to share with them the discoveries I had begun to make about the reality of God and the possibilities of being human. In this chapter I have tried to state my own beliefs. If I had made a traditional statement of Christian faith I should not have been honest about the real difficulties of believing, nor would I have said anything to help people who are caught in the tensions of living and do not see anything in Christian faith to meet their needs. I have described Christian faith as it has struck home to me in the circumstances and events of my life. As I test this faith against situations in which humanity is most threatened, however, I am forced to ask what there is in it that can strike home in the lives of people in these situations.

Could the man in the rolling mill hear and respond to the invitation of God to realize his humanity not only in retirement but in the mill? Is it possible for people who spend their lives in purposeless jobs to discover fullness of life? What could make it possible for the different groups in industry and politics, to share a worthwhile purpose, rather than tearing each other apart? Can we do anything to make our world more human? Again and again I am forced to ask these questions.

Has Christianity anything to offer in these situations or anything to say? Have the churches ever done anything to help people in these tensions to see that Christian faith is about their lives? Can a faith that has meaning for me stand up to life as it is experienced by people in the typical situations of our society?

In order to answer them, we must look more searchingly at the actual experience of people in our world today.

II This is Our Life

'I'm often reluctant to mention God by name to religious people –
because that name somehow seems to me here not to ring true, and
I feel myself to be slightly dishonest (it's particularly bad when others
start to talk in religious jargon; I then dry up almost completely and
feel awkward and uncomfortable)' *(Dietrich Bonhoeffer).*[1]

1 *North East England*

I have spoken of my belief that God comes to us in life offering us our
humanity. But I feel oppressed with the fact that the way in which life
is experienced and understood today makes this belief seem out of
touch with the realities of life and impracticable as a way of coping
with these realities. I have to face the question whether this faith can
stand up to life as it is. Can this faith enable the girls in the basement
club, the men in the rolling mills and the shipyards, the unemployed
youngsters and a host of other people to live with purpose and hope?

In order to answer this question I must examine in more detail life
as it is experienced by people in some of today's situations. To talk in
generalities would only lead to facile answers. In this chapter I shall
therefore describe how particular people in specific places are experiencing life, and I have chosen that part of the world that I know best
– North East England. I have not chosen this area because it is different
from anywhere else, but because it is where I have been living and
working for the last ten years. I realize that I run the risk of confusing
the main argument of the book in a mass of detail, so I must underline
the fact that my aim is not to give a gazetteer of one particular region
but to expose human questions that are common to us wherever we
live.

I must say more about why this approach seems to me to be both
necessary and right. This book is concerned with God and his meaning
for our lives. It is therefore a theological book, and if I am to arrive at
theological conclusions I must follow a theological method. The
method I follow is this: I start with certain presuppositions from my
own position of faith which comes to me from the Christian community
and my own experience of life. These have been outlined in Chapter
I.

God is acknowledged by the Christian community as revealing himself in the world and supremely in Jesus Christ. His concern is with

humanity. Contemporary life with all its pressures on the human is therefore essential data of theology. It does not stand alone, but stands with the Christian tradition of the revelation of God in the history of the Jews and in Jesus Christ. Contemporary life is understood in the light of that revelation, and the Christian community's understanding of that revelation and its demand in terms of present response is constantly reconsidered in the light of contemporary experience. Theology consists of wrestling with the interaction of these two ways into a knowledge of God and of his call to obedience.

> Theological language and discussion which does not have built into it a continuing element of an attempt to become 'earthed' in the here and now of human questioning and practice as they exist in the world at large (and not solely within 'religious' questioning and practice) will not have 'substance' and will not be theologically valid.[2]

This process underlines the necessity of giving attention to present facts and of making some analysis of the present situation. Different kinds of analysis are appropriate to different purposes. My aim here is to uncover some main issues for human living and believing in our industrial world. In order to do this I must speak about actual people. Statistical facts have a necessary place, but unless what they stand for is seen in quite limited areas of life and in terms of individuals, they can be positively misleading. On the other hand, in the description of one event of a limited nature it is possible to glimpse the real meaning of what is happening on the larger canvas. This is what I hope to achieve in this chapter and why I am going to speak in some detail of life in North East England.

Before I came to live in North East England in 1969, I knew very little about it. I will therefore assume that there are others who are unfamiliar with the region, and will start by giving a few basic facts.

North East England includes the counties of Northumberland, Tyne and Wear, Durham and Cleveland (1974 local government reorganization). It is work that has shaped the area, and its particular characteristics, and it is in work that the people of the North East have found their sense of purpose and belonging. Work and life have developed around the region's three main natural resources: the rivers, the coalfield and the countryside. The main concentrations of population are in the two conurbations around the river estuaries: the Tyne and the Wear in the north and the Tees in the south. During the nineteenth century, the rapid development of the coalfield, which covers a large part of the region, led to a wider distribution of population. The region is now pepper-potted with mining and ex-mining communities. In the run-down of the industry, especially in the 1960s, mining was concentrated at a few large coastal pits. There is therefore a contrast between the decline and depopulation of West Durham and the comparative prosperity of East Durham, which in addition to having active pits, is nearer to alternative work. The outlying districts of the region are 'characterized by rural problems frequently accentuated by height above sea-level, severity of climate and remoteness from regional markets and services'.[3] Apart from an increase in the amount of land under afforestation, there are declining opportunities for work in these districts. The rural areas have become resources for the urban areas for water, leisure and second homes. Many villages, including some ex-mining villages, are completely changing their character as they become places of residence for commuters.

There are different opinions about how far the region should extend, especially in the southern direction. Regionalism in England is an arbitrary matter, but in the North East there are some natural boundaries, with the sea on the east and stretches of high moorland on the other three sides.

The development of the North East during the nineteenth century was spectacular. Its success depended on coal-mining, the traditional shipbuilding industry and the railways. With the discovery of iron ore in the Cleveland hills, iron-making was added to this impressive combination. The North East became pre-eminent in Britain's economic life as the centre of heavy industry. The entrepreneurs, landowners and capitalists who led this development were comparatively few in number: Armstrong who with his engineering works created modern Newcastle; Lord Londonderry, who built Seaham town and harbour for the export of coal from his own pits; the Furnesses, the Peases, the Vaughans, the Bells and the Bolckows. Between these families there was competition, but there were also overlapping interests, so that when occasion demanded they could present a united front.

Against these giants the smaller local industries – glass-making, pharmaceuticals and others – found it hard to compete and many went out of business. As a result the North East became dependent on a few employers and a few industries. This remains a feature of the region, though the private ownership of the big industries has been superseded by nationalization.[4] Some people suggest that this has led to a lack of enterprise among North Easterners.

The majority of the population were manual workers and it is only recently that the small proportion of professional and white-collar workers is beginning to increase. Trade unionism in mining and the craft unions of shipbuilding and engineering grew strong. There were few jobs for women, and many went into domestic service in other parts of the country. There were always ups and downs with long periods of unemployment and acute hardship. Though the depression of the 1930s was the worst, it was far from being the only period of mass unemployment.[5]

Today the North East is going through traumatic changes. By the turn of the century the major industries had reached their peak and thereafter decline set in. One major new employer came to the region when the chemical works of Brunner Mond (now Imperial Chemical Industries) was opened in Teesside in 1923. ICI now employs about 20,000 people on two sites, one on each side of the Tees. The overall decline was partly masked by two world wars, and revival after the great depression of the early 1930s was mainly connected with the rearmament drive. The post-war economic expansion until 1957–8 helped to continue the wartime prosperity in all the old basic sectors of the economy, and some important new growth industries were introduced. After that there was a rapid decline and with rising unemployment the North East became decisively a problem region. Prosperity derived from heavy industry alone had gone for ever. The need was to establish a completely new base for the region's economy. It is this process of change that forms the background to life for people in the region today.

I do not want to suggest that economic change, work, and the lack of work, important as they are, form the only shaping factor in the region's life. Durham City stands in the centre of the region. It was until recently at the heart of Durham's mining life, though the decreasing size and importance of the Miner's Gala which takes place there each year symbolizes the fact that this aspect of its life lies in the past. It is the cathedral that dominates the city. It stands as a witness to the long influence of Christianity and to the many saints known and unknown who have lived and died in the region. The cathedral stands on a hill, beautiful but remote, and to many people what it offers is inaccessible. What we have to discover is whether it witnesses only to the past or whether its faith can be a source of purpose, belonging and feeling for people today.

It is against this background of economic change and against the question as to what hope Christian faith can give us in economic change that I describe some aspects of life in more detail. This does not aim to be an exhaustive account of life in the region, but my choice of subject is not arbitrary. I have chosen to describe those things that seem to me to present the greatest challenge to people's humanity. There are factors which exert powerful pressures upon people, determining their way of life and their understandings of life not simply as individuals but as groups and classes.

Technology is one such factor – indeed it is the main factor affecting us all. Can we say that God is coming to people in the technological change of North East England? How can the depression of the region possibly convey an offer of greater humanity? Are there any real choices, or must men submit to the force of circumstances against which they can do nothing? It is with these questions in mind that I

describe the responses that are being made in the regional policies of
the North East.

My concern is with people and with the realization of their full
potential. There are different views of man, varying from extreme
optimism to utter pessimism. Politics is not concerned with the ideal
man, but with the behaviour of actual men and women with all their
unpredictability. In describing in section 2 the politics of the North
East, I ask what assumptions are being made about man and his
possibilities. The Christian is committed to a recognition of the dignity
and possibility of man, his flexibility, inventiveness and toughness. Of
course man can lose the use of these characteristics – just as he can
misuse them – through his own fault as well as the pressures of his
environment. For men today, life is dominated by structural and political forces. It is sheer nonsense to oppose an inward gospel that calls
for repentance and faith with an outward gospel that calls for social
action. Inward and outward belong together. We cannot know the
inwardness of the gospel except from within the struggle to grapple
with these external forces.

Thirdly, I examine some of the goals and purposes of various forms
of collective power, noting their positive and negative aspects. We
want a more human world, but there are glaring examples of man's
inhumanity to man. Some of these are described in the fourth section.
This should be sufficient to open up questions about the meaning and
possibility of Christian faith in our world.

In this reflection on life I find it is increasingly hard to answer these
questions. As I put questions to life in the light of my faith, I find that
life itself puts questions to my faith. If I am honest, I have to admit
that between Christianity as it is understood and life as it is experienced
there are tensions.

2 *Choices for greater humanity?*

For the first time since the war, the North East was beginning to
suffer from widespread unemployment and oppressive fears of a
return to the hungry thirties which had produced the Jarrow march.[6]

That was the situation Lord Hailsham described in 1962. The post-war
boom was over, and for the North East there was no possibility of a
return to 'normal'. Technological change and world-wide competition
demanded a radical transformation of the economy. That change with
all the disruption of human life and communities it involves is still in
process.

Can it be that in this change God is offering us greater humanity? I
have said that I believe God comes to us through the events of life. I
now ask, 'Can this faith stand up to the realities of life?'.

An essential sign of humanity is the fact of choice. In this section I ask what choices are open in the North East's response to change. The changes are due to forces from outside; technological change and a shrinking world, as well as to given factors of the North East's condition; its geographical position and past history which has shaped it physically and culturally. Choices are limited by these factors, and it is even arguable that there are no choices.

From the start we must be clear that we cannot get to grips with the future of the North East on the basis of purely individual choices. What we are concerned with is social choice. What economic policies will be put into operation? What planning decisions will be implemented? These are not matters for individual decision but for governments, local authorities and committees. To ask what choice a government or local authority has is quite different from asking what choice a woman has who is trying to bring up a family on social security, or a man who has been made redundant from an engineering works, though it is conceivably possible that they might influence these decisions.

It is not adequate to bring individualistic solutions to social questions. Yet this is precisely what many Christians do. It is suggested, for instance, that poverty is due to personal inadequacy and can be overcome by 'trying harder'. Not only is this cruelly unjust, but it blinds us to the reality of the social forces which we should be tackling. My concern is to know what social choices there are for North East England. I want to know what part institutions, including the church, can play in shaping the region's future and what part individuals can play within these social and political moves. In order to do this I look in some detail at the regional policies of the North East.

There were people in the early 1960s who believed that there were social choices and who in their determination to prevent a return to the massive human suffering of the 1930s said: 'It shall not happen again.' Lord Hailsham's visit to the North East was not only the beginning of new policies for the region, but also an example of the deep human concern that inspired and to a large extent continues to inspire these policies. Lord Hailsham was commissioned in 1962 by the Government to study conditions on the spot and to make recommendations for action. His aims were 'nothing less than the improvement of the whole quality of life of the region, and not simply the propping up of dying concerns'.[7]

In his view there were certain priorities for action. A co-ordination of effort was needed. The different government ministries concerned had little communication with each other, and there were over fifty local authorities in the North East with no adequate means of working together. There must be an improvement in local morale. The sense of past failure needed to be overcome by the realization that a new future was already taking shape. In this observation Lord Hailsham put his finger on the basic need for people to gain a new vision of themselves and of the possibilities of life. Some forward picture is needed if men are to wrestle with all that is involved in bringing a new future into being. The picture of the kingdom of God provides in Christian faith a goal and promise. Men have to visualize something that can begin to approximate to it in their own circumstances and work for its realization in concrete terms. The image of the North East that was projected by the media was of slag heaps, derelict housing and unemployed men. This must be replaced by a picture of new trading estates, new towns and new shopping centres.

Communications with the rest of Britain and the world needed to be opened up by better roads, airports and seaports. Nor must the North East be seen as being in competition with other parts of Britain which were also in need, such as Lancashire, Wales and Scotland.

There had to be realism in the use of the limited money that was available. It should only be spent on things that could survive and which could become points of new growth. 'It was necessary to write off somewhat brusquely various concerns which could not have survived as viable entities.'[8]

During his brief visit to the region Lord Hailsham did something unusual:

> For the first and only time in my political life, I enlisted the churches on my side, and called meetings of the clergy of all denominations in each of the dioceses concerned. I tried to explain to them what I was about. I asked them frankly to call upon the people to pray for the success of my enterprise. I believe myself in the efficacy of prayer. But even on the purely natural and psychological level, I felt convinced that, if people pray for a thing, it helps to put heart into it, and to identify their individual purposes with that of the enterprise as a whole. I see nothing wrong or cynical about this. At the deep level at which prayer operates, there is no contradiction between the natural and the divine.[9]

Policies in the North East since 1962 have followed the pattern that was set then. In 1964 Regional Economic Planning Councils were set up. The Northern Economic Planning Council is responsible, in consultation with the Government and its representatives in the region, for policy in the Northern Region, which includes Cumbria along with the four north eastern counties.

The main strands of their policies have been growth and modernization. Growth, it was conceived, could not take place everywhere, so the region was divided into growth and non-growth areas. The growth areas were the river estuaries Tyne and Wear in the north and the Tees in the south. These are linked by a growth corridor along the north/south motorway, A1 (M). For the rest of the region a defensive strategy was proposed. It was, for instance, pointed out that 'in the circumstances the only sensible assumption for West Durham is that the area will continue to lose population'.[10] The theory was that though this might be hard at the time for certain areas, the policy would in the end be in the best interests of all. Growth industries were to replace the declining industries. Although many growth industries, such as petro-chemicals, brought few jobs in relation to their massive capital investment and land use, it was believed that they would have 'spin-off' or 'multiplier' effect.

Three kinds of modernization were considered to be necessary: modernization of the economy, of the region's 'image' and of people's skills and attitudes. The region's economy was seen to be backward in its exclusive dependence on heavy industry and comparative lack of light industry and services. Diversification was vital. To this end a number of new industrial estates and advance factories were set up. The Team Valley Trading Estate in Gateshead had in 1938 been the first of its kind in Britain, so there was precedent in the North East for this development.

In addition to the financial incentives offered by the Government for the re-location of industry in development areas, the local authorities spent vast amounts of money on producing an infra-structure conducive to the needs of industry. Efforts were made to get some of the government offices re-located in the region, resulting in the Department of Health and Social Security head office being sited at Long Benton in Newcastle, the National Savings Office in Durham and in 1978 the promise of the Property Development Services in Middlesbrough. (This promise was revoked in 1979).

There was a continuous effort to promote the region as a modern and attractive place. An improved 'image' was considered to be essential not only to attract new industry, but to stem the drift of population away from the region. The County Planning Officer of County Durham asked 'what to do with the dreary former mining settlements . . . the nineteenth-century scatter of straggling industrial villages located on a dying coalfield'. The region's five new towns were designed in conscious contrast to the mining settlements, to represent a carefully integrated pattern of living, working and leisure. Killingworth, for instance, is constructed to represent a medieval city with a central citadel and the suggestion of a moat in the pleasure lake that lies by the side of the road that leads into the town. All its industries are of a non-polluting kind; and twelve of the industrial buildings have received national design awards.

The third aspect of modernization was the need for a change in the skills and attitudes of the people of the North East. Workers must acquire new skills needed for modern industry, a technological university should be established in Teesside, and the development of

entrepreneural skills should be encouraged: 'There must be change in
the accepted traditional working habits of the region, and above all,
changes in the attitude of resistance to new ideas.'

In the earlier documents there is an optimism and an evangelical
fervour and appeal:

> It is above all on the people of the North themselves that success
> in building a strong and prosperous region must depend . . . We
> have fallen behind some other regions and an all out effort is needed
> if we are to catch up.[11]

Real hopes were kindled. A man who in the 1960s was a young local
councillor told me of the excitement he and his colleagues felt in being
caught up in new objectives for the whole region: 'We felt we were
creating a new world and really doing something for people.' Today
that optimism is less evident and the same man went on to say: 'Now
there is a stodginess about things. There is no leadership or charisma.
No one spells out the issues or says what has to be done. There is
disillusionment with democracy. It leads only to disorder and becomes
a matter of reconciling minority group demands. Moreover, people's
sights are so low that they cannot see the need for change. When we
got residents transferred from some condemned housing it cost us
seats and we lost control in the Council.'

In the 1960s local expansion seemed possible. Today, partly as a
result of pursuing the vision of a new economy, other realities have
emerged. It is now clear that it is not within the power of the people
of the North East on their own to make their future, nor does the
future as it was projected by the policy makers now look feasible.
Factors outside the region have to be taken into account.

How are we to understand this failure of dreams? How are we to
respond to our present situation? These dreams were of a more human
world, and that surely is part of what the kingdom of God is about.
The promise of the kingdom of God is a call to work for a world in
which there will be justice and in which all men will have enough.
Many secular agencies are doing the work of God as they attempt to
improve opportunities for employment and give a better environment.
Some things have been achieved, and in that the kingdom of God is
partly realized. But there is also tension. All that was hoped for has
not been achieved, and a number of new factors make them more
difficult to achieve. It is this that causes questioning and recriminations.
To change course is not easy. There is a tension between the planning
that has led to large sums of capital investment committing us for
many years ahead to decisions which cannot now be reversed, and
what we might now judge to be right.

Yet, though individuals may live only for the day, responsible politics demands long-term planning. This means that certain options

have already been closed for us, and that we in our turn are closing down some options for future generations. The kingdom of God points to the fact that some things are realizable by human effort and others are not. The history of mankind suggests that God is continually inviting man to push the boundaries out with regard to what he can achieve, while at the same time man should acknowledge his ultimate dependence upon God. In the immediate situation of the North East, as we continue to ask what choices are open, it may be that the present policy is best, even though it is more difficult and limited in potential than was at first imagined. We must see whether a case has been made for a different policy and what responses are in fact now being made.

The latest policy report looks at the record of achievement and concludes that 'remarkable progress has been made, but the region has not developed to the point at which substantial assistance from the national government can be removed'.[12] Many of the old problems remain and new ones have emerged. Unemployment remains high (9.3% in the northern region against 6.2% in the UK as a whole in February 1978). Male unemployment is higher still (10.9%), and school leavers are among the largest single group of unemployed. Inequalities within the region have increased. Though some parts are better off, others are considerably worse off. Hartlepool, Sunderland and West Durham are particularly hard hit. The only improvement in job opportunities is for women. In the attempt to attract light industry it had not been foreseen that many of the new jobs would be for women.

Another unforeseen consequence of the initial policies is that many of the new firms consist of branch establishments of larger national or international companies. These tend to be no more than production units without the higher jobs that are part of a total enterprise. In addition, these units are the first to be closed down in bad times. The fact that this is mobile industry means that it is as free to go as it was to come. This also increases the trend for decisions that were previously made in the region to be made elsewhere. I was told that in 1974, of the sixty largest firms in the North East only eight made their decisions locally.[13] This trend is borne out by information given in a study made in Sunderland in 1978.[14] A cross-section of seventeen firms was selected as part of a survey of participation in industry in the town. Apart from four or five of the smallest ones, all these firms are now part of a nationalized industry, or of a national or international company. Only one has its headquarters in Sunderland. There is obviously a problem in sharing in decision-making from a distance, not least in the fact that the better a local manager is, the more likely he is to be promoted to some other location. The actual situation is, however, more complex. There is an indication that people in the North East have never felt that they could decide their own future. They have been too much at the mercy of the economic ups and downs of the region to feel that they could do much more than accept what came to them. What demand there is for more participation is largely stimulated by people who come from outside the region, and in fact it is the firms who have connections outside the North East who have the best participative machinery.

A further area of concern was the conflict that had emerged between modernization and jobs. We only have to look at the modernization programmes of, for instance, the British Steel Corporation to see that it is precisely in the process of modernization that jobs are either lost or transferred elsewhere. But it is equally certain that jobs will be lost if there is no modernization. We may look for jobs which are labour-intensive, but it is only a matter of time before they too will be changed by new technology leading to labour shedding.

The introduction of micro-processors, the 'chip', signals an immense speeding up of this process. It has been said that the North East 'is unlikely to benefit from the new technology but cannot afford to ignore it'. The North East in fact stands to lose for a number of reasons, not least because it does not have the appropriate skills and because the labour-intensive industries it has managed to attract into the region are those that will be most affected.

> Companies find it easier to close factories in one area and open electronic factories in another . . . A limited number of geographical areas have people with the necessary skills, and it is no accident that Bristol should be the site of the new Inmos plant. There highly skilled workers are being shed from the aerospace industry and it is a desirable residential area. None of this augurs well for inner-city areas and peripheral areas like the North East, where the skills of workers are not appropriate for the electronic industry.
>
> The use of word processors in offices increases the productivity of clerical workers and far fewer will be needed. Newcastle, Liverpool, Blackpool and Swansea, to which government routine clerical work has been dispersed from London, are likely to feel the effects the most.[15]

The expected growth has not taken place in the way that was hoped. In the 1960s the British economy was still expanding and there was considerable mobile industry that could be attracted to the region. Today, when the British economy is in depression, it is clear how dependent the fortunes of the North East are on the national and indeed on the international economy. One result of the general depression is that other regions are competing for whatever industry is available. Voices are demanding that the policy of growth and non-growth areas should be applied not simply within a region but within the country, and indeed within the EEC.

Cuts in public expenditure are a serious blow both to jobs and to the quality of life in the region. The North East has a backlog of social deprivation, but the 1977 report conclusion about this is in line with previous policy:

> Certain aspects of social conditions, such as lower standards of educational attainment and of health and a greater incidence of deprivation, are essentially consequences of the nature and performance of the economy over many decades. Therefore they are not amenable in the long term to solution simply by increasing the social programmes concerned, but rather by improved growth and other changes in the working of the economy.[16]

The main modification this latest report makes to previous policies is to place greater emphasis on the need to encourage the development of local firms and entrepreneurs rather than on the attraction of new industry to the area. It points to the need to change the attitude that makes people passively expect other people – the Government or the big firms – to provide jobs. In spite, however, of growing recognition of the difficulty of achieving the prime aim of 'modernizing' the economy, regional policies remain in their essentials unchanged.

These policies have been presented with a certain air of inevitability, as though they were the only possible policies. We should be concerned about this attitude, for, as I have been insisting, choice is an important aspect of being human. We know that choices are limited by many factors; but if there are no choices, we can hand the running of our affairs to the 'experts' and the computers. If there are choices, we must make up our minds what values and considerations should determine our choices. In the North East there are people who say that other policies are both possible and preferable. What they offer, does not in my view add up to an alternative policy, but is rather a critique of present policy.

One proposal is that social reform rather than modernization should be the dominant aim of regional policy. Let us look at this criticism of present policies and then see what is offered in their place. Social reform is defined as the pursuit of the interests of the most disadvantaged sections of the community. In this policy the aim would be to use national and local government expenditure to alleviate poverty and social and geographical inequalities and to increase the degree of community control over decision-making. Priority would be given to social justice and quality of life. The proponents claim that this form of politics has a long history in the North East, despite domination since the mid-fifties by the politics of modernization.

This social reform policy is advocated by the North East Area Study (University of Durham) in its critique of County Cleveland's structure plan.[17] The writers maintain that regional policies have failed on four counts:

(i) They have failed in terms of their own economic goals, and this is largely due to a failure to understand how things work.
(ii) Adverse social consequences have resulted. These policies have especially led to greater social and geographical inequalities.
(iii) Social objectives have not been tackled. The long-standing social deprivation of the North East in comparison with the rest of the country will only be overcome if priority is given to social need.
(iv) Decision-making is increasingly being taken out of the hands of local people.

But what would a social reform policy mean in practice? In this report the alternatives are only stated as general aims. What we are not told is how these could be put into practice. Social reform, like everything else, needs money, and one objective of the modernization policy is to have more money available for social purposes. Without economic revival, where will the money come from? In reply to this obvious difficulty, the social reform advocates point to the vast amount of government money that has been poured into the region. This, they say, could have been spent in a policy of positive discrimination in favour of the disadvantaged. There are strands in government policy and within the region's life that are supportive of a broader human concern. There must be persistent pressure for these strands to be strengthened and developed as a basic element of official policy.

In this document, social reform is presented as a critique of official policies rather than as a coherent proposal for action. Many would agree with its basic claim that the criteria for action must be human well-being, with special consideration for the poor and the powerless. But the responses that are being made in this direction are piece-meal, being concerned mainly with single issues such as housing, environment, or services for rural areas. It is a matter of experience that when issues are tackled in isolation, greater problems are often created elsewhere. Attention is drawn to the symptoms, but fundamental causes remain untouched.

Another critique that does stress the need to tackle the causes of industrial decline comes from a group of community development workers involved in the government's urban programme. In the mid-1970s there was a switch from concern with regional to inner city problems. Twelve neighbourhood-based experiments were set-up to look into Britain's 'pockets of deprivation' and to work with local people to find solutions. A report analyses findings in five of these areas, two of which (Benwell in Newcastle and North Shields) are in North East England.

For a start, the writers point to the dubious assumptions that lay behind the setting up of the programme and note that these are similar to those of the regional programmes:

Poverty, bad housing and so on, it implied, were residual flaws in a society that had solved its basic problems . . . Poverty and deprivation were allegedly the fault of individuals. The solutions then were supposed to lie in self-help by the poor.[18]

Specific areas, in the first place the depressed regions and now the inner cities, 'lagged behind the rest'. These assumptions suggested that the problem was marginal, in the sense that it was not directly caused by the workings of the economic process.

In contrast, the writers themselves believe that the problem of declining industrial areas is a structural problem which is the direct outcome of a capitalist system of production. It is characteristic of capitalistic industry, they say, to move through phases of development and decline in one area after another, as profits made in one area are reinvested elsewhere. Today areas like Coventry, which ten years ago seemed settled in their prosperity, are following the pattern of decline. Mergers and take-overs make it all the easier for companies to choose where to develop and where to cut back production. The larger firms have plenty of choice within the European Economic Community and across the world. In this process, the North East and other depressed areas are used for branch production units which are the first to be closed in bad times.

The report concludes that local questions must be seen in national/international terms. The solution offered is a political one. Government must cease to rely on persuasion and must take responsibility for actually controlling the location of industry:

There is so little mobile industry at present that a successful 'work to the workers' policy is nothing more than a liberal utopian dream . . . The most relevant measures are not to be found in tinkering with housing or labour markets . . . but with measures designed to control the activities of capital. In this respect, the National Enterprise Board proposals, whatever their inadequacies, pointed a way forward. Until policies are implemented which seriously challenge the rights of industry and capital to move freely about the country (not to mention the world) without regard for the welfare of workers and existing communities – who end up carrying the cost under the present system – the problems of inequalities generated by uneven capitalist development will persist.[19]

In coming to this conclusion, the authors have accepted a traditional Marxist analysis of industrial development and of capitalism. They assume that the process would be different under a socialist system. But there are today – notably in the USSR and in Eastern Europe – highly industrialized socialist states, and the evidence is that they experience similar problems. This suggests that criticism should not be levelled so much at the system – whether it is capitalist or socialist – as at the common approach to technology and industrialization.

The Marxist philosopher Herbert Marcuse points to the

> fateful interdependence of the only two 'sovereign' social systems
> in the contemporary world . . . When capitalism meets the challenge
> of communism, it meets its own capabilities: spectacular develop-
> ment of all productive forces after the subordination of the private
> interests in profitability which arrest such development. When com-
> munism meets the challenge of capitalism, it too meets its own
> capabilities: spectacular comforts, liberties, and alleviation of the
> burden of life. Both systems have these capabilities distorted beyond
> recognition and, in both cases, the reason is in the last analysis the
> same – the struggle against a form of life which would dissolve the
> basis for domination.[20]

Domination is the characteristic of both systems. First, domination
of nature through technology; and second, the domination of man by
means of technology. This domination has reduced man's freedom,
taking into itself all forms of opposition and domesticating protest. It
has produced 'one-dimensional man'. Political and social change will
only be possible when the attitude of domination towards nature is
changed. Christian faith is relevant to this matter in at least two ways.
First, there is some evidence that Christian faith has some capability
of opposing oppressive societies. We need to ask how far our faith has
this prophetic quality.

More pertinent to this discussion is the fact that many people believe
that there is a link, though exactly what that link is is not agreed,
between Christianity and the development of science and technology.
Some people have suggested that 'Christian faith is a direct cause of
a disrespectful, reckless technological exploitation of nature'.[21] Others
say that the Christian understanding of an orderly world is a necessary
presupposition for technological progress. Both views over-simplify
what is a more complex relationship.

Christians affirm the material world as expressing the goodness of
God and as given by God to be used for man's good. Man has been
given rule – 'dominion' – over nature. This is to be understood as a
command to care for nature, to 'husband' it, a stewardship under God
rather than a licence to exploit. Technology can be used, and is essential
to the fulfilment of this command. We recognize that technology has
in fact produced suffering and inequality, but this is not due to technology as such or to some political system, but to the choices that
mankind has made and is making about the use of technology. These
choices are made within political systems and require political systems
for their implementation, but behind these systems lie fundamental
assumptions, and it is with these that we must get to grips.

We have to work on at least two time-scales. There is a long-term
job of changing the fundamental attitudes that lie behind all political
systems and policies; and there is the immediate job of carrying on the

business of living. Though there are radical gestures in the critiques of the present regional policies, no positive alternatives are offered.

The Community Development report that we have been discussing does not go so far as to call for revolution – and in the North East there is little sign that such a call would be heeded. It points instead, in its reference to the National Enterprise Board, to the radical strand in British socialism. Leaving further political implications open, it comments that labour organizations have a major task to perform if change is to be achieved. Whatever one may think of the political conclusions, we are left in no doubt that local problems must be considered in their world context. We not only have to work on several different time-scales at once, but on a variety of geographical scales.

The choices that have to be made in North East England appear in a different light when they are seen in a world perspective.

The world is in the midst of an explosion of productive capacity. That explosion brings with it, of course, stress and strains, as well as immensely exciting possibilities of cultural and material liberation and enrichment.[22]

In a world in which more than half the population is under-nourished, the choice lies between that of using this productive capacity to meet the essential needs of all people or that of increasing hostility between nations and classes as the poor struggle to get their share of material wealth and the rich try to hold on to what they already have. This is not simply a technical choice – as some would have us suppose – but an ethical choice.

I have been describing the economic policies of North East England and searching for an answer to the question, 'Can we possibly discern in the changes that are happening, God offering us our humanity?' What choices, if any, are open to us in responding? It seems that we are being pressed to look at things in new ways. I want to suggest directions in which I believe we are being pressed, by pointing to three further questions that need to be considered. The first two concern the goals of our economic policy. 1. If the aim is to enhance life, are we clear whose life is to be enhanced? 2. Do we know what is most needed by human beings for the enhancement of life? The third question is even more fundamental. Given clarity about what we should do, are we able to achieve it? Are there any real choices? I propose to look at each of these questions in turn.

First, whose life is to be enhanced? Within the region it is obvious that some people benefit more than others from regional policies. It may even be said that some people benefit at the expense of others. There is competition for jobs between different parts of the region as well as between the North East and other regions. It is not, however, national but international competition that is hitting the North East hardest. If we see things only in terms of competition we may enhance the life of our nation but depress that of others. Another way of looking at the matter would be to ask what would constitute justice between nations.

The world context puts our problems in a new perspective. From a national point of view full employment seems to be a possible target, but it is not possible to provide jobs for the millions of unemployed throughout the world. We become anxious when other nations take 'our' jobs from us, but we should be asking more fundamental questions about the place of work in man's life. Now that technology has changed the nature of work, should work continue to dominate our lives in the way it does? Do people need work?

This leads to my second question: What do we judge human needs to be? Some things are, of course, necessary for survival. In the 1930s a primary cause of death for many people in the North East was undernourishment; but the loss of self-esteem which work gave a man was almost as destructive as hunger. In the 1960s and 1970s the welfare state has reduced, if not eliminated, the threat of starvation. Other needs are now more pressing. What we have to decide is which needs are now the most important. When it ceases to be a matter of mere survival, what are the priorities?

We can learn a lot from the work of psychologists, and I have found Abraham Maslow's analysis of human needs helpful in many ways.[23] Maslow claims that most people have too low a view of man's possibilities, aspirations and needs. We should not measure man by his past achievements, but make room in our thinking for new developments in the future. Those who propound social theories, Maslow says, are themselves the products of technology. Being deficient themselves in aesthetic and emotional qualities, they discount these aspects of man's nature and think of men as 'higher' animals who should be satisfied with food and shelter. Maslow sets out a wide spectrum of what he considers to be human needs. These include physiological needs: food, rest, shelter, sex; security needs: from threat, danger, deprivation; social needs: love, friendship, acceptance; 'ego' needs : self-respect, self-confidence, competence, status, recognition, respect; and the need for self-realization, which has no bounds. Man, says Maslow, is never satisfied and he never should be satisfied.

Maslow is less helpful, and in fact he is positively misleading, when he suggests that these needs are experienced in some sort of order or hierarchy, so that men only seek to fulfil the higher needs, like self-respect and self-fulfilment, when the 'lower' ones like food and security have been satisfied. It is, of course, true that if a man is dying of starvation the need for food will tend to dominate every other thought. Even, however, in the most extreme circumstances and often precisely in such circumstances, men assert their dignity as human beings and are capable of complete self-sacrifice for people and causes. It is true that a prolonged struggle for survival tends to cramp man's growth, so that people who have known long periods of deprivation may become content when they attain material comfort, but on the other hand creativity may actually be stimulated by deprivation.

Man responds to his situation as a whole person, and his many needs are woven together and must be satisfied together. It is *in* his dealings with material things and *in* his social relationships that he finds self-realization. This brings us into the realm of values, intentions and attitudes. It is not only a structural change in the economy of the region that is needed, but new understandings and values that must be incorporated into the structures. For example, a main aim of regional policy is to bring work to the area. It is work that has in the past given purpose to the lives of communities and individuals, and helped them to discover who they are, but current developments in technology suggest that this may not always be the case. There simply are not enough jobs to go round, and already there is discrimination about *who* shall work: people in West or in East Durham, school leavers or married women? Bristol or Newcastle? Brazil or Britain? Moreover, there are people who having been released from monotonous and pointless work are now discovering themselves for the first time – in unemployment. We must ask questions about the values that are expressed in work and give due weight to other aspects of life.

What bearing has all this on our regional policies? It is not a criticism of the goals that have been pursued, but of the fact that other things were not taken into account at the same time. It is not enough to say that we will *first* meet man's physical needs and *then* deal with his 'higher' needs, as if dignity, creativity and self-respect could be added *after* everyone has a job. There are conflicts between the different things that man needs. For instance, there is tension between on the one hand efficiency in the economy and getting jobs to the region, which has often been served by small 'quangos' working closely with central government, and on the other hand local democratic initiative and participation. Man is a whole person; all his needs must be seen as belonging together and the tension between these needs should be creative. There must be a conscious effort to incorporate human values into all that is being done to provide for physical needs. What is needed is not one revolution but two – a revolution in the economic structures and a revolution in the values embodied in those structures.

This brings me to my third question. Are there any real choices? If we know what we should do, are we able to achieve it? Is God offering us in changing technology the possibility of greater humanity, or is the technological world we have created carrying us along with such force that we have no option but to go along with it? This latter is in fact how things look and feel. In theory we may know what we ought to do, but in practice we seem to be trapped. Of course choices of a kind are being made, but the 'sin in the structures seems constantly to make destructive choices inevitable. And as the opportunities before us are immense in their potential, so are the consequences of the wrong choice in their destructiveness'.[24] It is not that technology is in itself wrong, but that we have built destructive values into the system we have created in our use of technology. Now we feel powerless under these systems.

There is an inertia in society so that there is massive pressure to continue in our present direction. In Western society, and not least in North East England, there is overwhelming support for policies that make jobs of whatever kind their prime aim. Environmentalists, for instance, who opposed certain industrial developments on the Tees estuary, were unable to make any impression in the face of the united stand of industrialists, trades' unionists and councillors. The argument against them was, moreover, put in emotional terms : 'Do you want people to have jobs or are you more interested in the birds?'

Politically, the widespread distrust of any increase in government control aligns itself with powerful vested interests and makes inevitable the defeat of any proposal to limit the freedom of industry. Nor is there any r nception of how things might be better organized, for there seems little to choose between the existing socialist or capitalist systems. Protest is rendered innocuous as environmentalists are labelled as cranks, und community development workers are dismissed for being 'too political'.

Every imaginable choice is not open to us. External factors and choices that have already been made limit our choices. But even if the range of options is limited, there are still choices. In fact choices about the future of the region are being made every day. These are *social* choices. They are decisions made within institutions and about institutions. At this very moment, as I am writing, every public institution is having to decide at what points to make expenditure cuts as a result of central government budgetary decisions. These decisions are being made by people in their roles within institutions, and within all the constraints that institutional structure implies. The head of a department in a college has to decide, with others, what services or staff will be cut. A hospital committee, and a local government education authority, must decide what services to curtail.

An individualistic solution that only takes into account the need of some particular known individual will not do. It must be replaced by a 'statistical compassion' that considers the situation as a whole, weighs up the different needs of different people, and considers the institution as a whole and the purpose for which it exists.

The problem is that all our institutions are in a mess. The service they are meant to offer has been lost sight of as they increasingly serve themselves and their own survival. As a result there is general disillusionment about the possibilities of institutions, and those who hold responsibility in them get disheartened. But it must be obvious that good institutions are essential to any society. The church as one institution among others shares the same problems, but all the same it has something to offer to other institutions; and it should be giving support to the people who hold responsibility in them.

When there appears to be nothing ultimately hopeful, it is impossible for individuals whose lives are bound up with these institutions to see how radically they need reform. It is 'the belief that Jesus is, in some sense, the Lord of history'[25] that makes it possible to face what is wrong with our institutions – with hope. This requires a certain attitude, a morality and a spirituality, that is appropriate to collective living. But the church only offers an individualistic spirituality which drives us back to the individual and the small group. It does not give a spirituality that relates to the realities of collective living.

There are people in the institutions which are concerned with regional development – economists, planners, officials, politicians – who are members of churches or believe that the church should have something to offer. Nearly all of them say that they get little or nothing from their churches to help them make a critique of the values that press upon them in their public responsibilities. It is not a matter of suggesting that there are Christian answers to secular questions, but of providing settings within which people can help each other and draw upon the resources that are in Christian faith for facing social questions. Questions about collectives need collective responses and people need to explore these questions together. What choices are available in the immediate situation, and within what long-term vision can these choices be made? How do we continue to believe that it is worth while trying to involve as many people as possible in these decisions? How can we keep the vision of a new and compassionate world when neither the situation nor the people respond to our efforts? How can we maintain our own humanity, charity and hopefulness on the long march? My last question here is a question to the church. It is a question that was put by Professor Charles Elliott to the bishops at the 1978 Lambeth Conference:

> How well equipped are we to sustain, nourish, envision, heal and restore those who are more directly involved in them (the revolution in the structures and the revolution in values) than we are ourselves? It is a profoundly theological task. For it demands the identification of, and engagement with, structural sinfulness. It demands prophetic action. It will exact a costly price. For to confront the prevailing value-orthodoxy of a rotten civilization costs much: and to live out an alternative set of values founded on an ultimate concern for Christ's poor and the deepest fulfilment of all men costs

more. What reserves, spiritual resources of grace, have we that will keep us all in this task? What is the ground of our hope when the technical analysis gives no ground for hope?[26]

Belief that Jesus is Lord of history makes it possible to endure what has to be endured and at the same time to maintain hope, discernment and integrity in a situation that is resistant to change. The church should encourage this faith in those who hold responsibility in our institutions. Let us see how far it is doing it for the politicians of the North East.

3 Politics and people

Who are the politicians? A local councillor today is more likely to be a Roman Catholic housewife or an agnostic polytechnic lecturer than a Methodist trade unionist, an Anglican landowner or a Presbyterian industrialist. When I think of the councillors whom I know, the first who come to mind are: a Roman Catholic housewife who, besides being a Labour party district and county councillor, is chair-person of one of the main regional councils; the owner of a small business who represents ratepayers on the district council; a polytechnic lecturer who is a Liberal district councillor; and a retired progress clerk representing the Conservative party. Councillors in the North East region are a mixed group, and quite different from those who in the nineteenth century gave the region its distinctive political traditions.

In the nineteenth century the divisions between employer and employee were clear, and for the employees life was harsh. It was this that forced people to recognize the necessity for collective action. If they did not stand together, they went down together. Today the lines between different group interests are blurred. The easing of economic pressures has tended towards privatization – a man's home is his castle, and there are more comforts and diversions in private life. This is not to say that fundamental divisions do not exist, but that they are obscured. The public are 'bought off' by offers of tax reductions and rate rebates, so that politics demands no more of a person than that he buy before the budget price increases. The real political issues are more complex than they were, and as no one helps people to understand what they are, people give up trying to understand. All the time the collective realities are increasingly dominating people's lives, so that the only way of gaining real freedom is by collective, political responses.

Today there is a cynicism about any form of institutional or representative authority. This continues in spite of the increasing collective pressures on people, for they do not see that either the politics or the politicians they have offer any hope. Cynicism is reciprocal, for the politicians themselves have little hope in people. For example an elderly man, who had served on his local council for many years, was speaking to a group of clergy about his work as a councillor. He endured their slightly critical questioning for some time and then exploded, pouring out his deep disillusionment. He had entered politics in the belief that he could do something for people. But people's lack of response made him feel completely let down. The 'image' he presented was of an old and rather pompous politician. Behind this 'front' was a man whose dreams had been destroyed. On the 'receiving end' the same cynicism is shown by the sheer indifference of the general public and by comments such as that of a planning officer: 'The council is as irrelevant as the church; both are well-meaning but irrelevant.'

How does this cynicism about politics and people square with the belief I have been expressing that choice and responsibility are essential characteristics of humanity? If this is true, then politics should not be left to the politicians but should be part of everyone's life. Our attitude to the possibilities of politics comes down to what we believe about the possibilities of people. I asked in the last section, 'How can we continue to believe that it is worth while trying to involve as many people as possible in political decisions?' In this section, by looking in more detail at politics in the North East and in County Durham in particular, I pursue this question. During the nineteenth century the North East and County Durham in particular developed a strong and in some ways unique tradition of political participation. If we are to identify signs of hope in our present politics we must look briefly at this background and ask, 'What has gone wrong?' 'What are the strengths and weaknesses of today's politics?' 'What should today's responses be?'

The masses of semi-literate people who came in the early years of the industrial revolution from all over the United Kingdom to work in the expanding industries of North East England were not the most obvious material from which to look for social creativity. Yet it was these people and their offspring who developed the strongest and best organized working-class electorates in the country.

The rapid development of the coalfield during the nineteenth century led to a kind of frontier situation. Villages sprang up almost overnight to house the workers as each new pit was sunk. These villages were simply rows of houses run up as quickly and cheaply as possible. Nothing else was provided, which meant that for many years the battle that had to be fought was for the basic decencies of life: water, sanitation and elementary forms of welfare. The 'get-rich-quick' drive of competing entrepreneurs became an integration of powerful interests which, though often in competition with each other, was united against any sign of unrest among the workers. In the face of the collective power of the owners the miners were driven to develop their own collective power.

> Collective action of a political kind took two closely related forms, the long and bitter struggle against hostile employers through the local Lodges of the Durham Miners' Association; and the development of a working-class political movement in favour of social reform which found expression in the Labour party.[27]

The nineteenth-century villages were small, tightly-knit communities having little contact with people and places outside their immediate neighbourhood. Each was more or less self-sufficient and self-contained. In addition to meeting the basic needs of life, the people had to provide their entertainment and leisure activities from within their own resources. The institutions which dominated life were the pit, the trade union, the co-operative society, the miners' welfare, the pubs and the chapels. There were 'natural leaders in every village, who were the public representatives in the Miners' Lodge, the Co-operative Store Committee and the Local Council'.[28]

Much of the inspiration that informed this movement came from the chapels:

> The chapel gave (these communities) their first music, their first literature, and philosophy to meet the harsh and cruel impact of the crude materialistic age. Here men first found the language and art to express their antagonism to grim conditions and injustice.[29]

Many of the elected representatives were Methodists. Religion gave the miner a sense of his own dignity and worth, so that he was able to face his employer without feeling inferior. It also gave him a view of society in which the determining factor was not conflict, but the ability of men to work together to shape their own situation for the common good. In the early days, especially where the pits were small as in parts of West Durham, the managers lived in the pit village and shared its social life, often participating in the chapel activities. In these circumstances each side could recognize that the other was struggling with the same situation, to which there were no simple solutions. It was possible for both sides of industry to understand and respect each other and work out their differences in the belief that a solution was possible – though without questioning the basic ordering of society.

It was recognized that religion led to integrity and honesty. In the handling of union funds it was important to have someone who could be trusted, and this quality was associated with the chapel man. There was a jealous concern to guard the integrity of the movement in this respect. A story is told at a later date, when in 1919, Peter Lee became the first chairman of a Labour-controlled Durham County Council. It was obvious that he could not cover the expenses entailed in this office out of his own wages, but when the question was discussed, he made it clear that though he was compelled by circumstances to accept expenses, he would not accept more than half the amount granted by the Council'.[30]

The close link between Methodism and the miners is one clue to the Durham miners' reputation for moderation both industrially and politically. Methodism and Liberalism, which held sway politically in the area until the 1920s, seemed to cling together. The *laissez-faire* doctrine of the Liberals tuned in with Methodist individualism, which looked for a new man rather than a new society: 'The individual stood alone not only before the majesty of God but before the forces of the market.'[31] Neither Methodists nor Liberals looked for structural social change. The miners' leaders, as well as being Methodists, were generally Liberals and opponents of socialism. It was the depression and unemployment of the 1920s that forced many people to question this philosophy and to seek radical changes in society. In this potentially conflictual situation a socialist philosophy was more relevant. The consensus philosophy of Liberals and Methodists made little sense of what was happening, and though other factors were involved, it was from this time that Methodists lost their influence in mining affairs.

Of course even before that time Methodism had not been the only source of vision. A minority had found that a Marxist interpretation made more sense not only of life but even of the Bible. A personal account survives of union activities at some of the more militant pits such as Thornley and Wardley (which was known as 'Little Moscow'). There is an example of how socialist and biblical strands of an alternative vision were interwoven on the occasion of a lecture given by a local trades' unionist. The title of the lecture was 'Isaiah the Bolshevik'.[32]

The leading trades' unionists put themselves to school to learn about economic and international affairs. Their grasp of the wider issues impinging on local matters permeated the movement, and helped local officials to maintain hope in spite of set-backs encountered in day-to-day negotiations.

Some of the younger people widened their horizons by further education. At first this was a source of enrichment to the villages, though later it meant that they moved away altogether. One or two young men revolutionized the thinking of a local Methodist Bible study group by introducing the thinking of Tolstoy and other radical writers with whom they had become acquainted in the course of their studies at Bede Teacher Training College in Durham.[33]

We should not idealize the past. Close-knit, highly integrated communities can exercise powerful controls over their members. The villages could become prisons and the leaders demagogues. But the overall effect was the development of a powerful working-class movement committed to work for a just and humane society – an ideal for which many people were ready to make considerable sacrifices.

In 1975 Durham County Council celebrated fifty years of continuous Labour control. Although this dominance has not been so complete elsewhere, the Labour party is extremely influential throughout the North East. Both gains and losses come from this success. On the one hand it has been possible to pursue policies without interruption over a number of years; and to do this on the basis of the vision and tradition that has been outlined. On the other hand, there is the danger of complacency and of the abuse of power. One remarkable feature of the election of councillors has been the significant proportion who have been returned unopposed.[34] This reached its peak in 1964, when 92 out of 106 Labour members of Durham County Council were either aldermen or unopposed councillors. The lowest number was in 1970, when only 49 out of 92 Labour aldermen and councillors were unopposed. This has led to a lack of involvement of the electorate, lack of political education and a low level of political debate. It leads to the isolation of those in control from the changing realities of the actual situation they are meant to represent. In 1973 the Labour Party received a rude awakening in the shape of the powerful Liberal challenge, made in the Chester-le-Street bye-election. Chester-le-Street is in the heart of the old mining area and has returned a Labour member to Parliament without exception since 1909 – with huge majorities. On this occasion the disillusionment of the electors and the changing social structure of the area contributed to make the Liberal candidature a real threat to the Labour succession. Although in the event Labour retained the seat, the Liberal revival has continued as far as local government is concerned, and is effecting some healthy self-criticism in Labour circles.

In view of the background of intense local loyalties, it is not surprising that accusations of 'parochialism' are levelled at North East politicians. There are also splits within the Labour party between the 'old guard' and those who try to introduce new ideas. Another criticism is that an understandable tendency to give jobs to local applicants and to party members turns into nepotism and the use of patronage in order to increase personal or party power.

A more serious charge is that of corruption. Corruption involving prominent North East figures made the headlines in the cases following the bankruptcy of the architect John Poulson. That the whole of public life is damaged by corruption in a few people was pointed out in a speech made at the time by Harold Wilson:

> If only a very small minority give way to the temptations which beset them for personal gain or other unworthy motive, then the whole of public life is sullied.
> The price we face is that fewer and fewer people will concern

themselves with local or national issues, with the workings of local or national democracy.

The price, too, is that for every case of corruption which comes to light, a hundred other devoted public servants find it that much harder to do their job. *Men and women of all parties who have given their whole lives to community service find their efforts greeted by cynicism. The dedication which inspires them no longer appears to their constituents to be the crusade which was proclaimed.*[35]

The bankruptcy of John Poulson brought to light a network of corruption that, though it was by no means confined to the North East, has very serious implications for politics in the region. In 1974 two of the North East's leading public figures, Alderman Andrew Cunningham and Councillor T. Dan Smith, were convicted at Leeds Crown Court with Poulson of conspiracy and corruption and sentenced to terms of imprisonment.

These were the two most powerful men in the North East, and that is why Poulson chose to do business with them. Cunningham held many posts, including that of alderman of Durham County Council, Chairman of Durham County Police Force, official of the National Union of General and Municipal Workers and member of the Labour Party's national executive. Smith was the most influential figure on Newcastle City Council and was known as 'Mr Newcastle'. His other appointments included that of chairman of the North East Development Council. Both men were among the comparatively few people in the North East who had real power at national as well as local level. Cunningham had this through his membership of the Labour Party National Executive and Smith through his chairmanship of the NEDC, which put him in frequent contact with various Government ministries. Poulson's policy was to build up a network of people who could open doors that would gain him local authority and government contracts. This network was extremely complex and widespread. The first trial in fact came in 1971, several years before the bankruptcy. On that occasion a member of Wandsworth Town Council was convicted and imprisoned for accepting a bribe from T. Dan Smith, who was himself charged but cleared.

All sorts of people got tangled in Poulson's net, not least the contractors and builders who were anxious to get work in the North East. Nor should we cast Poulson himself as the arch-villain, for he too was caught in the net of his own dreaming with all its limitations. Those who suffered were inevitably the people of the North East whose money was misspent by the uncritical preference given to Poulson in many prestigious building contracts. Those who suffered most were the people who raised their voices against what was going on. The Wandsworth Town Clerk who asked for further action to be taken lost his job. Eddie Milne, MP for Blyth, who continually asked for an enquiry into the Labour party in the North East, was expelled from the Labour party and lost his seat. He commented:

> Anyone who dared to demand action or investigation was ruthlessly dealt with. People in high places moved in swiftly to protect the wrongdoers, and above all to prevent further disclosures . . . the casualties . . . came from the ranks of those who were from the corrupt or the corrupted.[36]

It is not easy to make black and white statements about corruption. Giving and receiving gifts in the course of business can be quite innocent, or it can reach the gigantic proportions of the Lockheed bribery case which implicated governments. 'Corruption is itself extremely hard to define, and almost as catching as smallpox.'[37] There has never been a time when public life was free of scandal, and there is no adequate way of preventing corruption. There is an obvious case for altering the procedures for financial checks, but against this is the ever-increasing weight of administration and bureaucracy. People can usually find ways of cheating the system if they want to. There is no doubt that the miners knew what they were doing when they appointed to look after their financial affairs Methodists whose convictions made it possible for them to be trusted without elaborate checks. The absolute integrity of these men was part and parcel of their whole outlook on life, but we should not imagine that faith in the abstract will produce this kind of character. The training ground was the Methodist chapel. These congregations were communal groups linked not only by belief, but by marriage and kinship. The members knew each other well, had specific standards of behaviour which they expected of each other, so that 'discipline was maintained mutually by sect members, and backsliding meant expulsion from the only community men knew in the industrial wilderness'.[38] If the Methodists were short on social vision, they upheld a strict standard of personal ethics.

The real problem in politics today is, however, not corruption but a disillusionment with democracy. Corruption is not even the main cause for the cynicism and lack of interest on the part of the public or for the politician's loss of faith in the democratic process. The main causes for the low state of politics today are: failure to grasp a vision of the whole, lack of belief in the possibilities of people, and failure to grasp the nature and necessity of politics that leaves the power-handlers and their policies without any general support. I look first at the need for a vision of the whole.

Labour politics developed as a protest against inhuman conditions. The vision of a different kind of society consisted of the dreams of those in opposition rather than the blue-prints of those in power. An attitude of 'This won't do' rather than a positive vision of the future was the spur to action:

> Action for change generated from the negation of extreme or obvious evils is likely to lead to the isolation of certain issues as calls for action.[39]

This leads to the impassioned campaigns for single causes which are in tune with common radical political moods in Britain since the sixties.

There were people in the 1960s who held a broad vision of a different future for the North East, who believed that others were capable of responding, and who actually aroused the enthusiasm of a number to work for it. Some worked to make Newcastle into a worthy regional capital, others in Teesside got together to make a community out of their new county borough. Today the things that were said then are still being said: 'A University of Technology in the Teesside region', 'Peterlee is the place to be', 'We are planning for people'. But they are being said without conviction. What started as a total picture has been reduced to a search for jobs at any price, while everything else must wait.

Some attribute the present lack of political interest to the centralization of political power and the fact that local issues have not been tackled. Participation, they believe, must begin in 'community politics', by stimulating concern at the 'grass roots', helping people to identify their own needs and discover their own power. Community development workers at a number of points in the region are following this approach with some success. A campaign inspired by the community development team appointed under the government urban programme in North Shields led to local people, who had been living in run-down housing in the centre of the town, being re-housed on the new estates of East Tyneside. During the campaign considerable leadership skills emerged, especially among some of the young housewives. A step forward had been taken, in that people who had felt themselves to be at the mercy of officialdom discovered power to control their situation. But the weaknesses of this approach came to light when the women tried to find a role on the estates. The only style they knew was that of protest, whereas what was needed now was a positive vision of a society of the future that would enable them to use power constructively.

There are two approaches to politics. First is the piece-meal approach that comes from desperation and attacks a specific wrong. This is a reaction to 'unfreedom' and it has in itself something of that same 'unfreedom'. In contrast to this is the politics of freedom which rather than simply attacking what is wrong dares to visualize a new society and to sketch blueprints for the future.

The following quotation from an article by Dr Haddon Willmer contrasts these two approaches and points to the fact that Christians easily align themselves with the piece-meal politics of desperation:

> Christian compassion for the suffering and the outsider has seemed to validate this way of drawing up the political agenda. Christian social thinking has not been sufficiently aware of the distinction made by Hannah Arendt between the politics of enraged misery producing revolutions and the politics of freedom which is able to make constitutions. It certainly has not faced the possibility that Christian thinking should positively aim for the public realm of freedom and not simply be driven by the 'rulers of this world', of whom the most powerful in Europe, as she argues, are the misery of the poor which makes the goal of 'abundance and endless consumption' compulsive. What is important about her argument is not that it might lead us to belittle the burden of misery, but that it makes clear that in both its destructiveness and its affluent-hedonist forms the impulse of misery is inimical to the politics of freedom. In that way she shows that we live in a tension and are faced with a choice. What we are to choose or whether we can choose the hard option of founding freedom is secondary to recognizing that we have a choice. It is important to recognize that we live in a political order where certain choices have been made for us or are being made, so that we cannot have all imaginable political goods. If we are desperate to escape poverty, we shall not found freedom. Not that freedom and wealth are necessarily incompatible; it is freedom and desperation which do not mix. . . . The reactive piecemeal 'This won't do' approach drives us into the politics of misery. It is only the daring of blueprinting that lays hold of that freedom to think, to speculate or fantasize and even to believe which is the theoretical counterpart to the politics of founding freedom.[40]

The single-issue approach to politics appeals on account of its simplicity, and for Christians it has a double allure if it can be presented in black and white moral terms.

In order to gain a view of the whole, there must be an analysis of the complexities of society, and there must be work on specific issues. But this must be done without losing sight of the wood for the trees by isolating any one issue from its place in the total picture.

'The Marxist critique seems to be the most powerful pointer to our sharpest present human contradictions and sources of inhumanity.'[41] Marxism commends itself as a serious attempt at social analysis and also for the role it sees for man and in its concern for the poor. Its solutions, however, are not as total as they claim to be, and though they offer some men in some situations a call to decisive action, they do not provide a general theory which gives light to *every* man in *every* situation. For instance,

> the idea of participation or of democracy before the revolution, which is where we are in England and probably will be for a long

time, is likely to be seen in Marxist terms as a deception. . . . The systematically pessimistic interpretations of those present possibilities that do not amount to the 'revolution' appear to many to be untrue, to discourage what good action is open to people in many situations.[42]

A doctrinaire Marxist interpretation of our situation and of what is possible in it is an over-simplification that forecloses choices that may be the right ones in our particular circumstances. What is even more damaging, and this relates to the second main cause of apathy in politics, is that the Marxist view of man presupposes a certain predictability about man's behaviour. In contrast to this view, one of the things that is hopeful about man is his *un*predictability. Men and women are capable of doing surprising things, for human beings are infinitely resilient and inventive. It is true that this inventiveness may be used for unworthy and wicked ends, but it may also be used for the creation of the good. If politics is to have any liveliness, there must be a belief in people.

I will sum up where this discussion about the causes of political apathy has led us so far. There is an absence of a relevant framework of ideas which could help people to gain a vision of the kind of society they might work for. There simply is no serious political debate in which people can share. The projections that are made are all in terms of the past or presuppose a situation other than our own. They fail to grapple with the questions of a different kind of future to which we might contribute. It is this lack, first of analysis and then of vision and 'blueprinting', that makes so many efforts inadequate.

The single-issue approach to politics comes from desperation and carries with it negative attitudes towards power and the power-handlers. The community development workers, for instance, are right to start with people's immediate problems, but their overall assumptions about power and people who handle power are negative; and they have no plan for the use of power when they get it.

A positive view of politics must be based on a positive view of man. The biblical view of man assumes the solidarity of mankind and the belief that power and responsibility has been given to mankind as a whole. All men are meant to share in political responsibility in some way. Those who are denied this power or fail to exercise it are in some way diminished as human beings:

God blesses the rest of his creation by supplying people, to control and develop it. These are going to be people with power, people who will be able to act in a co-operative and purposive manner to control their environment . . . Man as a whole is given this mandate both to work and to exercise power; and any system which deprives healthy and adult people of the opportunities to work and to exercise political power is to that extent failing to measure up to the Creator's mandate.[43]

The Bible reckons with the tension between man as a sinner who is capable of wilful destructiveness and self-seeking, and man in the image of God who is capable of extraordinary acts of self-sacrifice and idealism. Christians have in fact often resolved this tension by stressing one aspect of man's nature at the expense of the other:

> The problems of politics were confused by the undue pessimism of the orthodox church and the undue sentimentality of the liberal church. In the one case the fact of the 'sinfulness of the world' was used as an excuse for the complacent acceptance of whatever imperfect justice a given social order had established. The fear of the possible disintegration of a sinful world into anarchy prompted a rather frantic and pious commendation of whatever order had been historically established. In the other case the problems of politics were approached from the perspective of a sentimental moralism and with no understanding for either the mechanistic and amoral factors in social life or the mechanical and technical prerequisites of social justice. . .
>
> Men whose very existence is imperilled and whose universe of meaning is reduced to chaos by the social maladjustments of a technical society, may be pardoned if they dismiss, as a luxury which they cannot afford, any 'profound' religion which does not concern itself with these problems.[44]

Politics aims to bring conflicting group interests into some kind of order through a variety of checks, to which politicians themselves must also be subject, through balances of power and through compromises. The ideal of love cannot be applied directly in politics as it might be in individual situations. But in political attempts to approximate to justice, love is held as the norm that characterizes the ultimate perspective.

The insights of Christian prophetic religion are needed in order to help people to hold a vision of a shared future that is ultimately hopeful, and for the creation of which all have a responsibility. While being realistic about the tension between man's actual behaviour and what he is capable of, prophetic religion enables a continuing hopefulness about the possibilities of people.

Only a sense of shared responsibility can lead to any general support for the power-handlers. This means that there must be more participation in politics. There are a number of reasons why this is a matter of urgency. From a purely pragmatic angle, a society in which people are not involved is open to manipulation not only by those who hold power, but by the extremes of right or left. 'The price of freedom is eternal vigilance' (Burke).

However, participation is not just a pragmatic matter, but concerns our deepest beliefs about ourselves as human beings and what is involved in responding to God's call to be human.

It is significant of the low ebb to which involvement in public affairs has sunk that the word 'participation' is today used in a semi-technical way for the exercises that are mounted in relation to local government structure plans. These are usually little more than a sharing of information with opportunity for comment. It remains an 'us' and 'them' situation, in which certain sections of the community are concerned to make particular points which touch on their own interests without consideration of the whole. In contrast to this, what I am concerned with is shared responsibility and shared power.

There are obvious problems which cannot be shirked. First, there is evidence to support the contention that people do not want to be involved. For example, at a certain conference everyone was invited to submit one problem experienced in their own job. The person who received the least sympathetic hearing was the local councillor who asked how he could gain more backing from his constituents. He was told firmly by the conference members that he should not expect other people to do his job for him.

Second, political questions in advanced technological society are on an unprecedented scale as regards both size and complexity. We have to deal with nationalized industries and multi-national corporations rather than with local managers; with central government departments and the European Economic Community rather than with the town hall. No one can handle all the information; and even those 'at the top' cannot assess the effect of their policies. Today's decisions commit us for many years ahead, and mistakes are proportionately costly. The 'lay' person feels and is made to feel inadequate. I was at a meeting at which the impact of North Sea oil on Teesside was discussed. When a housewife ventured a query about a possible rise in rents she was told by a trade unionist to keep out of a discussion which was none of her business. No wonder that the man or woman in the street leaves it to the 'experts'.

In fact it is precisely because no one person can be *the* expert in what it means to be human in our complex society that all sorts of people must be involved. In a technological society power is collective power. People in the North East have to learn again in a new situation, which presents new questions, how to respond collectively.

4 Collective power, purpose – and some irrationality?

The question, 'How can we realize our humanity in a more human world?', must be answered collectively. Individualistic answers are inadequate. In the nineteenth century, industrialists and workers were forced to recognize this fact and built up collective institutions for the achievement of their purposes. For the industrialists this meant using nature and people to increase their own wealth and prestige. For the workers it meant counteracting the collective power of the industrialists with their own collective power in order to maintain their humanity. Today, organizations that were built up to serve human ends are crushing the people they are meant to serve. In this section I examine collective power in our society and ask: 'How rational is our collective behaviour?' 'Have we a gospel for collectives?' All institutions face similar problems, but because technology and its changes have such a profound effect on the distribution and shape of collective power in all its forms, I confine this discussion to industry and the trade unions.

I turn first to the collective power of the industrialists. The men who gained power in the North East during the industrial revolution were those who had the capital to sink mines or build iron and steelworks. Having gained power they combined with each other to keep their power. For example, Dorman Long & Co, in addition to its main business as an important iron and steel concern in Middlesbrough, owned in 1939 eight pits, coke ovens, by-product plants and ironstone mines. Its most important connection was with Horden Collieries in County Durham, via a directorate association. The 'family' tree below illustrates the extent of these relationships.[45]

The industrialists' philosophy of *laissez-faire* made it inevitable that in practice it was a matter of every man for himself. The associations that were made were associations of convenience, in which the chief aim of each participant was to maintain the viability and increase the

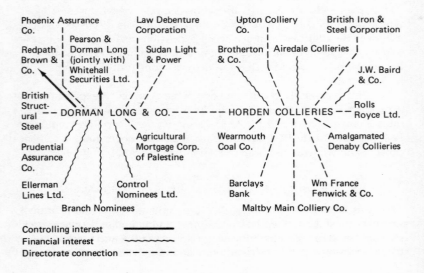

Controlling interest ————
Financial interest 〰〰〰
Directorate connection — — — —

profitability of his own concern. There was enough co-operation to keep the workers in their place and to maximize short-term profits for the owners, but not enough for the long-term development of the industries' capacities. In the years prior to nationalization the effects of this short-term policy became acute in the form of worked-out mines and aging machinery. No amount of persuasion, however, could get the owners to combine to put the necessary capital into the modernization of plant and equipment that was vital to the long-term viability of their industries, and nationalization in one industry after another became essential if anything was to be salvaged.

The power the early industrialists exercised over the lives of their employees was arbitrary and unchecked, and the effect in many cases was crushing. We have already noted how the workers' realization that if they were to preserve their humanity they must confront collective power with collective power, led to the creation of trade union and political organization.

In more recent years the demands of developing technology for massive capital expenditure has among other things led to an increase in the size of enterprises, a growth in the complexity of inter-relationships and a concentration of power. Whether this is a necessary outcome of advanced technology is now being questioned.[46] The fact remains, however, that these are the trends and they must be reckoned with. A few facts and figures should be enough to make the point. The coal and steel industries are now co-ordinated by nationalization under their respective boards. These industries employ:

NCB nationally 290,000 (1977–78), locally 32,000
BSC nationally 186,000 (July 1979), locally 24,000 (approximately: an ever decreasing figure).

The largest local employer in the North East in the private sector is ICI which employs:

nationally 90,000, locally 20,000.

The headquarters of all the above enterprises are in London. One local company that managed to make a stand against the trend towards centralization, and to maintain local autonomy, was Northern Engineering Industries, which was formed in 1977 by a merger between the Tyneside companies of Clark Chapman and Reyrolle/Parsons. It should be noted that this merger took place in defiance of a government recommendation that they should become part of the giant company of GEC.

The collective power of industry is recognized by Government in its regular consultations with the CBI together with the TUC. This is one of the visible aspects of a network of formal and informal relationships. A diagram of the inter-relationships that exist today would show a far greater concentration of power in particular organizations and people than the diagram at the beginning of this section.[47] Without going into more detail I want here to underline the strength of the collective power of industry, not only over people's jobs but over their whole lives, and to go on to ask questions about the nature of that power and the goals to which it is directed.

In contrast to earlier industrialists, the men who appear to hold the reins of power in industry today feel under pressure from forces which they are unable to control. They do not choose their own goal, but feel bound to pursue the goal of survival for their company and for themselves. In the present situation of industrial decline and recession, there is acute agony for those who hold responsibility. I have heard senior managers who in an atmosphere of confidence and trust have been able to say how trapped they feel. One who had to make a number of men redundant said, 'I felt this was so contrary to my human and Christian instincts that I could not mention it even to my wife. But I have no choice.' Industrial life becomes a battle in which only the strongest can survive. There are some for whom this presents a certain exhilaration – as one man put it – 'in the fun of the chase'. But it has obvious disadvantages in the price that is paid in terms of personal and family life.

The understanding of the situation as a competition or even a battle comes out very clearly, for example, in the 1978 annual report of GEC, which is one of the largest companies in the United Kingdom, employing 156,000 people in about 100 establishments in Britain and with a spread of subsidiaries overseas:

> The future is likely to produce . . . ever tougher competition abroad as other countries fight even harder to top-up their order books . . . To prosper in the big league of world electrical and electronic engineering, we now have to accelerate our efforts to raise efficiency . . . (The Chairman).

From the Managing Director comes a comment on what this means in practice:

> We don't want to change just for the sake of it. We *have* to change . . . To secure a future in a fast-moving world, we have to go on changing and adjusting, aiming to get one step ahead of the competition . . . But in the cut and thrust of competitive life, it is inevitable that not *every* GEC activity will *always* turn out to be a winner . . . No one pretends it's easy for the people involved in the processes of change, in moving jobs or learning new skills. But we cannot escape the realities of the world about us. Nobody owes us a living. No one can honestly promise jobs and prosperity for all – it doesn't lie in the power of any person or government to deliver . . . It's up to us all (his italics).

This philosophy contains considerable elements of determinism in the light of which choices seem to be limited or non-existent. What is said is stated as though there could be no disagreement about the nature of the 'realities' of the world, or the course to be taken and its obvious rationality. But these assumptions are debatable, and we must discuss first the question of rationality and then the question of determinism and choice.

Technology is only a possibility where man uses his reason, but in many ways technological society is totally irrational:

Is it rational for the world to spend 'as much on arms as the 2 billion people in the poorest half of the world's population earn in a year?[48]

Is it rational to have a vast productive capacity that is under-utilized when at least half the world lacks the necessities that technology could produce? Is it rational to develop technology for socially trivial objectives when there is so much human need which it could supply? Is technology being used to make life happier and to make the world more human – or is it contributing to the destruction of life? Is this the rationality of the madhouse?

These competitive goals are only rational when they are considered in terms of a limited aspect of reality, the efficiency of technology and the system within which it operates. Account is not taken of the realities of human nature and the wider purposes of life. In consequence some people have concluded that our industrial society, far from being rational, is:

a mindless juggernaut . . . leading to . . . depersonalization, meaninglessness and repression, until it has destroyed all meaning and all life.[49]

This society is irrational as a whole. Its productive capacity is destructive of the free development of human needs and faculties, its peace maintained by the constant threat of war, its growth dependent on the repression of the real possibilities for pacifying the struggle for existence – individual, national and international.[50]

We have already noted that there is a special quality about collective irrationality which is different and more complex than that of individual irrationality. Because of the inclination of Christians to think in purely individualistic terms this must be emphasized:

There has been little suggestion in modern culture of the demonic force in human life, of the peril in which all achievements of life and civilization constantly stand because the evil impulses in men may be compounded in collective actions until they reach diabolical proportions.[51]

There is an irrationality in both individual and collective action that needs for its resolution more than a process of reasoning together. This does not, however, mean that human beings have no control over the course of society. Our particular kind of technological society has not come about by chance or simply by the operation of outside forces. It comes from the values and decisions of people. The particular meanings and values people hold are embodied and expressed in their institutions. These institutions then gain a power of their own, so that instead of men controlling them they dominate men. They cannot easily be changed, but they can be changed. Just as they were created by people, so they can be changed by people. This must be done not by individual but by collective action. Nor can it be done by human will alone. It requires grace.

I have spent some time describing the collective power of industry, for, while one hears many tirades against the power of trade unions, the power of industry is often taken for granted. I want now to show that the same questions apply to the trade unions.

The original motivation of trade unionism lay in opposing the philosophy of competition with a philosophy of co-operation – 'all men are brethren',[52] and the goal to be pursued is 'justice for all men'.[53]

Trade unionism started from a position of powerlessness. Those involved knew that their only strength lay in their unity. Today it has attained recognition as being of equal significance with the CBI in tripartite talks with the Government. So changed is the trade union position that people are now saying, 'The trade unions are too powerful'.

In order to look more closely at this power and the way it is being used, I will describe a conversation with some shipyard workers on the Tyne. First I must briefly sketch in the background of trade unions in shipbuilding. In the construction of a ship very diverse skills are needed.

> Traditionally each trade or group of related trades was organized in its own trade union. In addition semi-skilled workers and labourers were organized by one of the general unions . . . (In spite of union amalgamations, the manual workers in the Wallsend shipyard are still represented by nine different unions . . .) Traditionally antagonisms between some of the trades have been strong. The sense of exclusive competence to do certain jobs, allied with the general insecurity of shipbuilding has in the past, led to frequent and long drawn out demarcation strikes. In recent years the incidence of demarcation strikes has diminished; in fact there were only two on the Tyne between 1946–61. The loyalty to trade and the protectionist attitudes stemming from this are, however, still present.[54]

In July 1977 the British shipbuilding industry was nationalized. Its first task was to gain orders in the worst shipbuilding slump of this century. One of the orders won in the face of hard competition and with the promise of considerable Government subsidy was for twenty-six ships for Poland. The Poles made conditional clauses which led to the orders only being allocated to those yards where agreements were signed to the effect that work would not be interrupted by disputes. Workers on the Tyne believed that their levels of pay were below that of other yards, including those on the Wear, where a new wage structure had been successfully negotiated. There was also a long-standing battle over differentials between the outfitters and the boiler-makers. This meant that when four of the Polish vessels were offered to the Tyne, there were difficulties about signing the agreement. Protracted discussions failed to get both the boiler-makers and the outfitters to sign and the orders were directed to other yards.

These events appear in a different light according to the position of the people involved. The men I spoke to, who were all members of the outfitting trades, showed that far from feeling powerful they felt threatened by the outside forces of international competition and by what appeared to them as collusion between their own full-time officials and the management of British Shipbuilders. This is what they said:

When vesting day came we thought it was the day of the Messiah.[55] Perhaps we expected too much. We put in a claim for parity with the other yards. As negotiations dragged on we increased our industrial action and our faces got harder. Then they used the Polish order to put a sword over our heads. We felt sure that the Government letter containing the conditions had been written in collusion with our own management. If only someone had asked us then how we felt about the final clause – that all restrictions should be lifted forthwith – we might have avoided a confrontation.

The full-time trade union officials don't understand the situation either. They came down from London and gave us a lecture on the state of the shipbuilding industry as if they were talking to yokels. After that we had a series of deadlines for accepting the order, and each time these were extended our members believed in them less and less.

The view expressed in the British Shipbuilders' journal – the official paper of the nationalized industry – is predictably different, and suggests that the stance of the unions is in effect an example of corporate irrationality:

Tyneside, the traditional heart of British shipbuilding, is bleeding to death from self-inflicted wounds.

Deep-rooted rivalry between trades has driven away much-needed work that was originally intended for the Tyne, and as a result 1,152 redundancies have been announced in an area of already high unemployment . . .

There is no point in complaining about what has happened in the past and using history to justify entrenched positions now. The industry is changing fast but the attitudes on the Tyne are not reflecting this.

Other yards have virtually eliminated damaging rivalry over pay by moving on to common wages structures which ensure common earnings for similar skills and effort.

There appears to be a growing awareness that the Tyne will have to follow suit. But will the urgency of the situation sink in quickly enough to prevent decimation of shipbuilding on the Tyne?[56]

Much more could be said about this situation. It is typical of what happens in many other industries. My purpose, however, is not to draw conclusions about the rights or wrongs of this particular situation, but to bring out points about the nature of collective power and the rationality and irrationality of collective action, and so to face some general problems concerning institutions in our society. In order to do this I point to three factors in this example.

First, rationality of response relates in some degree to a group's perception of reality and of the facts of the matter. There are vast differences between the situation of British shipbuilding in the nineteenth and early twentieth century and the present day. Previously the main force that confronted the workers was the collective power of management and owners. Today outside forces, changing technology and a shrinking world, threaten management and trade unions alike. A main event that changed the world ship-building scene was the change in Middle East oil policies in 1973/4. This was only indirectly connected with shipbuilding, and no one in shipbuilding could be held responsible for it. But the effect was to make nonsense of everything that was going on in the industry at the time. The boom in giant tankers that was in full flood stopped abruptly, so that some of the tankers then under construction have never been used. Today shipbuilding throughout the world is in trouble; a quarter of the world's ships, especially the large tankers, are idle, and demand is slack. Britain long ago lost her world lead in shipbuilding and, though in the last few years she has maintained her percentage of the trade, the total amount is shrinking.[57] These are new realities that create a new situation in which (as *Shipbuilding News* pointed out) it is no good simply appealing to the past. Among our collectives it is not only trade unions that tend to be dominated by the past.

Tradition, however, has an essential place in helping us to face the future. In the traditions of trade unionism the concepts of co-operation and brotherhood have a greater relevance today than the industrialist's philosophy of competition. A prophetic approach to tradition purges it of false accretions and enables its essential meanings to find new expression. A purging of trade union tradition is needed, from its identification with the philosophy of competition and with the goal of

'abundance and endless consumption'. Its philosophy of the 'brotherhood of all men' needs to be opened out so that it really does mean
'all men' and not just those who belong to 'my' union.

A second factor relates to the question of size. How far are large
institutions able to respond to the real needs of those they are meant
to serve? Is it inevitable that they should become paralysed by bureaucracy, and end by simply crushing individuals? It is hardly helpful to
talk about seeing things in world terms, when people already feel
oppressed by the size and facelessness of the operations in which they
are involved. There is an indication of this in the shipyard workers'
attitude to their full-time officials, whom they saw not as 'brothers',
but as 'boss-men' from London. Some quite senior managers in big
firms feel they have no real authority, and many workers see their
union not as a liberating force but as one more restriction on their
freedom. There are a number of processes at work in smaller firms.
One of these is that not only are the managers in many of these firms
opposed to unions, but a number of workers choose to work in them
as a way of escaping from what they feel to be union restrictions. At
the same time, other workers who are less secure, including many
women and immigrant workers, realize their need for collective action
and are seeking to get union recognition. It is not collectives themselves
that are wrong, but the kind of collectives we have.

A third factor relates to one of the greatest social changes during this
century – the change of attitude to authority. Today people will not
accept orders from others without question. They are not prepared to
be pushed around by others, however good their cause may be.
Reactions to this kind of direction can be seen as mindless anarchy,
but more positively there is a necessary step towards maturity for
individuals and for society in which people take responsibility for their
own lives. If this is to happen, everyone must in some way be involved
in decisions that affect their lives. This demands a complete change in
the style of organizational behaviour in all institutions, and for industry
a change from an authoritative to a participatory style of industrial
relations. The foregoing considerations about perceptions of reality,
size of organizations and attitudes to authority have bearing on the
question of irrationality in group behaviour, and therefore on the
responses of the shipyard workers to the Polish orders. Rationality is,
however, a relative matter:

> Rationality in social action cannot be evaluated against any absolute
> standard. It is not a question of all or nothing, but rather of more
> or less. . . . In assessing the rationality of an action (or perhaps
> more appropriately, a series of actions), there are numerous dimen-
> sions which need to be considered.[58]

Among these is the dimension of the demonic which, as I have already indicated, is a factor in human behaviour which is intensified in collective behaviour. Irrationality in trade unionism is no stronger than in any other collective. The fact that people do not believe this is in itself due to some irrationality:

> Strikers are often credited with less rationality than is justified. 'People cannot allow deviation to threaten their picture of what their society is about' (Cohen, 1971:19). To admit the rationality of strikes is to accept that strikers have a case, that genuine deprivations underlie industrial conflict.
>
> Those who deprecate industrial conflict – employers, and in some cases, sections of workers also – have a powerful incentive to deny that it is rational or meaningful. Such obscurantism must of course be transcended by those whose aim is to *understand* reality.[59]

I want now to leave this particular example of collective behaviour in the shipyards in order to face basic issues it raises for any kind of collective.

In a complex technological society the quality of personal life depends increasingly on the quality of institutions. A concern with persons demands a concern with institutions.

Social goals can be pursued effectively only by collective action; and individual men and women can only discover their full humanity by relating in some way to institutions. We must have collectives.

The question we have to face is, how can collectives be developed that, (a) embody values and promote goals that are truly human; and (b) instead of crushing individuals, free them to become more truly themselves? If we accept that what is wrong with our collectives cannot be dealt with simply by 'reasonable people' coming to 'reasonable' agreements, and that our institutions cannot be healed by our efforts alone, we may frame the question in this way. Have we a gospel for institutions? Can our collective behaviour be redeemed? What hope is there for our collectives when we look at them in the light of belief in God and in his kingdom?

In order to grapple with this question, three points must be discussed. First, many positive responses are now being made, and in this sense secular agencies are doing the work of God by contributing to the creation of a more human world. Secondly, much more can be done and people need encouragement to do it. Thirdly, some things cannot now be changed and these we must help each other to endure, being alert to what God wants us to do, which is most certainly to trust him. In the final part of this chapter I briefly say something about these three points.

Among many positive things that are happening in collective behaviour is a movement towards greater participation. This movement is not confined to industry, but it is industry that is being most innovative in the matter, and it is from industry that I take my examples. One of the firms most committed to participation is ICI. Its present programme of change started in 1965, in an attempt to introduce a weekly staff agreement as a productivity agreement of a relatively limited sort. In 1975 a book was published telling the story of this process. Many things have, of course, happened since then, but the summary in this book is enough to start with:

> The obstacles (to the WSA agreement) encountered were immense and unexpected, and in trying to overcome them the company found itself engaged in the biggest programme of organizational change that had ever been carried out. More than that, it was a programme of total re-education in which thousands of managers and tens of thousands of shopfloor workers were required to think about their work from first principles, and by a process of shared learning to bring about improved attitudes and working practices. In order to do this they had to look in an open and constructive way at the nature of their jobs, at their relationships with the people in other organizations whose work affected those jobs, and at the management organization which made decisions about those jobs.[60]

The process was far from easy. There were enormous risks for the organization and for the individuals and groups concerned. The security of working within traditional role concepts had to be abandoned and there was a fear of losing control of the situation, and of losing one's own identity. The undoubted success of the venture, which has led to a new kind of sharing on the job and a transformation of the confrontational style of industrial relations, has not been achieved without personal casualties.

Once change has started it is impossible to know where it will end. The aim was to improve industrial relations, but the change has spilled over into the community. Now ICI personnel are giving support to similar changes in other institutions – education, social services, hospitals and other industries. A more disturbing 'spin-off' is that people have not stopped at questions about industrial relationships but are asking 'What is involved in being human?' and 'Should the whole of life be sacrificed to work?' Some have concluded that however much industrial relations may be improved, their own job will still be unsatisfying. Of these people, some have left the safety of their employment in order to discover themselves.

In other parts of the North East the meaning and needs of participation and power sharing are being tackled from different angles. There are, for instance, a number of common-ownership firms, in which all members share to some degree in financial and planning decisions. Among these firms I came across a common-ownership grocery business owned and run by a group of young working-class women, who, because they had small children, were not free to take up traditional employment. The idea had come from one of the women whose husband worked in a common-ownership firm. As they set up business, applied for loans and guarantees, they had been forced to question many of the traditional assumptions about the place that women should occupy in industry and business. They had also discovered untapped resources in themselves: for instance, the young woman who talked to me said how much she enjoyed doing the accounts and how she was studying the subject so that she could do the job better.

An example from the Midlands of how trade union patterns of behaviour are changing is afforded by the Lucas Aerospace shop stewards. As a result of reduced demand for the firm's products, the management put forward a plan that involved large-scale redundancies and plant closures. The shop stewards, instead of fighting a rearguard action that could only have ended in the acceptance of redundancy payments, produced an alternative plan. This plan was based on two principles: first, the belief that the combined skills of the workforce should not be dispersed; and second, that these skills should be used to make products that were socially useful. In their attempts to develop this alternative plan the shop stewards are co-operating with the Centre for Alternative Industrial and Technological Systems, whose aim is to develop different kinds of technology for different purposes.[61]

These examples show that changes are being made in the behaviour of collectives and in their values and goals, and that this is contributing to a more human world. The gospel in relation to these events consists first of all in the acknowledgment that what is being done is in line with the purposes of God. It is therefore an encouragement to continue these efforts. After this, and only after this, it is the church's task to help these ventures stay on course by providing a critique of what is being done in the light of its gospel. Pitfalls, dead-ends and idolatries endanger new movements as they do the old ones. Enthusiasm for participation, for instance, can lead to the imprisonment of the individual in a new and even more powerful group control than any of the old collectives. Concern with its internal life may make the group insensitive to outside realities and needs. The purpose of the group may become no more than the service of its own life and its members. Participation, instead of leading to collective action, may lead only to collective insulation against reality and against the call of God in that reality. At this point the gospel for institutions is a word of judgment.

Secondly, the gospel encourages us to believe that even more is possible, and gives a vision of what these possibilities are. There is evidence that the expectations of people in the North East have, by many disappointments and hardships, been reduced to an incredibly low level. Jesus' promise is that to faith 'more is possible' (John 4.12; Matthew 17.20). It is in response to faith that new possibilities are opened up. This is a reminder of Lord Hailsham's request to the churches in the North East to call on the people to pray for the success of his efforts. Concern for the health of our institutions and for those with responsibility in them should not be a mere formality, but should be at the heart of our prayer. In doing this our expectation should not be that God will miraculously change the course of events, but that he will make us more receptive of his redemptive presence with us all the time, and that we may receive from God encouragement and grace.

Thirdly, there are things that cannot now be changed. The North East region is at a disadvantage in what is now seen to be a world recession. Attempts to revivify the region and to get new jobs are meeting with increasing difficulties. During a period of comparative success there was a spirit of buoyancy, but now it seems that nothing really works. People are dispirited and cynical about institutions and those who run them, and collectives become defensive. The gospel in this situation is belief in God who through suffering brings new life. It is in the strength of this belief that we can sustain each other to continue to do the things that continue to need doing in and through collectives in a society for which there is no easy way forward.

If we are to speak of new life coming through suffering, we must be clear who is to suffer and who is to have new life. There is a way in which the suffering is endured by certain groups of people while others enjoy the new life. We are concerned to tackle the causes of this kind of injustice.

5 Man's inhumanity to man – the outcasts

What does it feel like to be a young unemployed person in one of the decaying villages of West Durham?

> 'Oh, it's boring. I used to play football or something like that, sit about the house and play me guitar, and I just got fed up. . . .' 'I had a job with a milk round. £7 odd. I got paid off. They give you work for six months and then you come off before you get more money, you know. They paid us off before we can get our award. . . .' 'I used to work at the steelworks, apprentice sheet metal. I got the sack. They said I wasn't brainy enough to do things like.'[62]

These are the actual words of three young men. Multiply that until you get 8991, which was the number of unemployed young people under the age of eighteen in January 1979 in North East England, and you will have some idea of the problem.[63]

This is not simply a matter of helping certain individuals to find jobs. It is a question of the structures and values of society. Our present society produces 'winners' and 'losers'. It creates a division between those who live in areas of growth and those in areas of decline, between those who are mobile and those without transport, the able and the disabled, the 'clever' and the 'not so clever', those who have and those who have not got a job. Disadvantages do not come singly, but together, so that although deprivation is to be found throughout the region, there are groups of people and whole areas suffering from multiple deprivation. In the ex-mining and old industrial areas and the inner cities the people least able to help themselves live together in the worst housing and the most depressing environment with the least adequate services. The sheer waste of the whole thing is staggering in its senselessness. Witton Park, which a few decades ago had a population of over 5000, now has only 500 inhabitants. The physical infrastructure of houses, public buildings and streets is crumbling. Not far away at Woodhouse Estate in Bishop Auckland, a new estate has been built to which the former inhabitants of Witton Park have been directed. The wasteland that is now Witton Park was once inhabited by a community in which over a number of years people who were not well equipped to stand on their own feet gave each other mutual support. Woodhouse Estate, on the other hand, is known as a problem estate. Thus both a place and a community have been destroyed.

This concentrated deprivation must be seen in the context of the fact that the Northern Region as a whole is well behind the national average in terms of all the main social indicators. The Northern Region Strategy Team statement on this is all the more telling in view of the fact that they are trying to paint an encouraging picture of the situation:

> Personal disposable incomes have remained some 12% below the national average since the early 1960s. The two most important causes of this differential are the lower demand for labour in the Region (resulting in lower pay for the same job, lower activity rates, and higher unemployment rates) and the structure of occupations . . . (a continuing preponderance of manual jobs both in manufacturing and service industries).[64]

A third cause mentioned later in the same report is the greater incidence of sickness, injury and disablement.

> The region has a fine record of housing achievement. . . . But . . . a large number (some 130,000 in 1976) of substandard houses remain, the majority in the privately rented sector. Most of the substandard housing is concentrated in riverside and inner urban areas and in isolated industrial communities, and in some cases they form a very high proportion (over one quarter) of the total housing stock.
>
> The standards of health – as measured by mortality rates, sickness, disability and industrial injury – in the North as a whole have long been appreciably lower than the national average, though there are significant variations within the region. The generally lower standards and the sub-regional variations reflect the historical pat-

tern of industrial development and the types of job available in particular places, the associated housing and environmental conditions, as well as dietary and smoking habits. . . .

Despite the Region's above average needs, the health service provision has been well below the national average. . . . The Region's share of national public expenditure on health is some 10% below its corresponding population share. . . . There are acute shortages of doctors and dentists in general practice in some of the older industrial areas of the North.[65]

The North has the lowest proportion of young people staying on at school beyond the age of sixteen, fewer people going on to higher education, higher teacher/pupil ratios and more obsolescent school buildings.

Because of the long-standing emphasis on manual jobs which do not demand high academic qualifications . . . perception on the part of young people, and indeed among the community at large, of the importance of education to long-run career development, is often poor, and is also an important cause of below-average educational attainment in the older industrial areas.[66]

The report divides those who suffer particular disadvantage into two groups – those who are potentially in the market for jobs, and those who are not and who therefore depend on welfare benefits for their income. The first group consists mainly of manual workers and notably the young manual worker. Their comment on the second group is,

With respect to the deprived outside the labour markets, a high proportion of the population of the North (some 20% above the national average) is in receipt of income supplements and disability and other society security payments . . . On the other hand local authorities in the North generally spend below the national average (an average of 7% less over the period 1969/70 – 1973/4) on the provision of social services for the disadvantaged.[67]

Many people find it hard to believe that with the welfare state there can possibly be any real poverty today. But a number of studies have been made which prove them wrong. It is true that the causes of poverty have shifted their order of importance, but even during the boom years of the 1960s there were more causes than might have been imagined:

	%
Inadequate wages and/or large families	40
Old age	33
Fatherless families	10
Sickness	10
Unemployment	7[68]

Today the percentage suffering deprivation through unemployment has vastly increased without decreasing the absolute numbers suffering from the other causes listed.

Standard diets have been worked out in order to prove that no one need go hungry.[69] These fail, however, to take account of the human factor and the accidents of existence. Supposing you have a sick relative to be visited in hospital, or someone needs a special diet? Supposing the children won't eat the six pounds of swedes that is included in the weekly diet?

> Mrs Coxon (whose husband is unemployed) had only £4 a week to spend on food for two adults and a child after spending on rent, lighting, bus fares for shopping and a clothing club. And out of this small amount she spent up to £2 a week on milk. 'You see my husband practically lives on that. In that pint mug he has that much, he has about eight mugs of tea a day. He has sugar and milk in that tea, and that really keeps him going, so if I cut down too much on that I'm really cutting down on the goodness.'[70]

It is easy to say that Mrs Coxon should have managed better, but those who say that don't live in a damp house which is always cold and dark with a husband who suffers from bronchitis.

This kind of deprivation is not caused by personal inadequacy but by the structures of society. The young men I quoted at the beginning of this chapter were 'losers' from the start. They had to lose in order that society could continue as it is. They were born into a certain stratum of society, about which there were certain assumptions about their future. These assumptions became explicit as soon as they went to school. For it is in the educational system that people are 'sorted out', labelled and moulded to suit the needs of society. I have already mentioned the low educational achievement of the North East. 'In the past, educational provision was shaped by employers' requirements for large masses of cheap unskilled labour power.'[71] With the cutback in the number of unskilled manual jobs, the low achievers leave school and go straight on to the dole. Naturally, parents are anxious that their children should be among those at the top who will get what jobs there are. Pressure to produce is put upon the school, by education authority, parents and employers (who in view of the increasing sophistication of technology now demand some guarantee of academic ability). It is the case of 'winner takes all, and the devil take the hindmost'. This goes not only for the pupils but for the teachers and the schools that fail to produce results.

In terms of preparation for life the system fails for most of the pupils. Yet the pressures are so great that it is extraordinarily difficult to make any change. One head teacher told me of his efforts to reshape the syllabus to include teaching about the nature of our present society.

He was meeting opposition not only from the parents, who felt that their children's competitive chances might be affected, but from many of the teachers. One cannot blame the teachers for the fact that many young people feel already when they leave school that they have been rejected by society as inadequate to its purposes. This sense of rejection is confirmed when they find that there is no job for them.

There are other deprived groups in the region. Many elderly people live in the old industrial areas (one vicar of an ex-mining parish told me that one third of his parishioners were pensioners). In these areas all the main services – health, social services and transport – are deteriorating. There is a lot of concern for the elderly, but much of it tends to underrate the contribution they can make to the community, often treating them as less than adult persons. I know one young social worker who fights a continuing battle for old people to be allowed to decide for themselves whether they stay in their own homes or go into care.

There are many women who are bringing up families on their own or caring for elderly relations. There are men who in early middle age have been made redundant and will never work again. I have, however, focussed on the young unemployed because it is their situation that sums up the waste and tragedy of society's rejection of so many of its members.

What kind of life can these young people have: and how much do we care? Many people do not see the seriousness of the problem, for they are shielded by the fact that they do not live in the main areas of unemployment.

The predominant feeling of those who do live alongside the unemployed in the inner urban areas is one of anger. Vandalism and destruction depresses already run-down neighbourhoods. The fact is driven home to them that the unemployed are an integral part of their society, and that they will inevitably drag others down with them. The one-ness of humanity is recognized as a painful and unpalatable truth.

Other people for a variety of reasons try to do something to help – creating jobs, providing leisure activities and setting up training schemes. Short-term and palliative though many of these things are, they can bring a ray of hope to an otherwise hopeless situation, and should not be despised. In these ventures some important new discoveries are made. People who were 'at the bottom of the class' discover that they have unexpected skills. Others who had been 'wage slaves' begin to open up as more complete human beings. Among those initiating the more imaginative schemes are people who believe that unemployment presents an opportunity to pioneer new life styles. They suggest that people 'content with unemployment benefits, leaving the few jobs available to those who are desperate', perform a social

service.[72] Unemployment, they say, should be welcomed as an opportunity to explore alternative ways of life.

But the fact that those who accept this philosophy reject traditional
offers of work in order to continue their new way of life could lead to
further divisions, rather than to the creation of a just society in which
everyone has a place. However liberating this approach may be for
individuals, it does nothing to tackle what to me is the central question
about work, how it can fulfil its proper social function. To answer this
question we need to explore work rather than unemployment, and I
shall say more about this later. There is, of course, a difference between
work and employment. It is employment, the work for which we are
paid, that gears us into the purposes of society, and it is the justice of
those purposes that has to be questioned.

The Old Testament is full of hopes for justice and the need to create
it:

> Here is my servant, whom I strengthen –
> the one I have chosen, with whom I am pleased.
> I have filled him with my spirit,
> and he will bring justice to every nation . . .
> . . . He will bring lasting justice to all (Isaiah 42. 1,3).

It is the same cry for justice that is echoed by oppressed people
throughout the world today:

> I do not want my country to be divided.
> There is room for us all in this land of mine.[73]

Jesus sought out the poor and the oppressed. He did not set up an
alternative society for them, but challenged the rich to accept that the
outcast, too, belongs and has rights in the same society, 'since he also
is a son of Abraham' (Luke 19.9).

It was the burden of humanity as a whole, not a section of humanity,
with which Jesus identified himself. If we are to share in his purposes
we have to break through the barriers that isolate us from our fellow
human beings and set ourselves to learn what is happening to people
in our society. This is a long process, in which mere good-will and
enthusiasm are not enough.

An example of the kind of thing that has to be done is provided by
a project among young unemployed manual workers in Manchester.[74]
This project began in 1974 and is still in process. Recognizing that it is
these young people who are most at risk, a team of workers is following
up certain groups through their last years at school and in the years
immediately after leaving school. They collect together the key factors
about the nature and causes of the problem of the young manual
worker, and provide a check-list that can act as a hard test for those
who say they care about the problem, but who continue to make the

same basic mistakes. It is those who are involved in the structures of society who must make the changes, so the team gives valuable information and support to teachers, employers and to trade unionists in the setting of goals and objectives in their negotiations. This project is not simply concerned with finding jobs, but with getting to grips with the forces that are thrusting these young people out to the margins of society. It is not the young people who are the problem, but the nature of our society.

The way in which our society operates pushes certain people to the margins,

> in the sense that they are left on the edge of the main activities of the society. . . . For example the old, those on fixed pensions, those who are handicapped by a physical disability, by being members of a one-parent family or by belonging to a so-called 'coloured' race, are often driven below the poverty line. Thus poverty is manufactured, for groups such as these, by the dynamics of the operations of society.[75]

The Old Testament does not only contain messages of hope, but prophetic denunciations in which the judgment of God upon society is pronounced.

> The oppression and neglect of the poor throws into relief those features of society which are contrary to the will of God for his covenant people. . . . It is by paying attention to those whom our society leaves poor or makes poor that we can be alerted to those features of our social and political life which are under the judgment of God. That is to say that it is the condition and treatment of the poor which point most sharply to those practices of ours which contradict the gospel of love, according to which all human beings are as human as all others so that no human being can be fully human without all being fully human. . . . Hence the poor and the marginals are not primarily objects of charity and compassion but rather subjects and agents of the judgment of God and pointing to the ways of the kingdom.[76]

I have spoken of some of the realities of life in North East England – of technological change, politics, collective action and deprivation. The main human questions that have been discussed are common to people in any part of our industrial society. But while holding on to the fact that this is illustrative, I want also to say that the North East has an importance in itself. There is a uniqueness about every place as there is about every person. Each has its own potential and its own history. When life is seen in the light of faith in God and of his purposes, each part of the world has a significance for every other part of the world. In addition, therefore, to speaking about what is common to all, we should ask: 'In what way is North East England significant for the rest of Britain and for the rest of the world?' I believe there are qualities in the people and environment of the North East that should not be treated with nostalgic humour but should be developed with confidence.

My main purpose in describing life in this part of the world has been to stress the fact that it is only by giving attention to life as it is experienced by particular people in particular places, that we come to know the reality of God: 'Sharing in Christ we stand at once in both the reality of God and the reality of the world'.[77]

My reflection on life in North East England started from the questions: 'Can we say that God is coming to people in the changes that are taking place?' 'How can we see in what is happening God's offer of greater humanity?' 'Can Christian faith mean anything to people who live in the stresses of life today?' I find now that the stresses are even greater than I had imagined. At the same time, I am forced to enter more deeply into a life of faith. By sharing in the reality of Christ we are able to accept the tensions of life, not as a final contradiction of our humanity or as a sign of God's indifference to us, but as a way in which we receive our humanity from a God who comes into life and suffers its tensions with us.

III Tensions and Dreams

'My God, my God, why hast thou forsaken me?' (*Mark 15.34*)

1 What we now see about the tensions

The questions that started me on my search, rather than being answered, have been intensified. My original concern was a longing to see people who were being crushed by life responding to God's offer of life. I was aware that in a fundamental way the message of the church was not getting to grips with the realities of life and I wanted to do something to overcome this gap.

My own belief that this is God's world, and that in Jesus God has committed himself without reserve to humanity, makes me look for certain things in life. I hope and expect to find signs of God's life-giving activity in the world, and my approach is therefore basically optimistic. What I find, however, is that although things are not totally negative, the threat to human life is so great that I am forced to think again about my faith. The more completely I commit myself to the people I am working among, the more serious do the pressures upon them appear to be. The tension between the realities of living and God's offer of life is not diminished but increased. The pressures of life threaten our humanity, while the pressures of God offer humanity. Under this pressure I have discovered that the struggle to be human is part of the struggle to know and respond to God. As I share in what is happening in North East England, I realize that my faith and the way I understand it must be deepened if it is to make any contact with the deepest needs of people in today's world. My human pilgrimage and my theological pilgrimage are one and the same.

Man is struggling between, on the one hand, the pressures of life which threaten his humanity and, on the other hand, the urge to fulfil his humanity. How are we to understand this tension in a human and a godly way? In what sense could faith in God give hope to those who are caught in these tensions? Before attempting to answer this question, I must sum up what we have learnt so far about the nature of these tensions.

In our technological society, fundamental contradictions have emerged between the possibilities and what has been made of those possibilities. Technology opened up hopes that man might control nature for human purposes, taking the drudgery out of labour, bringing water to dry ground, supplying the basic needs of all and lifting men out of the realm of necessity into the realm of freedom. But today many people feel that man has lost control and that technology, far from freeing man, is menacing and enslaving him. 'The world and its inhabitants are threatened by the way in which science and technology are being used.'[1] The quality of life and even human survival is threatened by population explosion, the squandering of non-renewable resources, and environmental deterioration.

There are people who see this as a reason for rejecting technology and returning to a pre-industrial state. But they forget that in many parts of the world man is still enslaved to nature, against which he has to struggle for survival. Technology is an expression of man's adulthood. It represents man's attempt to take responsibility for his own life and for the world. The fact that it has led to the exchange of one servitude for another is no reason for retreat but rather an incentive to continue to struggle – forward.

Some people would like to hold things where they are. They call for a halt and suggest a no-growth, low technology policy. But those who take this stance are from the rich countries and those whose personal background makes it possible for them to contemplate their own future without fear. To people in under-developed countries and those in our own country who are living from hand to mouth this appears as just one more attempt to keep them down.

It is possible for individuals in affluent societies to drop out of the main activities of their society, or to attack isolated symptoms of its disorder, but people with responsibility aware of the potential chaos of changing direction redouble their efforts to keep things going in their present direction. There is on all sides a reluctance to face the stark reality of the situation.

Our attitude to technology and how we feel we should treat the earth and its resources depends on our understanding of the relationships of nature, man and God. The biblical view that man is part of God's creation conflicts with the way in which people experience themselves today:

> Modern man does not experience himself as a part of nature but as an outside force destined to dominate and conquer it. He even talks of a battle with nature, forgetting that, if he won the battle, he would find himself on the losing side.[2]

Christians have not been consistent in their attitude to material things, and in their sweeping condemnation of 'materialism' have often given the impression that they had nothing to say about man's treatment of the resources of the world. In fact the Christian's attitude to the material world is fundamental to his faith. The world is the self-expression of God, and men are in the image of God. God makes himself known to us and we must respond to him in and through what is physical and material. Matter and spirit cannot be separated. The way we treat the material world is a spiritual concern. It has been said that it is possible to see bread for oneself in solely material terms, but bread for one's brother is a decidedly spiritual affair. The problem does not lie in the fact that man is over-concerned with material things, but in the values he brings to this concern. The goals of our society are set in such a way as to suggest that the whole aim of life is the production and consumption of goods, and that the success of society is to be measured solely by its trading figures and its Gross National Product.

If people really knew how unequal our society is, they would be more angry than they are. But there is enough evidence to make many people feel that they deserve more than they actually get. Small wonder that those who know what deprivation is and who for many reasons feel insecure and under-valued as people, compete for their share of the national cake, for guarantees of security and for the acquisition of material possessions to the exclusion of less tangible goods. Simply to condemn this as 'materialism' is a failure to understand the pressures society exercises upon people and to miss the core of what is wrong.

Another tension is caused by the sheer size of today's organizations. Technological society has accentuated and intensified the extent of social cohesion so that the happiness of any individual depends increasingly on a just organization of the political and economic mechanisms by which the common life of man is ordered. But these mechanisms have in fact become a further means of oppression. Many people do not know who their bosses are, or who makes the decisions that affect their lives. They feel they are at the mercy of bureaucrats who are neither willing nor capable of any real appraisal of the situation. Any sense that a community or individual has responsibility for its own life atrophies, and there is a sense of powerlessness, a cynicism about institutions and a retreat into private life.

Yet there is a potential to be realized in the fact that men can relate to each other in large complex organizations. No doubt we should question some of the assumptions that lead people to suppose that bigger is in every case better, but those who wish to return to small self-regulating communities are blind to the cultural benefits open to them as a result of world-wide communication. Mankind is interdependent, and God's promise is for the unity of mankind. It seems that it is God who is pressing upon us to find more creative ways of realizing our one-ness so that the individual, instead of being crushed, can be more truly himself.

Change may be exhilarating, but when it threatens society's basic philosophy of life it is traumatic. A basic assumption that is put in question by today's technology is the dominant place of work in life. There are people who speak nostalgically about the decline of the 'work ethic', but when one reads about work in the 'good old days' one wonders what connection there was between work and ethics. Writing in 1912, the secretary of the Cleveland Association of Blastfurnacemen had this to say about work as it was in that area until 1897:

> The furnaceman only wore his 'best' suit on the occasion of a wedding or a funeral; for his working hours were eleven on days and thirteen on nights on alternate weeks throughout the year, with a 24-hour turn each fortnight which left little time, or inclination, to change from working clothes. The brutalizing nature of the work made itself expressly felt at that heart-breaking moment when one struggled to one's feet after the meal break on the long turn to commence the second half of the shift's work.[3]

Now, with one and a half million people unemployed and the likelihood that this will increase, circumstances are forcing us to ask questions about the place of work in life. To talk about the 'leisure society' leaves many questions unanswered. There is an immense amount of work to be done if human existence is to continue, and much more if life is to be fulfilling. God himself is believed to be continuously at work in creation, and we speak of Christ's work of redemption in which man is called to share. Work is by the nature of things an essential part of life. What we must ask is: What work needs to be done in our society? How can technology be used in order to release human beings for those tasks that require human imagination, ingenuity and skills? How can technology be used so that men can be free to develop in other ways? How can we learn to appreciate other aspects of life and get work into proper perspective? How can the work that needs to be done be shared fairly between all members of our society, so that we do not have some people working excessively and others left idle? What connection should there be between work and reward? How can everyone share in the planning and organization of their work? How can we make the transition from our present understandings and practices into something different, without a complete breakdown in the organization of society?

Conflict arises from the very nature of technological society with its differentiation of people by skills and classes, all with conflicting interests, and from its competitive philosophy which sees life in terms of 'winners' and 'losers'. The gospel speaks of reconciliation, but too often this has been a matter of upholding the interests of the powerful against the less powerful in the name of law and order. The response of the 'losers' has understandably been resentment and social aliena-tion. On the world scale, facility of communications has increased the possibility of conflict. The poorer nations strive to get their share of the world's wealth and to attain national and racial recognition.

To face the causes of conflict and to make decisions about how to handle it takes courage. People fear the unpredictable results of any initiatives they may take – the setting up of precedents and the opening of the flood-gates to change. So they prefer to 'buy off' those who have power to oppose the *status quo*. In view of what seems to be the inevitability of events, it is easier to believe in fate than in a world that has meaning in which man can make real choices about the future.

These are the kind of tensions I have tried to identify in my look at life in North East England. It is clear that changes are happening that have a far-reaching consequence for the future. The issue is being decided where the struggle is actually going on – among people, especially among those who are at the points in life where the pressure is greatest and where humanity is most threatened.

Many positive things are happening, which prove the resilience and inventiveness of man. It is often when things look most desperate that man asserts his true nature and projects a different future, showing that, far from being a 'cog' or a slave, he can rise above physical, cultural and psychological threats and affirm truly human values. The oppressed negroes of America dreamed of and suffered for a world in which 'people everywhere can have three meals a day for their bodies, education and culture for their minds, dignity, equality and freedom for their spirits' (Martin Luther King). The poverty-stricken labourers who came to the expanding North East of England, far from being crushed by their harsh conditions, asserted their dignity as men by envisioning a new society in which there would be justice for all, and they worked collectively to create it.

But dreams do not retain the same quality when they begin to be put into practice. The working man's dream of a new society is now buried under the economics of local administration, and the struggle for justice is less evident than the struggle to stay in power. In the face of many frustrations, men's sense of their dignity as free persons turns into bloody-mindedness. The revolutionary youth becomes the hard-faced industrialist. The idealistic politician becomes the cynical and self-seeking councillor. The hopes and plans of the 1960s become the tired slogans of the 1970s. Institutions which grew out of a concern for people serve only themselves and their more influential supporters. There is a circularity about it all – so that the brave new movements of yesterday are the main hindrances to today's advance. Men really are trapped.

A division of opinion appears between those who blandly maintain a confidence in human nature and those who have discovered that the facts cannot support such optimism. Rather than make a choice between optimism and pessimism, however, we should accept the fact that tension exists and that it is a positive and creative factor in society. Tension is, moreover, basic to the gospel. The gospel is about crucifixion and resurrection, about the tension between what life is and what in God's grace life can be. The church should be with the people who are caught in the tensions of life. This is where for good or ill the dynamics of change are at work, and this is where the activity of God is to be discerned. It is the tension itself that is creative, and it is God whose pressure we experience, urging us towards the fulfilment of our humanity.

But the church, too, is trapped. In spite of the different historical relationships of the denominations to society, all the churches today face the same problem. Religion of whatever kind is seen to belong to the fringes of life. It appears as a private matter for the individual, with nothing to contribute to the main questions of family or society.

Many people in the churches are painfully aware of this separation of faith from that which most affects our lives, but they lack the theological understanding and the skills that are needed for permeating a secular society. The models of the church's relationship to society that most readily come to mind are inappropriate, for they presuppose a different situation. They conceive of a church that either has a more powerful voice or takes up an isolated position in society. The creative tension of the gospel is lost, and responses veer from the over-optimistic, in which nothing but good is seen in technological development, to the pessimistic, in which everything new is rejected. In these responses, the prophetic tension of the gospel is lost and people are left struggling without help and without hope.

I find myself caught in this tension between life as it is being experienced and faith as I understand it. This tension increases as I enter more deeply into what is happening in the world. The more one is exposed to what is happening in the world, the less possible it is to accept faith in an unquestioning way. I find myself saying, 'I believe, but how can I believe?'

But it is when one is at the point of despair that the realities of faith are revealed. God is not a 'God of the gaps' simply waiting to step in when men's powers fail, nor does he come to us in those luxurious moments when we are sufficiently disengaged from life to indulge in fantasies. He is known in the midst of life, when tension is most acute. It is only possible to catch glimpses of what this means, but it is out of this tension that I must speak, however inadequately, of faith and of hope.

2 *The heart of the matter*

(i) *Dreams of a better world*

Hope is to be found within the tensions in the fact that, in spite of the failure of dreams, men continue to dream of a better world. There is a choice of dreams. Different situations stimulate different dreams. The dreams of making a fortune by one's own enterprise which inspired men in the time of Britain's industrial expansion have been replaced in our time by dreams of winning the pools or, more modestly, of acquiring a colour TV or a new car. But these are not the only dreams. Some people continue to hope for a return to full employment and a recovery of our former industrial success, based now on diversification and an increase in small firms and service industries. Some picture their own part and power in bringing about this recovery. At the same time, others dream of a world in which work will no longer dominate life. Some men seek to humanize the present system, by introducing more participative styles of work, breaking down the impersonality of large firms into manageable units of co-operation. Others have set up their own small businesses. Such enterprises are inspired by a variety of dreams – to use one's skills to the full, to have control of one's work, to make money for oneself rather than for someone else – or to try out new ways of working, which may vary in style from the ultra-authoritarian to the totally participative.

Some people believe that high technology applied without discrimination is destructive of human well-being. They look for a changed attitude towards technology in which there is the recognition that there are choices concerning which technology to use in each situation. Newcastle University has become a centre of discussion about appropriate technology, and within this discussion the idea that 'small is beautiful' plays a major part.

Disillusionment with industrial society has led some people to reject the goals of affluence in search of more human values. They have dropped out of the 'rat-race' in order to find ways of deepening their experience of personal relationships in encounter groups or some form of communal life. Others seek 'the good life' in a rural setting, even if this involves leading the double life of the commuter. Others seek religious experience by an exploration of Eastern religions.

Among the young are the flower children, the Jesus people, the punks and the rockers. There are also those who feel oppressed by the needs of the poorer nations. During my time in Hong Kong I met young people from Europe and the United States who, rather than follow traditional paths to success, were espousing the cause of the poor in Asia. They are among those who dream of food, justice and peace for all men. There are others who commit themselves to work among deprived people in this country, aiming in various community work projects to enable the voiceless to speak for themselves and the powerless to control their own lives. Others find that Marxism gives them a more capacious view of world history, in the light of which they commit themselves to the overthrow of the present system. At the same time, others dream of the recovery of lost values of national discipline, solidarity and greatness.

Not all dreams are good. Some dreams are best described as nightmares, representing the suppressed fears of what may lie ahead – the completely automated world of 1984, the post-nuclear wilderness or the over-populated world with standing-room only. Dreams perform different functions. They may provide an escape from life or an encouragement to make something of life. Fantasy withdraws energy from living, but when men are committed to dreams that illuminate reality, they receive power to transform reality – to go beyond what now is and to realize new possibilities.

What is important, in our philistine society, a society in which dreams are out of court, and in which everything seems to go on without any basic questioning of values, is that people still continue to dream. If people ever ceased to dream, we would truly be trapped in the present. Dreams are needed to project alternatives and to keep alive hope and striving by which we can create a different future. The fact that there are different kinds of dreams means that there are choices to be made. The dreams we accept as our own represent the values we hold and the way we understand and are prepared to relate to reality. Dreams are essential, but they are not all of the same worth. We need some criteria that will help us to distinguish between the fantasies that cut us off from reality and the dreams that illuminate reality and help us to live more fully.

In fantasies we picture an idealized self in an idealized world. Unconscious desires well-up in 'fairy story' pictures in which the dreamer may appear as a 'giant-killer' earning the admiration and gratitude of all, or in imagination he receives the gratification of all his wants. This is an avoidance of everything unpleasant and resistant in life and a refusal to face ourselves as we are. In its extreme form it removes the dreamer from reality into a personal cocoon which cuts him off from others and blinds him to the truth about himself.

There are many ways in which dreams can fail to match reality. The dreams of 'living happily ever after' as a result of winning the pools does, in the event of a win, touch down on reality. Then aspects of reality that were not reckoned with in the dream make themselves felt. Personal relationships may be dislocated through other people's envy or embarrassment, and through the winner's changed life-style. It may be discovered too late that money alone does not bring human happiness.

The dream of bringing jobs to the North East also has to be checked against reality. It is possible, though improbable, that full employment can be brought to the region. It seems right that a lot of energy should be spent on this objective, but the danger arises when the need for work in the North East is the only reality that is taken into account. Other regions see a different reality that is constituted by their needs, so that one region's gain may mean loss to others. Even, however, if full employment were achieved, in the light of the possible effect of micro-processing, it can only be a short term solution. Of course we must deal with short-term needs, but it would be wrong if we did not at the same time begin to tackle longer-term issues. The time to cut overtime working and to devise ways of work-sharing is not tomorrow but today. The time to consider what kind of jobs are essential to human well-being, how people can find satisfaction in doing the jobs that really need to be done, and how life can be fulfilling in a world that is not dominated by work, is now. These are realities which, in addition to the immediate need for jobs, should be faced now.

Of course no human beings are capable of comprehending the whole of reality, nor can we see into the future. But we can be alert to a reality that is changing, and we must adapt our dreams accordingly. If dreams are not adaptable they become obsessions. If we do not shape our dreams to reality, we end up by trying to force reality to fit our dreams.

This leads to the question of what kind of commitment we should have to dreams. Dreams should act as spurs to hope and action. They should embody values such as justice, love and peace, that contribute to human fulfilment. These values are pictured variously according to the pressures of the immediate situation, so that justice may appear in a picture of the unity of working men, the beauty of black people, or the greater participation of women in society. The particular picture will change with circumstances, but the basic values will remain the same. What easily happens is that people become more attached to the picture than to what it represents. This makes for inflexibility, so that instead of facing present needs, people go on fighting yesterday's battles. It is not a matter of a simple 'either/or' situation. We need both the picture and the value. There must be a real commitment to immediate concrete tasks if anything is to be done at all, but we must always be aware that what we achieve is always a provisional not a final solution. The sacrifices we are prepared to make for immediate ends will be greater, not less, if we see that these are not ultimate ends, but that they have value in relation to an ultimate end. We need this understanding of reality if we are to be saved from the kind of fanaticism – idolatry – which can destroy both ourselves and others.

Hitler provides a warning of the terrible power of fanaticism. One interpretation of the complex workings of his mind suggests that he began with the reality of unemployment and the dream of economic revival in Germany. In his failure to achieve a stable economy he embarked on the conquest of much of the rest of Europe. In pursuing this dream of German greatness he saw himself as a saviour, and gradually lost touch with reality so that from obsession he passed to madness.

Because dreams have power to change things for good or ill, we must ask questions about our dreams; and we must be clear about the reality-criteria against which we should judge them. Do they bring us into touch with the realities of the world, of people and of ourselves? Do they embody values that will lead to human fulfilment? Do they allow us to take account of reality in its entirety, so that we do not exclude whole aspects of it, and so that we are able to respond to new revelations of reality? Do they give us encouragement to hope and work for their realization, and in doing this to discover not only that we are touching reality, but that reality is touching us? Are we sufficiently committed to our dreams to die for their specific embodiments, but not to despair if the particular embodiments we espouse seem to end in failure?

The Christian believes that God is ultimate reality and that everything else depends on him. Dreams in this context have a foundation in the reality of God and his promises, and will therefore be fulfilled. Dreams in the Bible help us to grasp this hope.

(ii) Dreams in the Bible

Many of the typical dreams of men are found in the Bible. Here are dreams of nomadic peoples for land of their own – land that will not only provide basic needs but will give a super-abundance of all that is good. This hope is projected in a picture of a 'land flowing with milk and honey'. Here also are the dreams of those who live in fear of attack or rebellion. Their hopes for security are focussed in pictures of men and women living to ripe old age under their own vine or fig tree.

These are not mere fantasies, for they are based on an understanding of life which sees God as the ultimate reality, and on the belief that these dreams represent promises which God will surely fulfil.

The pictures in which the hopes are focussed give an important clue to the way dreams function. What was pictured was never fully exhausted by what came to pass. That is not to say that what came to pass fell short of what had been hoped for, but rather that what came to pass opened up new possibilities which still lay ahead. Pictures like the 'land flowing with milk and honey' were not literal descriptions but symbols which, in this case, pointed to God's graciousness in nature. This picture and that, for instance, of men and women living to old age in a settled community, always remained open to change and development in the light of new events. They had the effect, therefore, of stimulating vigorous action in the belief that the future held more than had yet been realized:

> time and again Israel experiences her history as a new intervention on the part of God. He revives ancient promises, but fulfils them in a way completely different from that which an earlier generation expected. Or he may refocus them so that they point to a fulfilment still awaited in the future. Each time, there is also a certain process of selection: statements once central become peripheral or vanish entirely; others, which were hardly noticed, come to occupy centre stage.[4]

The biblical symbols stand for values which are to be established in concrete ways, but are never exhausted by their particular embodiments. They remain provocative, stirring the imagination and inviting each generation to strive in their particular situation for new embodiments of these values.

One of the most persistent dreams of Israel was that of the kingdom of God. The idea of the kingdom of God took shape in the experience of Israel around the idealization of the reign of King David. As Israel looked back on her history. it seemed that David's reign had been the high-point of their national unity, prosperity and greatness. In time the idea of the kingdom became the focus for everything that was good, symbolizing a future that would include all that they longed for, a future which the Jews believed God himself would bring into being.

Dreams easily run into the danger of getting out of touch with reality. It was the prophets who confronted Israel with the question, 'Is what you want and hope for the same as what God wants and will bring about?' They made it clear that any hopes for the kingdom of God must tally with the character of God, and that in fact Israel's behaviour was in flagrant contrast with God's character of justice and compassion. Those who would not face this truth were living in an unreal world from which they would be rudely awakened.

The question of the relation of dreams to reality became even more acute as national fortunes declined. The Jews found it increasingly difficult to see any basis in reality for the hopes they held. Those who had taken the prophets' words to heart and had tried to live up to God's calling were dismayed because they still saw no evidence that God was doing anything to make his kingdom a reality:

> These are the wicked; always at ease, they increase in riches. All in vain have I kept my heart clean and washed my hands in innocence, For all day long I have been stricken, and chastened every morning (Psalm 73.12–14).

The question that now had to be faced was whether an understanding of life which saw God as the ultimate reality was in fact true. The awful possibility had to be faced that God might be no more than

wishful thinking – a projection of man's own sense of need and not a
reality at all. If he were real, why did he not act?

Why dost thou hold back thy hand,
Why dost thou keep thy right hand in thy bosom? (Psalm 74.11).

It is in the context of this hoping and questioning that the significance
of Jesus' life can be seen. Christian faith springs from the conviction
that God has acted in Jesus, that in Jesus God has fulfilled his promises,
and that what he has begun in Jesus will be completed. The whole of
Jesus' life, culminating in his death and resurrection, are evidence of
this. To put one's faith in God and to hope in him is therefore a matter
not of wishful thinking, but of committing oneself to what is most real.

To speak of evidence should not suggest that in Jesus there was
some obvious proof of God's presence and power. Reactions to Jesus
varied. He was ignored and rejected by those in power, and though
at first he attracted a large popular following, only a few people continued with him when things got difficult. Even they were bewildered,
and it was only after Jesus' resurrection that they were convinced that
God was in Christ:

> There can be guarantees – more or less – for the durability of a new
> steel bridge, for the truth of a mathematical proposition, for the
> washability of a fabric. But there can never be guarantees for the
> things that really matter in human life – for the beauty of a picture,
> for the enthralling power of a sonata, for a woman's true love . . .
> How could it be any different with God?[5]

The writers of the gospels do not speak of proof, but point to what
Jesus was and what he did as signs of the reality and presence of the
kingdom in their midst. Jesus himself emphatically refused to give any
kind of proof that might save men from thinking things through for
themselves. Instead, he asked them to use their eyes and senses in
order to identify those signs, to assess the values he stood for, the
truth of their situation, the powers that were at work, to weigh this up
for themselves and to make their own decision about what they would
commit themselves to. This is what he asks of us.

(iii) Transformation of our dreams – a question of values
'Are we hoping for the right things?' is the first question we have to
answer. Are our efforts for the regeneration of the North East in line
with God's purpose. Is God as concerned as we are with the plight of
the unemployed? Or does our frustration come from the fact that we
are heading in the wrong direction?

It is blasphemous to suggest that God does not care as much as we
do for human life. Jesus was deeply concerned with the hopes and
needs of men, and he picked up the most urgent dreams of his own

day when he made the kingdom of God the central theme of his message. He showed that he was on the side of men by taking their longings seriously; but, far from accepting their expectations as they stood, he transformed them. In the things that are now happening God may be putting questions to us and asking for a transformation of our dreams.

The kingdom of God is not an individual dream but that of a society. Our dreams for the North East are also dreams for a new society. But we should not therefore equate our dreams with the kingdom or see this likeness as a guarantee of their fulfilment. We must look again at the nature of our expectations. Who, for instance, is to benefit from the future we project? Do our dreams promise something for everyone in the North East? Do they go beyond this region to include our suppliers and 'competitors' in other countries? Are our dreams, like the kingdom of God, large enough to include all people?

In the many pressures constraining us to realize ourselves in a wider framework of relationships, we must try to understand what God is saying to us. The fishing community, for instance, is having to reckon not only with pressures from Iceland but from our membership of the European Economic Community; and industry increasingly has to be concerned with the international scene. The question of our wider relationships is at its sharpest in the issue of immigration and of Britain's development as a multi-racial society. Although North East-erners may feel that, with comparatively few immigrants coming to the region, they can ignore the question, it does in fact have implica-tions for us all. The point becomes clear in a report of a British Council of Churches' working party on the subject:

> The basic issue is not a problem caused by black people: the basic issue concerns the nature of British society as a whole, and features of that society which have been there long before the recent phase of black immigration . . . In certain very revealing ways, they (the black communities) are holding a mirror to British society, in which members of that society can see themselves. The urgent question, therefore, is not 'What shall we do about the black problem?' but 'What is British society like? and 'What sort of Britain do we want?'[6]

A document submitted to the working party spells the problem out in this way:

> Britain saw black immigrants as little more than second-class pro-duction factors . . . it was felt that it was quite acceptable to consign them to urban areas already disintegrating with decay, and rum-bling with the conflict generated by dispossessed groups aspiring towards a more humane way of life. Black people were lumped lock, stock and barrel with the white working class. The society then turned round and blamed the blacks for the urban decay and

for the results of social inaction and unplanned urban growth on the part of successive governments.[7]

The report comes to the conclusion that though racist attitudes are an issue, 'the main problem is the pyramid shape of British society itself. This condemns large numbers of people to a permanent position of disadvantage. These form the base of the pyramid . . . and although the privileged minorities depend so greatly on the rest for their privileges, the large number who constitute the broad base of society are always made to feel "outsiders" – and it is at the base of the social pyramid that the overwhelming majority of black immigrants have found themselves'.[8]

Enoch Powell and the National Front, in their attacks on black communities and government immigration policies, are picking up real problems. Tensions are being caused by the meeting of different cultures and ways of life, by pressures on scarce resources such as housing and jobs, and by the further depression of the lives of those who are already disadvantaged and struggling to keep their heads above water. We should not underestimate the difficulties or ignore the fact that the burden is being pushed on to those least able to bear it. But if we are to discover what God is saying to us in these events, there is more to be added. On this question, too, we may learn something from God's dealings with Israel.

The question of her relationship with other nations was critical for Israel. Her law commanded love of the stranger in her midst, for she was to remember the times when her people had known what it was to be aliens in a foreign country (Deuteronomy 10.19). It is possible for the aspiring working class of Britain to see immigrants as a threat to their own hard-won gains, but equally they may, on the basis of their own experience of deprivation, acknowledge a solidarity with all depressed groups and help to lift them up. Which attitude we take is a matter for us to decide.

The question took a different form in the later history of Israel. As she experienced God's power in the events of her life, she came to see that there could be no other God like this – and that God must be God of the whole world and of all people. This produced a tension between her pride in being the one nation whom God had chosen as his own and the potential claim of other nations. In this tension she was being urged to change her dreams of national exclusiveness to hopes that included all mankind. It was Israel's determination to exclude other nations from the kingdom that led to her own exclusion and to her refusal to accept the open invitation that God made to all mankind in Jesus Christ. The society that Jesus stood for – the kingdom of God – is for all men. The openness of Jesus' invitation appeared as a threat to many, but in fact what Jesus was offering was fullness of life. We, too, may see a multi-racial society as a threat, but it may be that rather than being a threat, it is an opportunity in which God is offering us a fuller life.

A second range of questions about our dreams comes from the fact that the kingdom of God promises the fulfilment of all needs. A transformation of our values is needed if our material and spiritual needs are to be properly integrated. Jesus had compassion on the hungry and the sick, and his acts of feeding and healing were taken to be signs of the presence of the kingdom. Men need food, jobs, fair wages, housing and hospitals, though we know that this is not all that they need. The question is not, 'What in addition to material things do men need?', but, 'How can material things be used in order to fulfil all man's needs and express his full humanity?'

The kingdom is about the fulfilment of the world's potential and the realization of man's full humanity. To say that we are concerned with people therefore puts us on the side of God and in line with his concerns. But it is possible that in meeting some needs we may deny others. It is, for instance, possible to care for old people in ways that lead to the severance of family relationships and the denial of their dignity as persons. All the time we have to reckon with the way a variety of needs are intertwined and work to a scale of priorities and values in relation to them. In a unique way we see in Jesus' temptation the kind of tension this involves.

A third question concerns the ways in which we try to realize our dreams. Throughout his life, Jesus rejected many of the ways in which people sought to fulfil their dreams. There were revolutionary groups in Jesus' day, but he did not join them. Nor did he make common cause with the political establishment, or the 'law and order' party. There were all kinds of religious groups, but Jesus did not fit into any of them. He stood outside every party and group. His own approach was more radical than any of them, for unlike them he got to the heart of man and so to the heart of the matter. Man's humanity cannot be realized by means that are less than human, and neither violent revolution nor religious blackmail will in themselves improve the quality of human life. Those who are working among oppressed people today are reminding us of this truth as they point out that simply to put power into the hands of a different group only produces 'more of the same'. A radical change in the quality of human life demands a change of consciousness and a change of values.[9]

The fact that Jesus did not fit into any political party should not suggest that Christians should not be involved in politics. It is essential that some Christians work within the party political system, and that the church enables them from their faith to bring to politics a critique of society that is not negative, but conveys a sense of freedom and hope for all. If God is ultimately concerned with man's life, his well-being must be worked for in specific ways, and this demands political action. It is this ultimate concern for man's life that Christians must bring to their political involvement, but they will recognize the provisional nature of all political structures, and will not be blind to the limitations and compromises of all parties, including their own. What they must do, and all that they can do, is to see that their party and what it does approximates as closely as possible to the purposes and values for which Jesus stood.

This means turning many of the values of society upside down, for Jesus, too, rejected many of the values of his society. We must follow him in reversing accepted understandings of authority and leadership, in putting service of others in place of self-seeking, regard for the abilities of others in place of arrogance, spontaneity and trust in place of anxiety and fear. This is the kind of transformation of values that Christians must aim to bring about step by step, by their involvement in politics and in society. It is again a matter of working for the two revolutions – in values and in structures – at the same time.

Even when our hopes come more into line with what God wants for the world, the promise of the kingdom should not lead us to believe that we can achieve all that we hope for. In the North East region, for instance, we have already achieved certain things, and there are other things for which we must continue to work. But there are some things in our present and our future that we cannot control. For what may come out of these things we must rely upon God. But faith in God is not a passive matter. The fact that we cannot readily tell the difference between what can and what cannot be changed by our own efforts produces uncertainty in us. Our faith is not a matter of handing over all responsibility, but of finding that God is with us in the ambiguities and tensions. God enables us to bear the tension without falling into resignation. He enlarges and transforms our dreams, and he continually presses us to test the boundaries of possibility.

If we are prepared to risk our present dreams for the sake of even more, we must also be ready to reckon with the cost. The cost to Jesus of opening up the dream of the kingdom of God to all mankind and of refusing to accept less than the best for men was crucifixion. Only the belief that in Jesus we see not only the love of God but the power of God at work can make this kind of risk a possible option.

(iv) Dreams and reality – a question of truth
We are forced to ask how far our dreams relate to reality – to the truth about man, the world and God. The truth about man is that he is unpredictable. This fact is recognized in such everyday expressions as 'the human element', which is taken to account for those (unfortunate) accidents which no amount of foresight can exclude.

Man is a contradiction. He is capable of the greatest heights of self-sacrifice and the lowest deeds of self-seeking. To put this in theological terms, man is at the same time sinner and in the image of God. Our problem is that we tend to emphasize one aspect at the expense of the other. The Western church has for many years put all the weight on man as sinner. Its theology underplays man, his dignity and his freedom. We need to learn again from the Eastern church that the most fundamental thing about man is not that he is sinner but that he is in the image of God. Our whole understanding of what we may expect from life depends on getting this right. We must grapple with the Bible stories of creation in which God is believed to express his own goodness in the material world. We must grasp the truth contained in the picture of God breathing his own life into man (Genesis 2.1). We must come to terms with the real humanity of Jesus Christ and recognize that in him all mankind has been lifted up to its destined glory with God:

> Only if we remember that it is a Man who sits at the right hand of the Father as Lord of all, can we have an adequately high view of the new humanity.[10]

At present, however, there is a tension between man as he now appears and what he really is by virtue of his creation.

It is in his freedom that man retains his God-like quality. Men know that they must live under many constraints, but when they feel their fundamental freedom is threatened, they have a way of hitting back. We resent attempts to categorize and label us, and we struggle to hold on to the dynamic of our lives so that what we may become remains open.

Man's freedom is a reflection of God's freedom. The Jews would not utter God's name, for to name him was to suggest that they knew God and that they had in some sense 'got him taped'. God always remains beyond human comprehension or control. As soon as we suggest that we know God, we reduce him to our own scale. Much of the cynicism about Christianity today stems from the feeling that the God who is so readily named in the church is inadequate to the depths of human experience.

Jesus appealed to men to exercise their freedom. He urged people to make choices, and he indicated that those choices were decisive for their future. When we take upon ourselves to make choices for other people, we threaten their freedom and dignity as persons. Our concern for others must not be expressed in trying to control them, but in letting them be what they truly are. The love of God is in contrast with the egocentric twist that is a feature of human love. God does not inhibit growth by seeking to possess and dominate, but is creative in that he gives man freedom to become what he truly is.

There are, of course, contraints that limit man's freedom, and in

order to avoid misunderstanding one point must be made clear at this
stage. An individual can only be free in a free society. The freedom of
man is not about individuals on their own, but about the freedom of
mankind. It is mankind as a whole in its freedom that is in the image
of God. It is not isolated individuals, but mankind together, that must
struggle to discover its freedom in the removal of constraints and in
the positive creation of good.

Man as image of God with freedom and creativity is one side of the
picture. The other side of the picture is man as sinner. The Western
church has stressed man as sinner to the extent of saying that man is
totally defined by his sin and that any goodness he has comes to him
from outside. I believe we have to look at things in a different way,
and see man as essentially good, so that it is evil that comes to him
from outside. This point of view recognizes that evil exists apart from
man's sin, and helps us to be much clearer about what it is we are up
against:

> Evil is prior to man, and has come to man from the outside. It does
> not belong to his nature, for nature is what man was created with,
> and creation, being an act of God, cannot be evil. Evil, which is
> external to the true nature of man, has come to him from outside
> as Paul says (Romans 5). Human freedom opened the door to evil,
> and evil became lodged within human existence. Evil cannot be
> eradicated without the assistance of the grace of God. Sin has gained
> mastery over man and man has become a slave of evil, unable to
> liberate himself.[11]

This view helps us to make a distinction between destructive things
like earthquakes and physical deformities which we did not cause, and
sin, which lies in the choices and acts of free human beings. Between
these two there is a large grey area – the wrong things which seem to
be outside the realm of human choice and freedom, but which are in
fact the result of the cumulative choices of many human beings. This
social evil is compounded not only of obvious social ills like starvation
and war, but of the whole atmosphere and pressures of a society going
in the wrong direction. We ourselves are part of it – and its power
should force us to realize that we cannot pull ourselves out of it by our
boot-straps.

If we can get rid of the idea that it is we who are responsible for all
the ills of the world, we shall be better able to identify those wrongs
for which we are responsible; that is to say, we shall recognize sin.
The word 'sin' is understood in different ways according to the frame
of reference within which it is seen. The understanding that comes
most naturally to us is that in which our own society or group is our
point of reference. Sin is then those defects which we see in other
people and in ourselves which contravene the norms of our society. In

this framework, all offences are judged in relation to the world of meanings constituted by man. The concept of sin becomes conventional and comparative so that it is relatively easy to think that we are 'all right', for we are no worse than anyone else.

Sin is understood differently when it is seen in the frame of reference of reality as a whole, which is equated by the believer as the mind of God. In relation to this order it makes sense to say that man fails, resists, refuses, and to realize that this is true of all men and of mankind.

There are important differences between these two understandings of sin. In the first sense, sin relates to a world in which man *is* the centre and judgment about the sinfulness of an act is made solely in terms of its effects on man. In the second framework, sin relates to a world in which man is *not* the centre – and judgment is in terms of the effects of an act on all possible reality, upon the universe and against God. There is an overlap between the two understandings, so that certain actions – rape for instance – would be considered sinful by both. In order to grasp the difference, we must concentrate on the frame of reference. Within the first reference rape is sin in that the man concerned chooses his own gratification against the dignity of another, of himself and of the norms of his society. Within the second reference the man chooses himself as he immediately experiences himself, against all reality, against the universe and against God.

A second difference is that the first framework does not help us to deal with the fact that there is a great deal of sin which cannot directly be attributed to individuals. It does not help us to understand the sin in the structures in which we are caught up against our wills. There are circumstances which we did not create; choice of action is not between 'right' and 'wrong', but between various shades of grey. Sin in the structures cannot be dealt with by individuals acting alone, but neither can it be dismissed as 'fate', for individuals share a communal responsibility for tackling what is wrong in their situations.

Both the differences we have noted between sin as it is seen in the two frameworks are concerned with our understanding of reality. In the assessment of individual sin we must ask, 'Against what kind of reality are we sinning?' In tackling sin in the structures we must face the reality of communal sin.

The problem for us in all this is that our sense of ultimate reality – that is, our sense of God – is weak. It is God who appears to us to be unreal. There is a sense in which men have no sin until they are alerted to the truth about life. Jesus made the reality of God present and vivid. In what he was and in what he did the reality of the power of God was at work, and Jesus showed people the possibilities this opened up. It was their refusal to acknowledge the truth, when it was presented to them, that constituted their sin:

> Some of the Pharisees . . . said to him, 'Are we also blind?' Jesus
> said to them, 'If you were blind, you would have no guilt; but now
> that you say, "We see", your guilt remains' (John 9.40f.).

Sin is the refusal to recognize reality when it stares us in the face. Sin
is indifference to the reality of the world and of ourselves. Typically,
sin is the assumption that everything is unreal 'other than the small
portion of it that one calls one's own and builds into immobility. Sin
is a monumental indifference to the totality of which one is a part and
is otherwise without meaning'.[12] This limited understanding of reality
leads man to try to build his own world with himself as centre and
without God. Not only is this sinful, but it is disastrous, for it is an
attempt to construct life on a basis other than reality. We need to be
sure that our dreams have some basis in reality. This means asking
the questions: Are our dreams bounded by horizons that are too narrow? Can we open them up to be enlarged and transformed in the
light of the reality of the universe and of God? If it appears that we
have been hoping for the wrong things, what may we realistically hope
for?

The refusal to acknowledge reality when it presses upon us is the
essence of sin. The result of sin is that we become entangled in a
fabrication of unreality and lies, and that increasingly we become
insensitive to what is true and what is real, and unable to respond to
it. It is this understanding of sin that enables us to see that man's
greatest need is for forgiveness, and to understand why forgiveness
– the opening of the eyes, the unhardening of the heart and release
from self-concern and perversity – is at the heart of the gospel.

(v) The power of dreams – a question of the gospel

In Jesus Christ, God's kingdom became present, and in him men were
confronted by the reality of God. They were not asked to assent to a
theory but to respond to an experience. To respond meant to be
released from a closed world, bounded by themselves, their past and
their own concerns. Limited horizons were pushed back, and they
were invited to realize themselves as part of a world created by God,
judged by the values and purposes of God and animated by God's
redemptive activity. To respond was to change one's point of view,
that is, to repent.

Though some people did repent, the most obvious outcome of this
confrontation was a mounting tension between Jesus and those who
resisted the truth that he revealed. Jesus is seen in tension with the
authorities, with pressures upon him to accept the world's conditions
of success, agonizing over the fate of the world, suffering from a sense
of failure and isolation – and all this culminating in his crucifixion.

It was the resurrection that led the first Christians to see this tension in the perspective of hope and promise. What they experienced was Jesus alive after his death and present with them in a new way. They saw this as a sign that God was at work not only in raising Jesus from the dead, but throughout Jesus' life. Through Jesus, God's power was at work in the world and in men in a new way. Jesus' resurrection was a break-through which was the beginning of the transformation of all things. They now saw that his rejection, suffering and crucifixion was not destructive, but creative of the change that was now taking place. Hope of future fulfilment, however, only heightened the tension for those who now believed that they were living 'between the times'. Today we still live 'between the times', and in our time too it is a matter of living towards the future in hope and tension.

Living towards the future gives us a different attitude towards the present. It does not devalue the present, but it makes us see it in a new light. Our thinking about the present becomes what Luther called 'expectation thinking' – that is, we see the present not only as it is, but also as, according to God's promises, it will be. We cannot say that if the world goes up in nuclear holocaust it is of no importance, for it is *this* world that is to be transformed. The future kingdom is not separate from the future of the material world, and it is *this* world for which we have responsibility.

> The orthodoxy of a Christian's faith must constantly *make itself* true in . . . his actions . . . because the promised *truth* is a truth which must be *made* (see John. 3.21 ff.).[13]

There is nothing static about this position of hope. The tension we are in is dynamic and powerful, urging us to make creative response in the present. We do not know what the future will be like. The kingdom does not give us a blueprint, but direction and a hope that has power to draw us forward. We must be clear about the distinction between fantasy, nightmare and dreams. Fantasy is based on an unreal world and withdraws us from life. Nightmare recognizes only what is destructive and has power to destroy. Dreams that are based on reality have power to create. This makes it essential that we check how far our dreams are based on reality. In order to do this the following criteria should be borne in mind.

The first criterion is that dreams should be based upon the ultimate reality of God and his promises. God's promises are summed up in the promise of the kingdom. Jesus' acts of feeding, healing, forgiving, freeing, giving new life are signs of the immediate presence of the kingdom and point forward to its fulfilment. In the light of this promise, men in every time and place have to embody the same characteristics in their own circumstances. An effort of imagination is needed to overcome the pull of the past and to picture a new future for which to work. The form dreams take will vary but, if they are based on the promises of God, they will have similar characteristics and will point forward to the same ultimate hope.

The second criterion is that dreams should take account of reality in its entirety. It is, of course, impossible for anyone to be aware of the whole of reality, but we can be responsive to new aspects of reality as it comes to us, and if we are not prepared for our dreams to be transformed by it, then they become fantasies and destructive fanaticisms. In so far as we are sensitive to the pressure of reality and to God's call to us in and through it, then our dreams have creative power.

Dreams should not be a means of escaping from tension. The coming of the kingdom involves struggle and sacrifice. We have failed to come to terms with reality if we disregard the powerful obstacles in its way. Many of these result from the accumulated effects of blindness, despair, presumption, division and deliberate rejection of what is good, that is, from human sin.

The pronouncement of God's forgiveness of sins was the most revolutionary aspect of Jesus' gospel of the kingdom. Forgiveness is at the heart of the gospel and meets man's deepest need. Evil and sin fester and grow if they are not dealt with, and man on his own cannot do what is needed. If in a divided world there is no forgiveness, things can only get worse. In *The Great Divorce* C. S. Lewis gives a picture of a community in which people would not forgive each other. What had begun as a small village became a great straggling city. Because there was no forgiveness people, when they fell out with each other, simply moved away to live in another street. Only one or two people lived in each street, and the city spread further and further into the surrounding countryside. This gives a terrible picture of what happens where there is no forgiveness. Where there is forgiveness people do not move away from each other, but move away from their past by facing what there is in themselves which makes things go wrong. Then it is possible to move into a different kind of future.

To forgive people means to accept them as they are, and to do this because we know that, with all our faults, God accepts us. The effect of God's acceptance of us can only be expressed in metaphor. It is the warmth that unfreezes the coldness of human hearts; the water that softens dry ground so that all sorts of things begin to grow; the graciousness that overflows in its generosity so that the meannesses of our responses to life are opened out and barriers break down. God's love and forgiveness effect a change in us which we cannot make for ourselves.

If we have only a conventional understanding of sin, we will fail to see how crucial forgiveness is for us, both personally and in our group relationships. It is not the criminals and meths drinkers, but the people who think they are right, who are most in need of forgiveness. In

Jesus' ministry, it was those who knew they were sinners who were able to accept forgiveness, while the self-righteous people were the ones who were condemned. In the world today there is nothing that divides men so bitterly as the conviction that they are right while others are wrong. It is the people who believe they are fighting for truth under the banners of democracy, communism, nationalism and so on, who are most merciless. Jesus' condemnation of 'good' people was levelled at their pride. Putting themselves in the place of God, they had become blind to the limitations and contradictions of their own position. Jesus confronted them with the reality of God's absolute righteousness in the context of which the difference between men and their causes was a relative matter.

Forgiveness does not mean ignoring these differences or suggesting that they do not matter; what it does is to make possible an attitude of humility and self-criticism:

> When life is lived in this dimension, the chasms which divide men are bridged not directly, not by resolving the conflicts on the historical levels, but by the sense of an ultimate unity in, and common dependence upon, the realm of transcendence.[14]

In this dimension society will continue to punish those who break its laws, but there will be a recognition that the society is itself more responsible for their anti-social conduct than it realizes. Men will engage in social struggles, but they will be aware that there are contradictions in their actions, and in the realization will lie the roots of the spirit of forgiveness. Faith in a God of absolute righteousness will make men aware that there is 'a goodness which not only fulfils, but may negate, the highest human goodness'.[15] God's free forgiveness does not do away with his judgment. There is no absolute divide between the 'goodies' and the 'baddies', and no one of us can have cause for self-righteousness. We all need to receive forgiveness from God, and to forgive and receive forgiveness from our fellow-men.

The dead grey city of C. S. Lewis's story is one picture of how sin cuts at the roots of all that is lively, warm and human. The recognition that we have a share, a solidarity in sin, should not lead us to disown any specific responsibility, but should lead us to a more objective analysis of exactly what part we ourselves and our own group play in dehumanizing our society. This kind of objectiveness about sin is just as vital for groups as it is for individuals, if we are to move away from the past into a new future. Repentance involves a change of perspective. Confession means, in the light of that perspective, getting down to the specific things that have to be changed in oneself and in one's own group.

No amount of argument and reasoning, however, will make us do this, for left to ourselves we are powerless to face the truth about ourselves. Man is in need of salvation, and it is God who meets this need: 'The confrontation between man the sinner and Jesus crucified is how salvation happens.'[16]

In this event we see that what is wrong with us in our refusal of the truth, is that we are actually willing death and contributing to death. In Jesus we see what man is meant to be and what we ourselves are destined to be. What we do in our sinning is not only to deny life to others, but to destroy the person we ourselves are destined to be. The gospel – the good news – is that in Jesus Christ the awaited action of God has taken place, and men who are sinners are assured of their acceptance by God and invited to share in the new life made possible through Jesus Christ: 'The time is fulfilled, and the kingdom of God is at hand; repent and believe the gospel' (Mark 1.15).

(vi) Commitment to dreams – a question of discipleship

To accept Jesus' invitation to share in a new way of life is to accept discipleship – to follow in the way of Jesus. At a comfortable distance from the events of Jesus' life this sounds obvious and easy – 'Isn't this what we are doing anyhow?' – or irrelevant – 'But Jesus lived in a different kind of world'. This shows how far we are from understanding what the New Testament is saying. We have not perceived the bewilderment and fear of the first disciples:

> And they were on the road, going to Jerusalem, and Jesus was walking ahead of them; and they were amazed (bewildered) and those who followed were afraid (Mark 10.32).

Nor have we heard the warnings by which Jesus turned away those whose half-heartedness made them inadequate as disciples:

> No one who puts his hand to the plough and looks back is fit for the kingdom of God (Luke 9.62).

Tension is writ large in every part of the story, and warnings that to accept discipleship is to accept suffering. The question Jesus puts is the question of commitment: how far are we actually committed to our dreams?

It is easy enough to make electioneering speeches about our concern for people. It is easy to demonstrate the genuineness of this concern when large sums of money are available to spend on new developments. But we are not now in a time of expansion, but one of recession and decline:

> Today the hopes which were invested in progress, growth and profit are turning into fatalism, suicidal despair and nostalgia. They have been deeply disappointed . . . *The power of hope* is only manifested in the crisis of progress today if it leads to life even in the face of deadly crisis . . . it must make people ready to act in time

and to make the necessary sacrifices. There will be no survival for mankind without the rebirth of the power of hope, which in the face of the possibility of the world's death wills to live and prepares to live. The rediscovery of *the capacity for suffering* is part of the will to live and the power of hope . . . The ideal of Western progress – to lead a life free from pain or suffering – is intolerable because it inflicts suffering and pain on others. We cannot just minimize this by talking about regrettable 'side effects'. This is the actual price that has to be paid. . . . Humanity only has a future if it looks to a *common* future. If humanity wants a common future, and if people are not to bring one another to suffering and death, then the people who are now capable of acting must rediscover the meaning of suffering. It is only the dignity of solidarity in suffering which makes people capable of fellowship.[17]

There is a price in terms of suffering that has to be paid if a more human world is to be created. There is no painless way into the future and to the fulfilment of our dreams. If we are not to push this suffering on to other people, we have to bear our share. The call to discipleship is the call to solidarity in suffering which is accepted as the way of hope and of life.

Every married couple and every parent knows the suffering that is part of loving and of creating a family life. Every manager and every trade unionist knows the agonies involved in not giving up but continuing to search for a way through problems of conflict and change. Every politician has lived through the destruction of things to which he has given his best years. It is easy to hope when things go well, but the question of how far we are committed to our dreams is only answered when things do not go well.

There are many mistaken ideas about the place of suffering in discipleship, and the cross has been interpreted as 'taking things lying down, lacking self-confidence, yielding, knuckling under in silence, cringing, complying, capitulating'.[18] This kind of interpretation is totally misleading and does nothing to encourage people to continue to struggle for the realization of their hopes in the face of disappointment. To see suffering in a positive way is to recognize that we live in a world in which all that is life-enhancing confronts that which is life-denying: 'the more strongly we insist on reality, the more we are immersed in it, the more deeply we are affected by those processes of dying surrounding us and pressing upon us.'[19]

The resurrection hope which draws us forward cannot be separated from the suffering that is caused by sin and evil . . . but it is always a joyful and creative suffering the symbol for which is the pain of birth.

(vii) Shared dreams – question of solidarity

Discipleship is not meant to be solitary. The description of a Christian as someone who sticks out like a sore thumb is as misleading as it can be. The invitation to discipleship is an invitation to enter a community in which dreams are shared, and whose dreams give hope to the world.

Some essential features of this community are:

(*a*) It is the community of those who put their faith in Jesus Christ as the revelation of God and who commit themselves to the cause of Jesus Christ as the cause of God for all men. The community acquires its distinctive identity and its name from Jesus Christ. In the Acts of the Apostles the story of the beginning of the community is told. It is not an absolute beginning, for it is the continuation of what 'Jesus *began* to do' (Acts 1.1). What Jesus began, the church continues in the power of the same Spirit. The community was not founded by Jesus Christ, but emerged 'after his death in his name as crucified and yet living, the community of those who have become involved in the cause of Jesus Christ and who witness to it as hope for all men'.[20] The faith that arose from the resurrection experiences is that Jesus Christ is the revelation of the same God who revealed himself in the history of Israel: the same Spirit was and is active in Jesus, who is active in creation and in history. In Jesus we come to know God.

> To name the name of Jesus is to point to him who is the reality of God. . . . This is the living reality and the dynamic energy of the God who transcends the universe, who pins himself to our reality in and as the crucified man, and who penetrates all the realities of history and of nature as Spirit.[21]

(*b*) It is the community in which God Himself is present through Jesus Christ in the Spirit.

We must pause here to reflect on what it is we are saying about God and about Jesus Christ. To say that Jesus revealed God assumes that we have some idea of what we mean by God. The Jews believed that God was active in their history, but they were forbidden to make any physical representation of him. They believed that he was present in the world as Spirit and they thought of him in terms of wind and storm, invisible and yet powerful, real and having real effects.

Unlike the gods of other nations, which could be carried from place to place and could be persuaded by special offerings, God for the Jews did not do as they willed but as he willed. It was this same God whom the disciples recognized in Jesus. After the resurrection Jesus was close to the community of faith, not in visible form and not through their memory, but with the same reality and efficacy – in the Spirit, through the Spirit and as Spirit. The Spirit is not to be separated from Jesus Christ any more than Jesus Christ is to be separated from God: 'The

Spirit is the presence of God and of the exalted Christ for the community of faith and the individual believer.'[22]

If we hold only to the person of Jesus without grasping his relationship with Father and Spirit, we lapse into sheer sentimentality. If we hold only to the Spirit, using him as a means to justify our mental laziness or our fanaticism, and without reference to Jesus Christ as the criterion by which all claims to truth are to be judged, we end up in a morass of subjectivity. If we think of God only as the creator, God who is over all, we cannot experience our day-to-day lives as personal encounter with him. So we need to do all these things if we are to know God. The last of these, in which we think of God as Creator, involves us in all the analysis of what is happening in our world which I have been talking about. It is this attention to the facts of our situation that is the antidote to sentimentality and subjectivism. This points us again to the fact that our faith depends on knowing God as Trinity – not as a matter of speculation but in order to know and respond to him as present with us.

(c) The community of faith is a provisional, flexible community, hoping and working for the future. The community's hope is not in itself and its own future, but in the kingdom of God. It recognizes that the whole world and all mankind are moving towards their fulfilment in God and that its own existence is relative to this purpose. The community is not an end in itself, but exists for the sake of the kingdom and will exist only until the fulfilment of that kingdom. Another way of putting this is to say that the community is one of hope and expectation.

There is a big difference between the way the church thought of itself in the first days of its existence and how it sees itself today. The first Christians believed that the transformation of all things that had begun in the resurrection of Jesus Christ would speedily be completed. They looked forward eagerly to the fulfilment of the kingdom of God and saw their own community existence as a very temporary affair. Nearly two thousand years have elapsed since then. Even within the period covered by the New Testament some people were beginning to say: 'But it isn't going to happen – all things remain the same.' The urgency had gone out of the situation, or so it seemed, and the tension of living provisionally – with 'bags packed' as it were – was relaxed.

The church began to settle down. Today it is even harder to hold on to the sense of the provisional nature of the church; indeed to many people the church seems to be the only part of life which is not provisional.

But if the church is to keep moving towards the future kingdom of God, and if it is to give courage and hope to the world to move towards its fulfilment, it must see itself as a provisional affair. It must be ready to have its present form broken and changed so that it can move into what is new. This is not a devaluation of the present but a way of seeing the present in the light of the future, that is, seeing it with expectancy and hope:

> Hope is a process of eliminating the provisional in order to make room for the radical and for the uncontrollability of God. Hope is an attitude in which we dare to commit ourselves to that which is radically beyond human control. . . It goes outward from itself to the uncontrollability of God. Only in this way do we understand who God is and that it is he who empowers us to self-commitment to the 'absurdity' of truth and love. It is an attitude to eternity which sets eternity 'in train'. . . The death of Christ was the most radical act of hope. The process by which hope becomes an achieved reality involves a permanent transformation of the framework of secular life, that is to say, Christian hope is a revolutionary attitude on the part of Christians to the world. It empowers an exodus out of the present into the future. Practice is not a mere execution of what has been planned but an attitude which dares to enter into that which has *not* been planned, which presses upon us. A worldly revolutionary attitude could mean ultimate value is given to some new structure. But to give recognition only to what can be controlled leads either to presumption or to despair. Christian hope subjects every structure to constant re-appraisal.[23]

(*d*) Besides being a community of hope, this is a community of thanksgiving to God and self-offering after the pattern of Christ and in Christ.

> I appeal to you, therefore, brethren, by the mercies of God, to present your bodies as a living sacrifice, holy and acceptable to God (Romans 12.1).

In these words Paul is not speaking of the offering of oneself in a church service, but of the day-to-day life of Christians and of the whole church. He is echoing the thought of the Old Testament, where it is made plain that the offering God wants from man is the offering of a life lived in obedience to God's will. There is, however, a big difference between Paul's position and that of the Old Testament – a difference brought about through Jesus Christ.

> Whereas in the old, the unconditional demand for a moral response from man came more and more to be felt as the unbearable burden of the Law, pressing externally on his conscience, never capable of fulfilment, in the new the perfect response has been made once for all. He (Jesus) . . . is God's Word; he is also man's only perfect response to the Word.[24]

By virtue of his union with Jesus Christ, the Christian can offer himself to God not in anxiety and guilt, but with thanksgiving, knowing that his offering is acceptable through Jesus Christ.

What is offered is one's life and the life of the community, and this offering must be made in the process of living. This radically new way of life must be lived in union with Jesus Christ. Baptism unites the Christian to the dying and rising of Christ, and symbolizes dying to the old life and rising to a new life of grace. In the holy communion the community constantly affirms and renews its unity with Christ. Thus there is a twofold movement and a continual interaction of faith and practice that informs the whole of life. The church is expressed both as gathered congregation, ever entering more deeply into the meaning of its faith and into the ultimate nature and goal of the world, celebrating and giving thanks for the present reality of the kingdom, and as dispersed in the world in fulfilment of its historical task.

(e) The community has a concrete historical task to perform, the precise nature of which will vary according to time and place.

Christianity is about the kingdom of God. The good news of the kingdom is that God can reign in human affairs through grace, and that therefore the world and mankind can receive their fulfilment. The church is the body of people which has the responsibility of directing people to this dream, showing the ways in which it can be realized, keeping people working for the dream and serving the world and all the dreamers in the world, whether they belong to the church or not. It has to orientate the world to its true goals, to influence institutions as well as individuals, and to subject them to appropriate critiques of the truth.

> In carrying out this task she is concerned with the whole of the world's life, from the quality of life and the decisions of the individual person through an immense range to the trends in human history . . . This is a task which can only be accomplished by the whole body of the church dispersed in the world in the form of her laity.[25]

How the task is done will vary in relation to different historical, cultural and geographical situations. In the same way that the work of Jesus Christ required the living of a concrete historical life, so the church, in order that dreams may be shared and worked out in a shared task, must have its own physical presence and, provisional though it is, must have some structural form.

(viii) What sort of dreams come true?

A just, compassionate society, in which human beings live in freedom, equality and community, realizing their full humanity, is what we dream of. The kingdom of God is the fulfilment of all these things, as everything is gathered into harmony and unity in Christ (Ephesians 1.10). But perfection will not come until all can share in it. In the meantime we must start from where we are – in our present society with all its flaws, contradictions and inhumanities, and with ourselves with our limited and biased vision. How can we possibly get from where we are to where we long to be?

We cannot even imagine what such a society would be like. But we must take the next step, and it is our dreams, crude and wrong-headed as they may be, that must give us pictures that are specific enough to enable us to do this. We need a rich variety of dreams if we are to move away from the present all-too-familiar patterns of thinking and living. A variety of dreams will help to enrich the vision of where we want to go, but – at the same time – some of these dreams will conflict with each other, so that all cannot come true.

Dreams picture what has not yet happened. Surely, therefore, they must remain vague, indefinite and unverifiable? What criterion could help us to know what sort of dreams can come true?

The dreams of the Christian are based on a definite reality and event in history – Jesus Christ. In the raising of Jesus, faith recognizes God's promise to transform all things. Dreams of the future are grounded in this reality and in this promise. It is the person and history of Jesus Christ crucified and risen who provides us with the touchstone by which to distinguish dreams that come true from those that are leading to disappointment.

The reality of Jesus Christ makes it possible for us to distinguish the spirit of promise from the spirit of utopia. Imaginary worlds constructed on the basis of how we would *like* life to be are a necessary part of dreaming. But they must be brought into touch with life as it actually is if they are to form the basis of strategy and action. Utopias that lose touch with reality and ignore the 'dark' side of life are impracticable and dull. Jesus Christ came to terms with the world and with human beings as they actually are. In him God promises the redemption of the world. This means bringing into the open much that is hidden and unacknowledged in our lives, so that all potentialities may be fulfilled, and so that what is evil and unresponsive can be purged or burnt.

Dreams that are grounded in the person of Jesus Christ are not simply projections of what at present obtains. Jesus' life was a contradiction of the *status quo*. He staked everything, suffering and dying in the process, on the belief that God's will can be done, and by doing this he cut at the roots of what upheld things as they were. His dream was not of continuation but of transformation.

In such dreams,

> man is not brought into harmony and agreement with the given situation, but is drawn into the conflict between hope and experience . . . Everywhere in the New Testament the Christian hope is directed towards what is not yet visible; it is consequently a 'hoping against hope' . . . The contradiction to the existing reality of himself

and his world in which man is placed by hope is the very contradiction out of which this hope itself is born – it is the contradiction between the resurrection and the cross. Christian hope is resurrection hope, and it proves its truth in the contradiction of the future prospects thereby offered and guaranteed for righteousness as opposed to sin, life as opposed to death, glory as opposed to suffering, peace as opposed to dissension.[26]

The dreams that come true are those that are based on the reality of God, what he has done in Jesus Christ and what he promises for the future.

We realize how limited our dreams are when we look back at the dreams of earlier generations. Who could have foretold, for instance, in 1825 the revolution that was foreshadowed in the first passenger train?

> When the steam-coach is brought fully into use, practice will teach us many things respecting it, of which theory leaves us ignorant. With the facilities for rapid motion which it will afford, however, there is nothing very extravagant in expecting to see the present extreme rate of travelling (ten miles per hour) doubled.[27]

Our faith in God promises his ultimate future and the fulfilment of man's humanity, but we must proceed step by step. Practice does indeed teach us many things of which theory leaves us ignorant. Dreams are essential if we are to move forward at all, but they can only take us so far into the future. It is as we meet reality and meet God in it, and as we try to put our dreams into practice, that our dreams are reshaped and our horizons expanded. If dreams can move us in the right direction, we should not be over-concerned if they do not come true, or if they only come true in some respects, for the promise that God holds out to us is always more than we can imagine. Yet we must continue to dream, and the end of dreaming will only come when there are no more horizons to open out before us. For each of us death stands for the final decisive limit, the crossing of the last horizon. This is for us the end of dreaming and entry into a reality beyond our control and given by God. The kingdom of God in its completeness stands for the same decisive limit to the world's dreaming. In the end, and there will be a decisive end, it is God who brings the fullness of the kingdom.

This discussion of tensions and dreams arose out of our consideration of life in North East England, and, in spite of the difficulties of making any predictions, we must ask what this discussion has to say about the future of the region. We have seen that our dreams come into touch with reality insofar as they are consonant with the promises of the kingdom of God. What, then, in the light of God's promises may we realistically hope for in the future of the North East?

There is no possibility of a return to the past, and insofar as this is what people dream about, there will be disappointment. But neither have all the dreams of a different future materialized. Things have been much harder to achieve than anyone expected. There is a painful tension between the high hopes of the planners and the actual results achieved. There are many difficulties outside our immediate control. But one of the greatest obstacles to a more human future is the sheer inertia of our society. People are not disposed to take new initiatives or to risk themselves in order to venture something new, nor do they welcome or support people with ideas. This is not simply a personal matter, but an inertia that is built into our institutions and our political life.

In our struggle against inertia, lack of vision, and a pragmatism that is indifferent to questions of justice, we are up against something that is too fundamental to be overcome easily. We must be prepared to pay the price involved in the realization of our vision. The gospel does not give easy answers, but gives us courage to face the reality of our situation with its long history of the deformation of people. It gives strength to endure and to keep on doing what is necessary so that by God's grace there may be a re-formation of people.

The pressures people are under in our industrial society have forced me to deepen my understanding of Christian faith. At the heart of this faith I find the cross of Jesus Christ. As I think about his life I ask, 'Is this what happens to those who really care about people?' 'Does discipleship lead us to see even more clearly the tragedy and waste of what we do to ourselves and to each other?' The tensions I feel are only faint echoes of the tensions in the life of Jesus Christ. To follow him is to accept a cross.

But the cross is not all there is. There is also a certainty, a new energy in living and hoping. Jesus' way is not a dead-end. He draws us out and opens up the possibilities of God's future. Resurrection is the beginning of new life that in and through all this struggling is given by God. There are signs of that new life now.

IV Signs of Hope

> "But that you may know that the Son of man has authority on earth to forgive sins – he then said to the paralytic – "Rise, take up your bed and go home" ' (*Matthew 9.6*).

---

1 Signs

If we are alert, we can see signs of hope in the world now. Though the kingdom in its fullness lies in the future, it is already breaking into life in unexpected ways. There are signs of the kingdom which should give hope and encouragement; and living by these signs and out of these signs enables us to share in the kingdom now.

In this chapter I look at signs of hope that are already present. I give first of all some examples of certain things which appear to me to be signs of hope. I then discuss the responsibility of the church to identify the signs of hope in the world, and to help people to recognize in these signs God's invitation. In the third section I describe what the church in the North East is doing in relation to this prophetic task; and in the fourth section I point to the fact that not only should the church identify signs of hope, but it should itself be a sign of hope.

Before developing the examples which are the subject of this section, I want to clear away a possible misunderstanding by dispelling any notion that we can equate the signs of the kingdom of God with some general idea of progress. We must beware of illusions. We should not expect to see steady progress towards a better world, or be surprised when the struggle between good and evil is intensified. The coming of the kingdom brings judgment on all that denies God's purposes of life and love. For those who are working for the fulfilment of humanity, judgment should be seen as a cleansing and a hopeful thing, and there are times when it must fall upon our own muddled attempts to do good. We must recognize that in the end the kingdom does not come through the sum total of our own efforts but through the activity of God. The signs of hope that appear are in themselves fragile and transient; their importance does not lie in themselves but in what they point to. The signs I am looking for are those that point to the reality of God and to his activity in the world.

Many people would not see anything especially significant in the

activities I describe. It would not seem to them that these things point
to anything beyond themselves. They stand in their own right as things
worth doing. If, however, hope is invested only in the events and not
in what they signify, there will be disappointment. There are destructive as well as life-giving elements in them. In some cases nothing
concrete is achieved, and in other cases what is achieved is uncertain
and temporary. The importance of these activities lies not only in what
is achieved, but in the possibilities of human living that are opened up
and the glimpses of the activity of God that appear in and through
what is being done. I take my examples again from North East England,
but I must emphasize that my purpose is to illustrate truths that are
in no way confined to this part of the world.

I have suggested that we should look for signs of hope at those
points in life where human beings are most under threat. I have
therefore drawn my first three examples from some of the blackest
points of life in the region.

(i) The right to useful work
Unemployment and the threat of unemployment faces today's workers
with as big a threat as that which faced the workers in the frontier
days of the region's industrial expansion. Out of a number of creative
responses to this threat, I will give one example.

For over a century West Newcastle has depended for employment
on the great engineering firm built up by William Armstrong and since
1927 merged with Vickers Ltd. The Newcastle works, which at the
time of writing consists of two factories, one at Elswick and one at
Scotswood Road, is famous for the design and production of armaments, its most notable contemporary achievement being the Chieftain
tank. On a less spectacular scale, work has always included commercial
products such as car presses made under licence from Schüler of West
Germany.

Since the end of World War II the numbers of employees at the two
works has been drastically reduced. In 1969 there were 12,350 employees, in 1973, 5,700 and in October 1977 only 1,850. Recent manpower
reductions have taken place against rising output, largely due to the
introduction of numerically controlled machinery in the machine
shops. At the end of 1977 it was made known that Vickers planned to
close the Scotswood works, transferring any remaining production to
Elswick or to factories outside the region. In an area of already high
unemployment this was bad news indeed. So much for the bad news
– now for the signs of hope.

In 1977, in view of the run-down of manpower and orders, and
before the projected closure of the Scotswood plant was announced,
the shop stewards of both factories formed a Combine Committee with
a view to proposing alternative products that might be made at the

works. They argued that the skills required to build a Chieftain tank represented a considerable asset. The value of this asset lay not simply in the skills of individual men, but in the combination of skills in a body of men trained to work together on highly complex tasks. The committee made an analysis of all the skills involved and listed other assets of the firm: 'large spaces, engineering skills and a custom-built approach.'[1] In their list of possible alternative products they comment that, 'Where possible the products have been related to local needs in Newcastle just as were the original hydraulic cranes built by Armstrong in the mid-nineteenth century.'[2] Having completed their list of useful products, they commissioned a research team from the University of Sussex to work out a feasibility study for their production. This study was duly presented to Vickers' management.

Before proceeding with the story let us identify what is hopeful about these moves. First, the shop stewards decided that it was possible to do something about their situation. Instead of simply accepting what 'fate' dealt out to them, waiting for someone to provide jobs or selling their jobs for the sake of a redundancy cheque, they took hold of their own destiny. Secondly, their decision to take initiatives forced them to entertain radically new ideas and to question many traditional approaches to work. The long history of craft unions in North East England has led to a fundamentally conservative attitude to work. The Vickers' shop stewards proposed a new attitude to the content of work and new relationships in the control of that work. As regards content they did not simply demand a right to work, but a right to work on socially useful products. Most people recognize the need for armaments in times of war, but the manufacture of armaments is a more questionable matter when they are being produced for oil-rich Middle East countries, and when employment depends on another war in the Middle East. The list of alternative products proposed by the committee included car presses, mining machinery, recycling equipment and brewing equipment, but no armaments.

As regards the control of their work, the committee recognized, that however feasible the making of these products might be on paper, the present structure of the firm militated against anything new happening. Vickers is too unwieldy. In the cause of 'rationalization' things that belong together – design and production, production and consumption, accounting and engineering – have been separated. Nor does the structure as it is allow for the initiatives and risks that are needed for change. 'To ensure that real needs are identified and social priorities shifted accordingly and that the productive and creative potential of workers is fully utilized, the system would have to be based on grass roots participation of workers and consumers.'[3] To tackle this problem the Combine Committee began work on a proposal for workers' participation at Vickers.

The third hopeful thing about the shop stewards' action is that in a society in which conflict between sectional interests is deep-rooted, horizons have been widened and new co-operations have been developed. There have, for instance, been extended conversations with other sections of the community in the consideration of alternative products, and the help of academics from Sussex University has been enlisted.

This particular story is far from finished and there have been a number of new moves. The announcement in October 1977 of the projected closure of the Scotswood works led to action which, while having the full support of the original Combine Committee, was separately organized. Two new committees were set up – a Corporate Committee, consisting of the Scotswood shop stewards including the white collar unions, and a 'Save Scotswood Committee', which included local political figures. More recently, in spite of months of activity by these committees, Vickers have confirmed that Scotswood will close. The firm has also rejected the proposals for alternative products as commercially non-viable. This means that jobs will continue to run down at Elswick, with no chance of alternative work being found there for the 700 workers from Scotswood.

In view of what looks like total failure of the shop stewards' initiatives, it may seem odd that I should continue to speak of this as a sign of hope. If I thought this was no more than drowning men clutching at straws I should not see hope in these actions. But this is only one example of something that is happening in many other places – and I see a recognition on the part of many trade unionists that they must get to grips with a situation that is new, and who in this process are beginning to change their attitudes to work and their thinking about the nature of work and the place is should have in life. In doing this they are discovering new possibilities in themselves.

Some of the things that are happening are exceptionally newsworthy and have captured the national headlines. The Upper Clyde Shipbuilders' Co-operative was one such initiative, and its leader Jimmy Reid became a household name almost overnight. On the other hand, many of the most creative things do not attract much notice. In another engineering firm in Newcastle, for instance, a corporate committee was formed as long ago as 1971 in order to face the threat of 1600 redundancies, due to falling orders. This committee, which is still working, brought together members of unions which traditionally had failed to co-operate, went out and found new orders for the company, and worked with management to resist a merger with a London-based engineering firm. We should not assume that only strikes and protests are happening, for there are many new and creative things happening in the trade union movement.

I should, however, be telling less than the whole truth if I did not say that along with these hopeful signs much that is negative has also emerged. The effect of operating under the glare of the TV cameras can be damaging to people who are trying to do their proper job in exceptionally difficult circumstances. The media can play upon natural human vanity so that personalities become more important than the issue that is being tackled; and the situation can become over-dramatized in a way that obscures reality. Another danger is that splits develop between people who had combined against a common threat. Men get tired of fighting what appears to be losing battles and are persuaded to settle for redundancy pay. Or, and this occurred in the Vickers case, as the threat to the Scotswood works increased and it seemed that Elswick had at least a limited future, divisions occurred between members of the two works.

The truth is that these new initiatives are so contrary to the whole character of industry that there are bound to be failures and casualties. The point I want to stress is that, even if what was intended is not achieved, these events contain signs of new life. What these signs point us to will be seen more readily when I have given several more examples.

(ii) Renewal in the inner city

My second example is of a community development project in a run-down inner-city area. Southwick in Sunderland is one of many similar areas in North East England. It is a community of 12,000 people, and lies to the north of Sunderland overlooking the river Wear. It used to be a separate village, but as Sunderland grew, Southwick became the home of the cream of the skilled workers from the shipyards and other industries. In recent years it has suffered many changes and now it is a decaying inner urban area. Eighty per cent of the housing is council-owned, and during the 1960s there was a good deal of rebuilding in which new ideas were incorporated with mixed success. Discussion about the remaining older property is concerned with the relative merits of rebuilding or renewal. Disruption of community life is further threatened by plans for new roads.

Today the population is becoming increasingly mixed as the original inhabitants move out to the new estates. An indication of the sort of people who now live in Southwick is provided by statistics which claim that sixty per cent – that is over 7,000 people – are in receipt of social benefits of some kind in the form of pensions, supplementary benefits, rent rebates, unemployment benefits and so on. Out of this number, 4,000 are wholly dependent on the state. Yet Southwick remains a community of contrasts, for some skilled workers still live there, and within its boundaries lies the most prosperous shipyard in the country, whose workers even in a bad week take home £100. For the unemployed man living next door to a shipyard worker the inequalities of life are made clear in terms of his neighbour's new car, his music-centre, holidays on the Costa Brava and children's pocket money.

But the really destructive aspect of life in Southwick is the massive dependence of the majority of people on the state. Not only do 'they' provide the weekly income, but 'they' decide where people will live, how the redevelopment of the area will take place and nearly everything else. Perhaps all that is left to decide is which horse to put your money on. The thing that threatens people's humanity is the fact that they become totally dependent and cease to believe in themselves or that they could possibly take some part in the management of their own lives.

There are, however, signs of hope which have appeared as a result of a community development project, Southwick Neighbourhood Action Project (SNAP). The attitude of dependence is changing, local people are beginning to do more for themselves and to recognize that the community has power to make something of itself. The project is run by local people through a management committee. For the first two years the scheme operated from the home of the first full-time worker. In the Spring of 1976 the project obtained its own base in what had been a hairdressing salon. This was turned into a coffee bar/advice/information shop. Although the project itself still only employs one full-time worker, others have been involved through the job creation and similar schemes. Two separate but related projects – the Southwick Youth Neighbourhood Project and the Southwick Village Farm – also have full-time workers. The task of the full-time workers is to give encouragement and back-up to work that is primarily done by local people. The work of SNAP falls into two parts – advice to individuals and support to local groups.

In view of the large number of Southwick people without work and dependent in some way on the state, it is not surprising that a large proportion (41%) of the problems with which individuals need help relate to the Department of Health and Social Security, with whom the project workers have excellent co-operation. In dealing with this kind of problem the project's aim is 'to ensure that those in need gain what is theirs *by right* from the state'. What is worrying is that still, despite what is said in the 'popular press', far too many people are not claiming what they are entitled to; this is particularly true of pensioners, of families with children who do not make sufficient claims for large items of expenditure, and for those at work whose wages are low enough to qualify for the family income supplement or for a rent and rate rebate.[4] Another area where advice is needed relates to housing repairs, allocations and transfers (31% of all cases dealt with). The third problem area concerns fuel bills (11%) . . . 'fuel debts are increasingly a part of life for working people.'[5] The total number of cases in all categories dealt with during the year was 1,532. This obviously involves a large amount of work not only with individuals, but with the local authority departments concerned, with the gas and electricity companies as well as with legal and tribunal work.

The second main aspect of SNAP's work is that of giving support and encouragement to local community groups; 'SNAP now has a commitment and responsibility to support, advise and encourage a growing number of community groups and initiatives.' An example of this comes from the groups represented on the management committee. (This list includes four tenants' associations, three play-schemes, the four main local churches – two Church of England, one Roman Catholic and one Methodist – the Southwick Village Farm and the Southwick Neighbourhood Youth Project.) In many instances SNAP provides the encouragement for a group to get together in the first place. It advises on community organization techniques, committee procedure, book-keeping and newsletter production.

> An interesting and welcome development is the growing 'habit' of local groups and individuals coming together on a Southwick-wide basis to take on agreed tasks and campaigns. Once again SNAP has very often acted as a catalyst for these developments which include – the revival of the Southwick Carnival – a massive undertaking in terms of organization – and the support of over 50 members of the Carnival Committee in their organization of this increasingly popular event.[6]

There is also a range of activities in connection with public participation in planning, where SNAP has enabled the local community to make its own proposals about how it would like its neighbourhood to be developed. Such proposals have included proposals for Southwick's riverside and the establishment of the Village Farm Committee.

Many people have concluded that nothing can be expected from people in areas like Southwick. 'There is no local leadership' they say, implying that people in this kind of area must always remain dependent on others. But despite this pessimism new hope is springing up, people are discovering that they have something to offer to the community and they are gaining confidence in themselves. Local groups are being helped to be more effective. People and groups across the community are co-operating with each other, and the churches, with one of the clergy chairing the SNAP management committee, are well and truly involved.

Much of what has been described is concerned with responding to immediate needs, but at the same time and included in this response there is a persistent process of adult education. The project is not just about the protest of the powerless, but is concerned that people should gain a mature attitude to the whole management of their lives and of their community. It is, for instance, easier to start a group in response to some obvious problem – such as vandalism on an estate – than to sustain it when the immediate problem has been dealt with. But if the quality of life on that estate is to be improved permanently, the tenants must continue to take some responsibility. The low-key participation that this entails requires a continuing community, a deeper under-standing of people, a wider knowledge of life and some general frame-work of ideas within which to operate. The project is concerned to develop this kind of maturity by long-term adult education. This means helping groups to keep together when there are no obvious issues to stimulate them and no obvious enemy to fight.

In this more fundamental process of changing attitudes and outlooks special attention is being given to the needs of women. Communities like Southwick, which have been based on heavy industry, have for generations been male-dominated. Women need to find a way through the mythology that surrounds ideas about their role in life, and to discover their full value as persons.

There is real hope in this project, but of course there are also diffi-culties. Not everyone approves of SNAP, and there is always the danger that a new kind of dependence on SNAP instead of on the local authority could develop. One difficulty is that the policy of appointing local people to employment in the project has given rise to unreal expectations. Some people have found it hard to accept the fact that because they have been able to help in certain ways in a voluntary capacity, they are not thereby equipped with the high degree of skill that is needed to take full responsibility for this kind of enabling work. We all have to learn not only what our potential is but what our limitations are.

(iii) A future for young people?

One more example should be enough to enable us to draw out the significance of these signs of hope. This example is concerned with the kind of education that schools provide.

If workers find their humanity threatened by the loss of their jobs, and if people in the inner urban areas are in danger of losing their humanity by becoming dependent on the state, many young people start their lives at a disadvantage.

A teacher in a large comprehensive school on a housing estate told me some time ago that of the 250 boys in his 'house', 170 had problems in their homes. Many of their parents were divorced, separated or on the verge of breaking-up and a typical problem was that of young people having to get used to new fathers or mothers or wondering what to do about the old ones. The teachers were dealing with young people suffering from acute emotional disturbance, and at the same time trying to prepare them for an unsettled future in which many would have no jobs, or at best would have to move from job to job.

If the educational system in the past was geared to meeting the needs of industry for large numbers of unskilled manual workers, there must be radical changes today to prepare young people for a different situation with different kinds of jobs, or no jobs at all, more leisure, and continual change and uncertainty. An urgent need is for young people to discover that they have certain resources in themselves.

A sign of hope is that a number of people, in different parts of the country, quite independently of each other, are tackling this problem. The teacher I have already mentioned is now head of a comprehensive school in a different part of the town and with a more mixed intake. He is working for the inclusion of a social education programme as a major part of the school syllabus. He argues that most teaching is a matter of handing on a tradition. The teacher in effect says to the young people: '*Your* experience and what *you* think about life is not important until you understand it in *my* words and through *my* interpretation.' This approach fails to take young people seriously, but treats them as subordinate beings, repressing the new realities.

Of course there is a tradition with which young people must come to terms, and there are knowledge and skills to be acquired, but there should be a creative relationship between the new and the old. This demands a different kind of relationship between pupils and teachers, in which the young people are able to confront the tradition with their own experience and their own interpretations of life. Only if young people learn that they have something to contribute that is valuable *because* it comes out of their experience, can they have any confidence in themselves and in their ability to live in a changing world. Older people are also in need of this exchange, for in the end it is only young people who will be fully able to adjust to the new things that press upon us.

Proposals for the social education programme are being prepared, and questions the committee is considering include the following. Can young people be helped to see and reflect on how the whole educational syllabus hangs together? Can they be helped to look at how they themselves are growing physically and emotionally? Can they discover things about their relationships and value judgments? The committee is also considering how learning can take place experientially as well as by more traditional methods, in groups and also individually, so that young people learn about their relationships with others and are also able to think for themselves and to make their own choices.

Although the social education programme is not yet in operation, changes are already taking place in the school. Any fear that a concern with social education reduces the level of academic attainment in the school should be allayed by the fact that all are on exam courses, and as pupils see that all are equally valued, any labelling of pupils as 'bright' or 'hopeless' becomes irrelevant. Because it is possible for all to gain something from education, few leave early. Hope is emerging in the young people themselves.

For the teachers it is an uphill task, but they gain encouragement by discovering that other people are working on the same lines. Some have found help not only from colleagues in education but from the church. The teacher I have been discussing has gained support from two aspects of the church's life. First, he has been linked with a project started by the industrial mission in which head teachers and industrialists share common questions. Second, he finds a parallel between his experiments in education and attempts by Christians to develop a style of theology which does not simply hand on a tradition but draws on people's own experience. It is this that has led him to share in some of my own activities. New ways of involving people in the learning process are being explored in schools, and in the churches I am working with others for changes, so that people can make their own contribution to the search for faith.

To return to what is happening in the schools. The proposed social education programme represents a major change in educational institutions. Many parents find it hard to accept change, and fear that their children will lose their place in the scramble for jobs. Some teachers also prefer to play safe, and educational administrators and politicans fear a loss of control and anarchy in the educational system. In fact what they should see is that a world in which large numbers of young people are unemployed and alienated from society is bound to become lawless and violent if changes which enable young people to make judgments for themselves, are not made.

(iv) Signs that point beyond themselves
I have described just three signs of hope which I have identified in places where there are great threats to human fulfilment. There are many other hopeful things happening which may be less obvious, but are just as real : where the hungry are fed, the stranger is welcomed, the naked clothed, the prisoner visited, where reconciliation takes place, where self gives way to the service of others and wherever hope is born in situations of despair. I have simply picked out three examples.

I now look at the significance of these signs. I must point out first of all that they need not be seen as signs at all. They are in themselves good, in that they are helping people to face what threatens them, to endure, enjoy and change things. There is no need to see them as signs of anything beyond themselves. All the same, it is possible to read them as pointing to something that has even greater significance and a more enduring quality. If we can do this, we come nearer to the truth and can be helped to respond more fully and hopefully to life.

I do not want to take away from the real value of the things I have described by pointing to the fragility of the results. I have already mentioned how many of the industrial co-operatives have failed, and pointed to the difficulties arising in the process of helping people to take responsibility for their own lives. Even where there is success the results represent no more than a temporary solution. A worker moves on to another job and the situation swings back to what it was before, or gets channelled into a 'safer' direction, or an area is redeveloped and yesterday's solutions become inappropriate in a changed situation. This is no argument for standing back and doing nothing. We must go on discovering new possibilities which in the short and medium term enable more humanity. It is, however, sheer fantasy to imagine that these moves will in time add up to a problemless society. We do not make progressive steps towards a perfect world nor is there any political programme for the achievement of the kingdom of God. For those who can read them as such, these things are signs of hope pointing beyond their own transience to something that will endure.

If we are to recognize signs of hope, we need some clues. Within the confusion of life there must be certain values which help us to identify a genuine sign of hope. It is the church that is interested in signs of hope as being signs of the kingdom of God. It is the church that has clues which make it possible to identify the signs of hope. The clues come from the gospel of Christ crucified and risen. It is the responsibility of the church to identify the signs and to point the world to what is ultimately hopeful in life. We must now take a closer look at what this involves.

2 Identifying the signs

The clue by which Christians interpret life is the resurrection of Jesus Christ. Resurrection faith is not primarily a matter of believing in life after death, but of believing in the living God and in his unshakeable faithfulness and total commitment to his creation and to man in life in death and beyond death. Resurrection faith is not concerned with the indefinite continuation of life, but with newness of life : 'new creation, new birth, new man and new world. That which breaks through the return of the eternal sameness of dying and coming to be.'[7] In his dying Jesus shared the common experience of men, but his resurrection was something new and unexpected. It was seen to be the act of God, who in raising Jesus from the dead put his seal on all that Jesus was and on all he had done. In Jesus' resurrection his manhood as representative of all mankind was taken up into the life of God. It was a definitive breakthrough into a new dimension of living.

Christians do not see the resurrection as an isolated event but as a sign of God's activity. First, the resurrection is the promise of new life for all men, God's invitation to men to receive their full humanity by sharing in his life through Christ in the community of faith. Secondly, the resurrection is the beginning of the renewal of all things and God's promise that this renewal will be completed. The resurrection is a new beginning, not an end. The risen Jesus still bears the marks of crucifixion, and crucifixion and resurrection remain inseparable. It is precisely in the tensions and in the face of death that the reality of God is to be known.

It is because Christians hold this resurrection faith that they expect to see signs of hope in the world as the kingdom of God breaks in, creating new life where things seem most hopeless. It is because Christians hold this faith that they are able to identify those things which constitute genuine signs of hope and understand that these signs point to the presence of God and to his invitation to man.

There is no easy way of reading the signs directly from our faith. We do not know what the kingdom will be like, but in knowing Jesus Christ we know the qualities of the kingdom. Our sensitivity to the signs of the kingdom depends not only on our intellectual grasp of the gospel, but on the knowledge of Christ that comes to us in our relationship with him in the community of faith. It is as we share in Christ's life, in his love of the world and his agony and near despair over it, that we also see what it is that gives hope. The qualities of the kingdom are the qualities of Jesus Christ as representative of true humanity, and the signs of hope consist of the emergence of true humanity in life and point to the activity of God as the one who bestows humanity. Wherever people receive their humanity we can identify the presence of God.

The examples I have given will show something of what this means in practice. In these examples certain things are happening, and in the context of these events, though not all the responses are positive, some people are discovering new possibilities of humanity. The trade unionists are discovering that they can take new initiatives; the people in the inner city are gaining confidence in their ability to make decisions about their own lives; in the schools young people and teachers are entering into a new relationship in which the young people are discovering that they have something to give to society.

If no action had been taken, if the trade unionists had not combined to resist the closure of their works, if the Community Development Project had not started and been sustained in Southwick, and if the head teacher in the comprehensive school had not determined to introduce a social education programme, things would have remained unchanged. On the other hand, the fact that these things are being done is not in itself a guarantee that through them people will discover their humanity. It is quite possible for new things to happen and yet for people to continue to operate on the same old assumptions, without any radical change in their perceptions about themselves or about life.

The signs of hope consist in the fact that people became open to new possibilities and powers in themselves and in life. They had the courage to put a question-mark against the past. Their response to the new possibilities, however, varied. A new sense of power can lead to a grasping after power; to greater humanity or to new forms of inhumanity; to fanatical and idolatrous commitment to specific objectives or to a recognition of God's grace in life and a radical change of attitude towards life.

It is the church's job to identify the signs of hope, to focus on the things that really are signs of hope and to keep men's various ventures on course. I have already mentioned how easy it is for activities to lose their original motivation and for extraneous or secondary motives to take over. For all of us there is the temptation to attach more importance than is warranted to the particular projects we are involved in, and to our own particular approach and methods. This can become not creative, but actually destructive of the purposes we originally set out to serve. We need continually to re-focus our aims, and to gain encouragement from identifying the really hopeful things that are emerging. It is this that can help us to avoid giving ultimate value to changing features which are relative to particular people and situations, and save us from being trapped by our own past successes. I shall return later to the fact that the church is in as much danger as any other body of people of losing sight of its true goal.

Cynicism and despair are the inevitable result of false expectations. A recognition of the enduring gains which are in themselves signs of the reality of God's activity in life is what gives hope to the world. The church's primary task is to bring to the world a spirit of confidence in the fact that God is at work in life and in our efforts to make a better world. The outcome is in God's hands and the future is assured. It is on the basis of this confidence that the church must also be an instrument of judgment. It cares too much about people to stand back and see opportunities being missed. The importance of the signs does not lie in the results achieved, but in the possibilities they open up for the recognition of the grace of God in life. The response that is called for is not anxious zeal but thankfulness, hope and expectation. It is the church's job to enable this change of attitude.

Belief in the future demands not only a renewing but an expansion of vision, so that men have a sense of anticipation and a belief that there is something more ahead of them. We must not be so concerned with signs that we fail to see what it is they signify; the purpose of signs is to point beyond themselves. The new relationships we have spoken of, the personal dignity and the expressions of self-giving for others that are being discovered, are under constant pressure, but they point beyond themselves to a reality that withstands all pressure. They point to the reality of God and to his invitation to men to receive their full humanity and to be built into a community which has a future. The church fails in its task in relation to the signs of hope if it stops short of putting people in touch with God as the source of hope.

In order to fulfil this task the church must maintain touch both with what is happening in the world and with the resources of the gospel. This is the double movement which I have referred to as the outward and the inward journeys.

It may help us if we look for a moment at how the Old Testament prophets went about their task of identifying the signs in their time. Their insights were given to them within a continual process of searching for the truth. They did not work in a vacuum, but stood within the religious tradition of Israel. They understood this to be a living tradition and used it with the utmost flexibility in order to interpret what they saw in the life of the nation. With their observation of events and their knowledge of their tradition as background, the word that they spoke came to them in their direct communion with God. In speaking the word of God their aim was not to give information but to call people's attention to their actual situation before God and to elicit a response to God:

> The prophetic word . . . has its origin in an impassioned dialogue; yet the dialogue never tries to climb into the realm of general religious truth, but instead uses even the most suspect means to tie the listening partner down to his particular time and place in order to make him understand his own situation before God. In order to reach this partner in the specific situation in which he has to make a decision and which . . . cannot be replaced by any other. . . . Their (the prophets') concern was to deliver a specific message from Yahweh to particular men and women who, without themselves being aware of it, stood in a special situation before God.[8]

There is debate as to the relationship of the prophets to the mainstream of Israel's life, but it is clear that they were not isolated figures, as was once imagined. They were actively or re-actively products of their own cultures and dependent on their own communities. In the same way today, identification of the signs is the responsibility not of lone individuals but of the whole church.

The church's ability to identify the signs of God's activity in the world depends on the same kind of faithfulness. Like the biblical prophets, the church must attend to what is happening in the world. It must reflect on its tradition, and it must wait on God in prayer and worship in order to know what his word is to the world and to the church.

The God who in the past spoke through the prophets and who has made himself known in the life of Jesus Christ, is the same God who invites us to receive our humanity in the present. The Christian gospel is good news because it gives hope to us in our actual situation. The church should point not only to what God has done in the past but to signs of his present activity.

3 The church and the signs

I have spoken about what the church *should be* and what it *should do*. Now I turn to what the church *is* and what it *is doing*. In order to do this I return to how the church appears to those who are outside. The majority of people are outside the church, and it is with them that I am primarily concerned. 'What goes on up there?' was an outsider's question about the church. From this girl's point of view, the church consisted of a small group of people, who were not representative of the people among whom she lived and whose concerns were remote from her experience. Whatever the church might believe and practice, it was inaccessible to her until she met those of us who were helping with the club. When she asked us what it was all about, we were unable to answer in a way that could make sense to her.

All the churches share the same problem. All have been pushed to the fringes of life, and to those outside they appear to be more concerned with their own life than with the common questions of mankind. We must enquire how far this is true of the churches in North East England. In what ways are they in fact going out in order to relate to the issues of life in the region? What signs of hope have they identified? How far are they helping people to recognize God as the source of hope and to respond to his invitation?

There is a considerable outward movement among the churches of which it would be impossible to give anything like a full account. What I intend to do is to give examples: first of how the outward journey is being undertaken, second of how the inward journey is being undertaken, and third, because there is a tendency to separate these two journeys, how both outward and inward journeys are being undertaken together. I start with the outward journey.

(i) Outward journey
Questions of technological change, participation and politics, collective power and deprivation cannot be tackled solely from a base in the local church. But this does not mean that the local church has no concern with these issues. If we are to have a personal faith, we must engage with the structures and issues of society. It is with the people who are seeking a personal faith and in the local community of faith that engagement with these issues must take place. A serious concern with the issues, however, soon pushes us beyond our immediate locality and demands co-operation across the boundaries of local churches and

denominations and more urgently across the divide between religion and everyday life. This means that whatever is done from a local church base needs the support of a wider framework.

Issues need to be understood from the inside, as they appear to those who are most involved in them, that is, from within the institutions of government and industry and from within the various collectives that operate in society. If the church is to gain a true understanding of the issues, it must insert itself into the life of society and appreciate from the inside the things that are affecting people in many different ways. Of course the church is already present in society. We are all affected in some way by the quality of our institutions, and there are lay people at work within these institutions. Just to be there, however, is not enough. There must be a deliberate effort to bring faith to bear upon the issues. This cannot be done by individuals alone, nor does it come about simply because church members happen to be present. The church as community has to work together to understand what is happening in the world in the light of its faith and to understand its faith in the light of what is happening in the world. It is this understanding that enables the church and its members to take appropriate action.

A ministry that is concerned with social questions must be a ministry of the whole Church. This is a prophetic ministry. That is to say, it is a ministry that is addressed to people in their responsibilities in society and asks questions about the values and goals of society. In order to perform this ministry the kind of question the church must ask is not, 'How many people are being brought into the church?', but, 'With what issues is the church getting to grips?', 'Does the church out of its faith bring anything distinctive to these issues?', 'How far are people being enabled to recognize and respond to God's invitation to them in these issues?'

Let us look at these questions in turn. Some of the issues have already been discussed: technological change and its effects on employment and unemployment, the possibilities opened up by these changes for the development of man's creativity in leisure, the quality of political life and others. These questions can hardly be avoided by anyone living in North East England. Many people in the churches are deeply disturbed by them, but there are others who think that 'political' matters are out of place in church discussions. Christian concern has in many places gone beyond discussion and local churches have set up job creation and youth opportunity programmes for unemployed people. The concern of some lay people has led them into full-time work with the unemployed or with the careers and other statutory services. I have already mentioned the involvement of the local churches in the Southwick Neighbourhood Action Project and, in the political field, one local clergyman was so unhappy about the state of local politics that he got himself elected to his District and County Councils.

Full-time appointments of industrial chaplains, social responsibility officers and a chaplain to the arts and recreation have made it possible for some clergy to perform a wider enabling role in relation to these issues. In their work, it has become clear that one function the church can perform is to bring Christians and non-Christians together across the different levels, parties and geographical areas to face common questions together. Because they spend most of their time in one sector of life and because they are not tied to one particular job, these ministers acquire a wide understanding of the issues of their sector. Individual ministers know a lot about technological change, about the tensions experienced by those who work in the town hall and about the possibilities for creativity opened up by unemployment.

But for most people there is a problem in actually getting to grips with an issue. I experienced this problem when I was invited to speak at a deanery synod meeting on 'A Christian Attitude to Work, Rewards and Industrial Action'. We only had an hour and a half, and there were too many other things to be dealt with for the discussion to continue at a subsequent meeting. A lot of information was needed, and we had to find some way of sharing the different experiences and points of view among the people present. Many people are concerned about social questions, but they need more than one discussion if they are to get to grips with a subject. There is concern, but there is also a feeling of powerlessness and a lot of confusion about whether these are things with which the churches should be concerned, and if so, what the churches' contribution should be. It is at this point that one question becomes urgent. Does the church out of its faith bring anything distinctive to these issues?

Let us, for example, take the question of young people who go straight from school to unemployment. The majority of those who are trying to get to grips with this matter are not consciously impelled by Christian faith but by their natural concern for humanity. They see more or less clearly that they are engaged in a project that is opening up possibilities for fuller human living. How does the Christian who believes he is engaged in God's project for the realization of full humanity account for this overlap of interest? Does the Christian, because he is a Christian, bring anything new to the matter?

The Christian first of all rejects any dualism between a spiritual and a material or a temporal and an eternal world. He believes there is only 'one single, God-fulfilled history'.[9] Whether he is named or not, it is the same God who is at work in men's concern for their fellow men. It is necessary to affirm the one-ness of life in the face of much of the church's recent past that has separated religion and everyday life. In the Bible, mankind as created by God is one and the world is one. The sense of solidarity with all men within the operation of God's purposes has led to the recognition that the things of the kingdom must be spoken of in the language of the world. Christians and non-Christians are in fact engaged in the same project and they must use a language in which they can learn from each other and which will enable them to co-operate.

But there are dangers in this position. If we are all engaged in the same project and we speak of this in the language of the world, we lose any identity as Christians and we are in danger of losing any belief that there is a gospel or that there is a God. In an analysis of South American liberation theology, José Miguel Bonino gives a clear warning of what is at stake:

> It is necessary 'to name the kingdom' in the language of everyday human history. There is no lack of precedents and possibilities. We speak of 'love', 'liberation', the 'new man', as the signs which allow us to identify the active sovereignty of God in history, the redeeming presence of Jesus Christ, and consequently, the call and the obedience of faith. This, we contend, is biblically and theologically legitimate. But a serious risk lurks in this option, because, as these terms are historicized in the general history of mankind, they run the risk of being uprooted, of de-historicizing themselves in the particular historical reference of faith. That is, we come to speak of a love, a new man, a liberation in which the reference to the history of Israel, of Jesus Christ, of the Apostles becomes secondary, or merely exemplary, or dispensable. If this happens, we have, in Christian terms, vacated any reference to God himself. What God and whose kingdom are we speaking about? At the extreme of this line, we would conclude by deifying man and history, and it would be more honest to call a spade a spade and to avow a total immanentism.[10]

Christians who immerse themselves in the cause of the world have not been equipped by the church with a theology that is adequate to this situation. Their intention is to overcome what they conceive to be a false dualism in their faith. But in practice the risk is that they will deny the reality of God.

The question that faces us is how, without slipping back into a false dualism, value can be given both to our present activities and to God as he has made himself known in Jesus Christ. Some theologians have tried to answer this question by using the history of the Jews and the life of Christ as illustrative of general truths of human life. Others suggest that faith's contribution to human activity is simply to provide motivation and dynamic for engagement in the issues of life. Both these approaches devalue either our present activity or the reality of what God has done and does in history.

If we are to get at the truth, I believe we cannot avoid a certain kind of dualism. Two histories must be taken into account, our present history and that of the Jews. Both are, of course, part of the one history of the world. But the particular history of the Jews (rather than some other part of history) is vital for us because it is within this part of history that God has made himself and the promise of his kingdom known to men. It is here that God has been named as the God of Abraham, Isaac and Jacob, and as the God and Father of our Lord Jesus Christ. There is tension in holding these two pieces of history together, but it is in doing this that we discover the significance of our own history and come to know who this God is, who calls us to share in his purposes in history. This way of looking at things gives real value to our present activities and at the same time makes it clear that we need to know *what* God and *whose* kingdom we are concerned with. From this it follows that it is necessary not only to obey but also to speak about God. The distinctive thing the Christian brings to the issues of life is a realism not only about the limitations but also about the possibilities of man's actions, because he knows that certain possibilities have been opened up by God and that God has given us a way of realizing these possibilities. It is clarity about this that enables men to see in their present activities urgency and hope.

An ambivalence with respect to Christian participation in the issues of life stems from the recognition that there is both continuity and discontinuity between our world and the kingdom of God. There is a tendency to solve the problem by coming down on one side or the other. That is, by claiming that there is complete discontinuity and thus robbing man's present action of any ultimate worth; or by claiming that it is man alone who builds the kingdom, thus making any reference to God irrelevant. A third way is suggested by the biblical pictures of the 'body' and 'resurrection'. St Paul uses these metaphors as an alternative way of speaking of the kingdom. The metaphor of the body illustrates the fact that in Christ mankind has a corporate identity (Romans 12.4; I Corinthians 12.12ff.; Ephesians 2.16; Colossians 3.15). The resurrection is not primarily an individual, but a corporate reality.

In a discussion of the nature of resurrection (I Corinthians 15), Paul pictures the continuity and discontinuity of the body in terms of the relationship between seed and plant. Visually the two things seem to have no connection, but there is an essential identity. Without the seed there would be no plant, and with a different seed there would be a different plant. This is the kind of relationship between what man does in his physical and historical existence and God's kingdom. Man has real responsibility and causality. Life is not a game, and the world is not a waiting-room. There are choices to be made and things to be done. It seems pretty certain that if there had been no attempt to revitalize the economy and to attract new jobs to the region, the North East today would be a more depressed and depressing place than it is.

People were encouraged by a new vision and real benefits have resulted.

Any idea, however, that it is possible to build the perfect world by our own efforts is an illusion. Some of the new housing that heralded the 'new Jerusalem' was so penny-pinching and jerry-built that it constitutes today's slums. Between all that we do and the realization of the kingdom of God lies the intervening fact of judgment. Mankind's activities are too muddy, mixed and evil to be equated with the kingdom.

> The kingdom is not the denial of history but the elimination of its corruptibility, its frustrations, weakness, ambiguity – more deeply, its sin – in order to bring to full realization the true meaning of the communal life of man. In the same vein, historical 'works' in all orders of life – social, economic, political – are permanent in so far as they belong to that order. At the same time, all possibilities of confusion are eliminated because in one case as in the other, there is the intervening fact of judgment which divides, excludes and cleanses ('burns') that which does not belong in the new age. The kingdom is not . . . the natural dénouement of history. Quite the contrary, history arrives at the kingdom through suffering, conflict, and judgment. But the kingdom redeems, transforms, and perfects the 'corporality' of history and the dynamics of love that has operated in it.[11]

It is out of this understanding of its faith that the church brings to the issues of life: discernment, hope and urgency. In the light of this faith it discerns the signs of God's present activity in the world. By its belief that new possibilities are opened up by God and in the assurance of the kingdom, it brings hope and encouragement to human action. By its understanding of the nature of the kingdom and the need for judgment, it exercises a critical function in relation to all men's activities. By its belief that God calls all men to co-operate in producing the kingdom it enables men to answer not only the question 'How do I know that there is a God?' but also 'How do I participate in the purposes of God?' It is this question that lies behind all our searching and it is so central that I want to deal with it in a separate section. At this point I want to pass from these reflections on the church's outward journey to consider what is happening with regard to its inward journey.

(ii) Inward journey

Jesus spoke of Christians as leaven, light and salt, and he warned that salt that loses its savour 'is fit neither for the land nor for the dunghill; men throw it away' (Luke 14.35). It is because of its gospel that the church has something vital to contribute to life. The gospel enables us to believe that things can be different. The gospel is not abstract information, but the living God as he makes himself known to us and calls us to obedience within the opportunities of our own situation. If we are to keep in touch with the gospel, an inward journey is also necessary. We experience this within a community of faith. Here is an example of how this inward journey is taking place in one congregation.

The vicar came to the conclusion that general exhortations to be involved in the issues of life were counter-productive. It only led, as he put it, to a hardening of the 'oughteries'. However worthy the cause might be, everyone cannot be involved in everything. There must be some discrimination about who is called to do what. What was needed, in his view, was for the congregation and the individuals in it to be sensitive to people's different gifts so that they could be helped to respond to their different callings. It seemed to this clergy-man that faith had impressed upon many church members a sense of their own worthlessness. Their negative attitude and lack of expecta-tion with regard to themselves presented a major obstacle to believing that they had anything at all to contribute to life. In order to tackle this problem he invited some members of the congregation to work with him to identify, not their sins and weaknesses, but their strong points. This involved commitment to a series of meetings in which they helped each other to come to terms with themselves as unique people with God-given gifts. Time had to be given to developing trust within the group, so that people could open up to each other and speak of their own feelings about themselves. Many misconceptions of Christian faith had to be overcome, and throughout the course there were periods of silent openness to what God might be saying to the members and simple meditations on passages of scripture.

To lead people in such a project requires pastoral skill. It was, however, not lack of skill but pressure of time that threatened this particular scheme. Two kinds of time pressures have to be taken into account. The first is the pressure that life puts on lay people. Young couples with children have little spare time and people in positions of responsibility are under continual pressure. If the church is not to consist solely of people who have time to spare, it must be sensitive to these pressures. There is, of course, good reason why we all plead lack of time rather than make time for something that is difficult. The 'gifts' course asked people to become open to new discoveries about themselves and about God. Even if one does not admit to being afraid, one may be glad of an excuse not to risk venturing out of one's depth. Fear in the presence of God is in no way out of place. Terror as the 'Hound of Heaven' pants behind us increases the nearer he gets to us (Francis Thompson). The call to discipleship is a call to the unknown, to self-offering and to sharing in Christ's suffering for the world. It is only God's grace that makes it possible for anyone to accept such a call.

The second kind of time pressure arises from the priorities of the church. The experience of this vicar when he came to the parish is typical of many other clergy. He found a full programme of activities in which the amateur dramatic club held pride of place. It took a great deal of determination and the endurance of considerable unpleasantness to get priorities redrawn. Most churches are not organized for the inward any more than they are for the outward journey. For many congregations this is not the result of their own choice, but of the situation they have inherited. I visited a vicar in a mining parish which had been amalgamated with two other church districts. He was responsible for three church buildings, a church school, two church halls and four separate communities which all saw him as *their* vicar. He told me that, having spent the first two years dealing with buildings and boundaries, he thought he could now get down to the real job. The next I heard of him, however, was that he had moved to another parish. He will be fortunate if the same problems do not await him there. This is not to say that the inward journey is not taking place, but that where it is happening, it is despite many difficulties.

It is not only fear and lack of time that keeps people from the inward journey, but sheer boredom. Some imagination is needed if people are to sense that there are depths in themselves and in life that are worth exploring. In Sunderland a week of activities of a carnival sort was planned under the title 'Sunderland Search'. The programme included a mini-pilgrimage through the town with stops at points where there were good views of the town, the river, docks, industry, public buildings and housing. At these points there were brief meditations on the life of the town and on the saints who had lived there. Among a variety of events there was also a series of meetings in which forms of meditation were jointly explored. Many people feel a need for time to be quiet. There is a search for spiritual growth in forms of meditation and relaxation. But the old ways in the form in which they have been received have gone dead. I do not wish to discount the importance of the different things that happen in regular church services, but if people are to discover the full possibilities of the inward journey, something more is needed. I have only given examples of the new life that is stirring.

A second essential aspect of the inward journey is reflection on the gospel in relation to contemporary experience. Christians believe things can be different because God is at work in the world. In order to identify God's present activity, there must be a continual wrestling with Christian tradition in the light of contemporary life. Without this kind of reflection, the church will get stuck in its past and will be unable either to move forward itself or to help the world to move forward. Reflection on faith and life is a matter for the whole church, and although it requires the help of professional theologians, it must not be left to them alone. The New Testament helps us to understand the struggles of the early church as it wrestled with the implications of its faith for the new questions that had to be faced. We must do the same.

In urging the need for reflection I do not refer only to intellectual knowledge, important though that is. Nor am I only concerned with what has been handed on to us in scripture and in the life of the church. The material for reflection comes also from the contemporary experience of Christ in the world and in our prayer, worship and life in the church. There are truths, too, that the church must learn from those who do not acknowledge God by name. Reflection on life in the light of Christian faith should be a regular part of the life of every congregation, and everyone should have opportunity to contribute. This is a continual job for the whole church, and we must ask, 'Where is this process actually taking place?'

In order to answer this question we must first observe that most congregations are not representative of their local communities. There are, for instance, more women than men in most congregations and a disproportionate number of older and retired people. There are less people in the middle age ranges, the thirties and forties, and an absence of manual workers.[12] Where there are people who have responsible positions in society, they are likely to remain on the fringe of the church's activities. Attempts to relate faith and life that are confined to the congregation therefore often fail to give a true reflection of the world as it is. We need to bring all the tensions and pressures of the outward journey to the inward journey if it is to lead us to the living God and not to be a withdrawal from life.

The difficulties of relating the inward and the outward journeys from within the life of the congregation has led some people to conclude that it is better to start from outside the congregation by bringing people together on the basis of their involvement in society. A social responsibility officer has been working for some years among people involved in local government. Many of these are in fact church members, but most of them say that they receive little help from their churches in knowing what it means to be a Christian in public life. In 1978 the social responsibility officer accepted an invitation to go with two local councillors to a national conference to be held in the following year. The aim of the conference was to bring together a number of Christians who were active in public life so that they could discover how their faith related to their responsibilities. The national project was important in that it set a programme and a timetable for specific preparation that would run up to the conference. This led to a definite commitment to give the necessary time to the task. Only two councillors were to go to the conference, but their first job was to invite eight other people to work with them in the preparatory discussions. The people they invited were also involved in local government and came from both major parties. In its monthly meetings the group first identified the tensions and possibilities they experienced in their work as councillors. They then explored insights about where Christian faith was relevant to these matters. The presence of the social responsibility officer was crucial in presenting aspects of Christian faith in ways that helped the members to make new discoveries. The fact that the group shared common experience and that the two who were going to the conference had chosen people they trusted to work with helped them to be specific about their situation and frank with each other. This example shows that however busy people are, it is still possible for them to carve out enough time for this kind of exploration.

(iii) Inward/outward journey

There is a tendency to force Christians into two opposing camps holding two different concepts of mission: Mission A is a calling out of the world, an inward journey. Mission B is a social gospel, an outward journey into the world. I take a third position which refuses to accept this kind of polarization.[13] Let us call it Mission C. Mission C recognizes that the inward and the outward aspects of the gospel cannot be separated. It is impossible to be gripped by the inwardness of the gospel unless you are engaged with the forces which hold people in their power. Neither inward nor outward journey can be undertaken on its own. They must go together. Let me give one example of how this is happening.

A Methodist chapel that had at one time stood in the heart of Middlesbrough's industrial life found itself in the mid-1960s in the eye of an area scheduled for redevelopment. Many people had already left the area, and those who remained lived in streets where half the houses were uninhabited and vandalized, wondering when the bulldozers would move in to knock down their own homes. This quite clearly was a 'dying' congregation. It had to be working-class, for only the less well-off had remained in the area. If anything, there were more old people than in most congregations. Its skilled people consisted only of one plumber, a draughtsman and one or two teachers. The church officials had to decide what the church should put its efforts into. The nature of the area meant that there was little scope for much growth in church membership. Were they simply to wait for the end? The decision they made was to stand with the people of the area, to share their tensions and to help them to make a positive contribution to decency of life in the present and the re-shaping of the area for the future. Having made this decision, the mid-weekly leaders' meeting took on a new lease of life. A systematic examination of the needs of the area was undertaken with the help of social workers and politicians. Debate was initiated about plans for the area. Demands were made to get definite dates for demolition and rebuilding so that people could plan the changes they had to make and not simply be pushed around by officialdom. People were living in the rubble of what appeared to be a permanent building site, from which most services had long since been withdrawn. The church set about providing an adventure playground, a children's holiday scheme, a caring scheme for families and a pensioner's luncheon club.

The crucial thing about this example is the interplay between the inward journey of the church and its outward journey into the community. It would have been possible for the church, like many congregations in similar circumstances, to have taken a self-pitying attitude and to spend its time looking back on the 'glories' of the past. Although I have described what happened in a few sentences, the leaders' meeting spent a whole year thinking the matter through before there was much active engagement in the community. All sorts of internal obstacles had to be overcome: 'I don't want to be involved with that type of family', and 'Should we not be preaching the gospel rather than doing social work?' These tensions had to be worked through by thinking about God's relationship with the world; and by bringing the social concerns into the worship and prayer of the church. Nor were all these doubts and difficulties cleared away once and for all. The minister said he felt there was a cyclic process in which people seemed to have overcome their doubts, only to come back to the same questions when there was a lull in activity or in the face of some difficulty or conflict. This congregation was not especially different from any other congregation, but it managed to combine the inward and the outward journey so that both were enriched.

There was a real inward journey in which the congregation wrestled with the question of what obedience to God might mean for them. Together they dreamed dreams and saw the possibilities of what could be. The essential material of this inward journey was their experience in the outward journey into the community. This was not a 'social gospel' but the expression of faith which enabled people to believe that God was present in events that were disturbing, and who, because they believed, not only recognized signs of hope but co-operated with God to produce signs of hope.

Today the area is still in the process of being rebuilt and the chapel has closed. Some of the things that were started, such as the children's holiday scheme and the pensioners' luncheon club, continue, but others, having served their purpose, no longer operate. In the engagement of the chapel with the community, signs of the kingdom and of the reality of God appeared. Like all signs they were provisional and temporary, but they were real enough. What was achieved was that

at a period of particular need some people were enabled to live hopefully. This is worthwhile in itself, and it brought something lasting
into life as it goes on in these people and through the community into
the life of mankind. The whole process, moreover, led some people to
recognize that more things are in fact possible than they had imagined.
A real contribution has been made to the kingdom, even though the
kingdom in its completeness is in the future.

I have given glimpses into some of the ways in which the churches
in North East England are seeking to recognize the activity of God in
the world. I now draw out the fact that not only should the church
point to the signs of hope, and help to produce signs of hope, but that
it should in itself be a sign of hope.

4 The church as sign

'The church is the church only when it exists for others.'[14]
The church as we know it is both a sign of hope and a counter-sign.
It holds out possibilities for greater humanity and at the same time it
appears to be against our humanity. There is an ambiguity in its
witness.

It is difficult to give a coherent account of the church in North East
England, for its most obvious feature lies in its diversity. I might give
an account of the life of the different denominations and their attempts
to work together, but this would not capture what is most true about
the church. Divisions between Christians do not run between but
across denominations. This point came home with some surprise to a
Roman Catholic layman and a Salvation Army officer when, in a discussion of their beliefs, they discovered how closely they agreed.

It has been suggested that throughout the world the Christian community is slowly re-grouping around certain foci which represent different ways of understanding the character and demands of the gospel
and of Christian life. As a result there are a number of different
'families' expressing different forms of Christian community. The main
'families' are the charismatic, the socially-concerned and the conservation-oriented.[15] It is from this angle that I look at the church in the
North East and ask in what way a church that is expressed in such
different ways is a sign of hope.

The charismatic 'family' includes a wide spectrum of positions:

> The charismatic movement takes into account the whole range of
> God's gifts to the church. These gifts vary from the sensational to
> the quite unsensational, from miracles to good teaching and admin-
> istration. God's gifts always take human talent into account, but the
> reality of his grace is much more than the simple embellishment of
> such talent. It is a gift, and as such marks those who receive it by

a new depth of faith, love and service and new openness to the action of the Holy Spirit.[16]

The movement is a sign of God's power to release springs in man's life that remain untouched by a purely intellectual approach, so that at the deepest level people are liberated to be themselves. The positive significance of the upsurge of the charismatic movement throughout the world is that it is a sign of God's power to engage and integrate the whole person.

> Dance, speaking in tongues and healing the sick . . . awaken confidence, make people feel accepted and loved by God. They strengthen trust in the inborn gifts of the people bestowed on them by the creator Spirit, and encourage them to recognize the organisational and liturgical gifts of their pre-Christian existence as gifts of the Holy Spirit. . . . They can liberate the people of God and free them from authoritarian structures. They create room for an oral theological debate. Thus they unfreeze the western liturgical formulas and replace imported ideologies (whether of a progressive or a conservative kind does not really matter) by a political literacy of the whole people of God, practised and learnt within the framework of an oral liturgy for which the whole congregation is responsible.[17]

In the Western world people are increasingly aware that they have lost touch with the affective part of themselves:

> Beginning with school, if not before, an individual is systematically stripped of his imagination, his creativity, his heritage, his dreams and his personal uniqueness, in order to style him into a productive unit for a mass technological society. Instinct, feeling and spontaneity are repressed by overwhelming forces.[18]

Attempts by people in the West to 'unfreeze' their affective natures tend to be outside rather than inside the churches, and take the form of behavioural and encounter groups, experimental life-styles, community living and exploration of the meditational practices of Eastern religions. Insofar as the charismatic movement has a footing in the churches in the North East, there are signs of a loosening of denominational barriers, in which the Roman Catholics are to the fore. In Newcastle, for instance, there are regular charismatic meetings of people from all denominations at the Roman Catholic College at Fenham. As well as meeting for worship, this group is active in the leadership of the Fenham Christian Council.

But the charismatic 'family' also stands as a counter-sign. Instead of being a sign of the creative integration of man, it often leads to new separations: between intellect and emotion, passion and compassion, church and world, and, in a contrary way, instead of enabling the whole congregation to use its different gifts in mission, it often leads to a greater gulf between minister and people in a new kind of authoritarianism.

In the article I have already quoted, Walter Hollenweger expresses his disappointment at the failure of Christians in the West to make a distinctive contribution to the charismatic movement out of their own traditions. What is needed, he believes, is a theological response in which new understandings of the Trinity, the church and the world are enabled to emerge out of Pentecostal experience. Instead, he says, Christians in this country have simply 'imitated the Pentecostal movement . . . on a higher social level',[19] and used it to reinforce their grip on the old ways.

The second 'family' is focussed around social concern. Most Christians are to some extent socially-concerned, but few understand or accept a theology that makes this central to the gospel. An example of how much this is a matter of division across the world was afforded by the visit of an ecumenical team of eight people from different parts of the world, who came to the North East in 1979. The purpose of their one month's visit was to give an outside view of the opportunities and needs of the region, and the strengths and weaknesses of the churches' responses. A main point made by most of the group was the lack of confidence they found among Christians in speaking of their faith. One member of the team, Anibal Guzman, however, was saying something rather different. He came from Bolivia and he directed our attention to a TV programme about tin-mining in Bolivia that happened to coincide with this visit. The programme followed the lives of two brothers who were typical of the men working in the tin mines. The older brother, aged 32, was dying from tubercular pneumoconiosis, the tin-miners' disease. The younger one, aged 24, was suffering from the same disease but had to continue working in order to support both families. The average life expectancy of men in the mines is thirty-seven years. Anibal's question to us was not whether we were articulating the gospel, but what we were doing about the injustices of the world.

Social concern is not something you do *after* you have received the gospel; it concerns the nature of the gospel. The theological focus of the socially-concerned 'family' is the belief that God makes himself known in history and that he demands a specific historical response. God addresses us in our own situation, and it is only within a historical obedience that the gospel can be known.

The socially-concerned church is a sign of hope in that it expresses the movement of God towards the world that is expressed in the historical life of Jesus Christ. It puts its faith in a God whose saving action is known in the world, and it is faithful in its witness by working with God for the reconciliation of all things in Christ. This church does not *take* Christ to others but *finds* Christ in others, especially in 'the

poor'. Its social concern takes two forms – encouragement of all that
is in line with God's purposes and judgment upon all that is against
God's purposes – and we must remember that judgment itself is cleansing, saving and hopeful.

It is a sign of hope that the churches in North East England are
genuinely concerned with the social issues of the region. The long
tradition of clergy taking a leadership role in the community continues,
especially in rural and mining areas, and in some urban areas new
styles of approach are being explored. In recognition of the complexity
of the issues, specialist appointments have been made in the form of
industrial chaplains, social responsibility officers, community chaplains
and others. This is hopeful in that it provides informed backing for the
involvement of the whole church, though a negative result is that it
makes it easier for the rest of the church to slough off its own social
responsibility.

What is not hopeful is the confusion that exists about what the
fundamental issues are, what relation they have to the gospel and
what the church's contribution should be. In order to illustrate this I
return to our Bolivian visitor. After preaching at a local church, Anibal
joined in a discussion with the congregation. His answer to questions
about the church's activities in Bolivia led to critical comments about
'encouraging violence'. What was striking about the conversation was
that even when Anibal spoke about the demand of the Bolivian poor
for proper prices for their raw materials that was being supported by
the church, no one saw that this must lead to changes in our situation
and in the response of Christians in Britain. This insularity constitutes
a real blindness to the nature of our world and to the demands of the
gospel.

Blindness, however, is not confined to those who reject social
involvement. It is only too easy for those who see the importance of
involvement in the issues of life to accept current definitions rather
than defining the issues from a perspective of faith:

> The Christian religion has lost the power, and also the confidence,
> to define the areas of public debate, even in moral questions.
> Instead, it follows the definitions made by others . . . The contem-
> porary debate about world resources, overpopulation, pollution or
> nuclear catastrophe, is according to the analyses of secular thinkers
> – although the churches tag along, offering a religious gloss to
> precisely the same ideas.[26]

There is a second-hand quality about much Christian 'radicalism' that
points to a failure to identify and get to grips with the actual issues of
our own society. We need to be clear what things in our society should
be supported and with what particular blasphemies we should be
taking a strong line.[21]

The church's self-alienation becomes painfully apparent to Christians who see social concern as central to the gospel. On the one hand, in their social involvement they find themselves in solidarity with those who fulfil the demands of discipleship without acknowledging God.

> The Christian finds himself as a member of a community of historical commitment which not only cuts across denominational but also religious boundaries. He deeply experiences the reality of love, fellowship, sacrificial commitment, solidarity, and hope within this community in which the name of Jesus is not invoked.[22]

On the other hand, he finds himself a member of a church that is ambivalent about its social involvement and out of touch with 'the poor' – the very people in whom Christ has promised to be present.

> The community of faith has become predominantly the church of the rich and powerful and consequently the poor have been alienated from an explicit recognition of the Christ.[23]

Two faces of the church appear: on the one hand in obedient disbelievers, and on the other hand in disobedient believers. There is a deep division in the life of the church, which makes it ambiguous as a sign of the reality of God. Christ's presence in the poor and needy is not acknowledged by that which is explicitly church; but Christ is served in the 'poor' by those who do not name him. This division endangers the mission efforts of the church, for the obedient disbelievers may be brought into this 'believing' church at the expense of their obedience, while the disobedient believers may become obedient at the expense of their believing. We must struggle for a unity in the life of the church, which is not a unity between denominations but a unity between believing and obeying, between Christ in the 'godly' and Christ in the 'poor'.

By far the largest Christian 'family' is the conservation-oriented. It is to this group that I now turn. In this group, rather than in the charismatic 'family', I place the strong congregational life of the traditionally evangelical churches along with the traditionally 'catholic' churches of the North East. The focus of the gospel for this 'family' is belief in an unchanging God and commitment to a received gospel and to the continuity of church life. This is an essential element in any Christian faith. Christian faith is founded on a historical revelation that has to be preserved and communicated. There is a stability and continuity in the life of the church that links Christians everywhere to one another and to those who went before and who will come after. All are involved in one and the same concrete project for human existence. The conservation-oriented church provides a 'zone of stability in a world that gyrates madly from extreme to extreme'.[24]

But as with the other 'families', this focus is subject to aberration. A concern for the preservation of the gospel can slide into a concern for the preservation of the church. Concern for faithfulness to the past can lead to the rejection of everything that is new. All fresh initiatives are submerged and we are encouraged 'to entrench ourselves persistently behind the "faith of the church", and evade the honest question as to what we ourselves really believe. That is why the air is not quite fresh . . .'[25] Hence also a continuing dependence of the laity on the clergy. These are not the intended results, but they frequently follow from this focus.

To give just one example of the way priorities can get twisted. For the last few months the whole effort of my own local church has gone into a stewardship campaign. This is a thriving and in many respects a go-ahead church, but in 1978 its expenditure exceeded its income by about £1,000. The fact that the campaign involved the congregations in discussions about the church's whole programme does not take away from the fact that its main purpose was to increase the income of the church. This particular church is not facing insuperable problems of staff, plant or finance. It can afford to be confident about its service to the community. For other churches, however, the burden of maintenance is so overwhelming that it colours their whole outlook.

A conservation orientation is not only or even mainly due to financial concerns. A friend of mine was appointed vicar of a dual-purpose church in a new housing estate. The bishop charged him to make bold experiments in this new situation. When, however, after several years there were few confirmation candidates, the bishop made it plain that he thought the experiment was a failure. How ever much the situation may change a conservation orientation tends to apply the same success criteria.

There is an inevitable tension between those who hold responsibility in the church and those who are involved at the 'grass roots'. In this matter the church hierarchy are caught in the same dilemma as those with responsibility in every other institution. But they and the church can be a sign of hope insofar as they can transcend the pressures of the past and live by the belief that the God who came to save in the life of Jesus Christ comes to save today. Insofar as the church looks only to the past it is a counter-sign.

The point that has emerged from this brief survey is that the church as a sign is ambiguous. It presents us with what is liberating and life-giving, and at the same time it is restrictive and life-denying. It is both hopeful and hopeless.

But why should we expect anything other than ambiguity? The church is like the other institutions we have considered. Like technology, politics, and every other human institution it contains good and evil. The wheat and the weeds will not be separated until the end, and until then we must live with this ambiguity (Matthew 13.30). The only time the church is really hopeless is when she thinks that she is 'all right'.

In a contrary way, a false confidence often emerges when it is obvious that things are going badly. Church membership is declining, fewer people offer for the full-time ministry, inflation makes havoc of church finances and theology is raising difficult questions. It is precisely when the church is being challenged in this way to rethink its mission that some people feel it necessary to protest that 'everything is all right'. But these things may be pointing us to deeper questions about the present condition and needs of people in our world, and they may constitute the pressure of God upon us to respond in ways that are appropriate to our own time and place. We need to have confidence, not in our 'successes', but in God's faithfulness, if we are to face the changes that need to be made.

The only hopeful thing in that kind of situation is that God will not let the church get away with its complacency. Throughout history the church has been broken, converted and purged, time and time again. In this we should see God's judgment and we should take this as a sign of hope. God confronts us with the chance to make our own judgment in the matter.

The church should stand as a sign to the world of what all human life is meant to be. Members of the church are the people of God in the sense that they have made a conscious response to God's invitation. 'The people of God simply seeks to realize the possibility of a true humanity that is in all people.'[25] The church should display, in the quality of its relationships, the direction of its concerns and the flexibility of its structures, signs that point to new possibilities. What the church does and what it is is on behalf of all people and is informed by a sense of solidarity with all people.

But the church and its members are under the same pressures as every other person and institution, and they are as liable as others to failure and sin. As a sign the church is ambiguous. The essential difference is that the church has in its gospel an understanding of how things can be different and the resources that enable the endurance, suffering and hope that can make things different.

We must not be blind either to what is wrong or to what is right about the church. Instead we must ask how we can deal with the church's ambiguity in a positive way.

The most hopeful thing about the church is that it is not static. It does not offer us a 'package' belief, but in its variety it shows that it is fluid and moving. It is possible for people to get into this movement at many different points, and from that position to work with others for the church's cleansing and reformation.

For those of us who are committed to the church, our failure is not that we are divided, but that we are indifferent or even hostile to other expressions of the church. Our need is to open our eyes to a broader way of looking at the church.

For those who do not see the church as a potential sign of hope, who have turned away in disgust at its weakness, trivialities and inhumanities, there is need to continue to look, and to look in a more sensitive way.

For those with eyes to see, there are many signs of new life in the world. Just as there is no proof that Jesus has been raised from the dead, so I cannot prove that new life has been given by God. What I have tried to do in this chapter is to point to the fact that life is springing up and is being experienced in many different ways.

I will add one more example that concerns new life in the church. After ten years absence I returned to the mining parish in which I had worked. In the crowded hall of the dual-purpose church that had been completed just before I left, I was greeted by many of the people I had worked with to build up a congregation on the estate. With them were many other people whom I did not know. It was evident that new life had appeared in that place. Struggle and suffering is not all there is. There is also joy and celebration.

The reality of new life is focussed in the church's worship especially in the eucharist. The New Testament stories of the resurrection show that it was in a shared meal that the risen Lord made his presence known to his followers, and it remains that way. In this service men and women offer themselves in union with Jesus Christ for the renewal of the world, an offering that is lived out in the world. Here newness of life is celebrated as men and women extract themselves from all the things that press upon them in day-to-day life, and open themselves to the mystery within which the whole of their lives are lived – God himself. Here for a short time the main concern is not with struggling but with thanksgiving.

The signs of hope in life are not obvious and self-explanatory. We must not only point to the signs of hope, but in spite of all the difficulties we must also speak about the God to whom these signs bear witness. It is the need to speak about God that I now consider.

V   Why We must Speak about God

'The day will come when men will once more be called so to utter the
word of God that the world will be changed and renewed by it'
(Dietrich Bonhoeffer).[1]

1 *The saving word*

There are good reasons for *not* speaking about God. Christians are
often told that they must 'bear witness' and 'not be afraid to speak
about God'. But there is too much speaking, and people feel battered
and assaulted by our words about God. Bonhoeffer spoke of his shrinking with religious people from speaking of God by name because in
the circumstances that name did not seem to ring true, and 'for the
religionless working man (or any other man) nothing decisive is gained
here'.[2] Some religious people speak as if they know all there is to be
known about God, and as if it is only through them that God is
'brought' to others. By doing this they limit God and reduce him to
their own size. It needs to be known that Christ is not the possession
of religious people, but is 'really the Lord of the world'.[3]

There are profound cultural, social and intellectual reasons why we
should hesitate to speak about God. These are not excuses, but valid
reasons that lay upon us the need to struggle to discover what the
'word' is that must be said. But behind all these reasons for our silence
is a fundamental religious reason. The Jews were forbidden to speak
of God by name. To name a person was, in their understanding, to
claim some control over that person. To make any such claim with
respect to God is blasphemous. God is free to speak his own word,
and he does this in the events of life as well as in what men say about
those events.

Jesus Christ is the word of God. He is the word that God himself
speaks. It is not what Jesus said, but his whole impact on the world
that is the Word of God. The content of this word is God himself in
his self-giving. The impact of it is the salvation of the world. This is a
word that we cannot discover, deduce or arrive at by intellectual
reasoning. Nor can we simply translate 'it' into modern language, or
encapsulate 'it' in a handy form for communication to others. (I once
heard a member of a religious broadcasting station speak of 'beaming

the word across China on five wavelengths'.) God's word is not in our control but breaks 'into the circle of our subjectivity, our questioning and our own answering',[4] assaulting us as God's question and as God's invitation to us. If anyone is to hear this question and receive this invitation, there are things that have to be said about God, but that is only part of the matter.

This book started with a question to which I could give no reply. What can possibly be said about God to people in whose experience everything denies the reality of God? How can God be known as loving and as saving when there is no evidence in the world of love and of saving?

Atheism is a more serious and mature response to life than much that goes under the name of religion. Atheism cannot be dismissed by simply saying that men have been seduced by affluence. There are deeper reasons for unbelief. A 'god of the gaps' is not needed in a scientific and technological world. It is not just 'intellectuals' who recognize this fact, but anyone who is shaped by our culture. In what way is it possible to speak of God as doing anything at all now that we know the cause of most things? Bonhoeffer is only one of the many people who have pointed to the fact that what is being said about God is not helping people to come to terms with the actualities of a scientific world:

> Religious people speak of God when human knowledge (perhaps simply because they are too lazy to think, has come to an end, or when human resources fail – in fact it is always the *deus ex machina* that they bring on to the scene, either for the apparent solution of insoluble problems, or as strength in human failure – always, that is to say, exploiting human weakness or human boundaries. Of necessity, that can go on only till people can by their own strength, push these boundaries somewhat further, so that God becomes superfluous as a *deus ex machina*.[5]

So long as we use God as a stop-gap it will be less and less possible for people who are at the centre of what is happening in life to know the reality of God. In the passage I have just quoted, Bonhoeffer goes on to say: 'I should like to speak of God not on the boundaries but at the centre, not in weaknesses but in strength.'[6] If we are to speak of God in this way we must know how in a scientific technological world God can be said to be *doing* anything; and how God and our belief in God changes anything. We must grapple with the questions raised by science and technology, and we must wrestle with what faith in God means in the light of science and technology.

Some people say that *faith* makes a difference and that they could not live without *faith*. But this is different from saying that they could not live without *God*. *Faith* can be no more than a re-affirmation of the world as we would like it to be. It is comforting in that it provides a different world into which we can escape from the harshness of the real world.

God brings us into touch with the world as it is. This world does not comply with our emotional needs, but contains people who oppose us and events that frustrate us. God does not always soothe us, but confronts us with uncomfortable truths about things that have to be changed in the world and in ourselves.

To speak of faith in the abstract suggests that religion is an attitude to life rather than a relationship with the living God. This kind of emotional dependence is recognized as being helpful and even necessary for some people. But it stops them from coming to terms with the realities of life and from attacking the things in life which inhibit full human living. Religion then appears as an opiate.

If our speaking about God does not help people to face life as it is, it will fail to touch the depths of their unbelief. For most people our talk will lead only to a further deadening of the ears, while those who do come into the churches as a result of our speaking will bring their unbelief with them.

Most serious of all is the fact that for many people belief in God is morally impossible. The world is too unjust, inhuman and cruel to be associated with the existence of a loving, saving God. This is no new cry, nor is it the cry of those who are indifferent to God. It is the cry of the most deeply religious people down the ages. The book of Job is a classic expression of the agonies of the man who will not believe in a God who is not worth believing in:

> Why are not times of judgment kept by the Almighty,
> And why do those who know him never see his days?
> Men remove landmarks; they seize flocks and pasture them.
> . . . From out of the city the dying groan, and the soul
> of the wounded cries for help;
> Yet God pays no attention to their prayer (Job 24.1f., 12).

The other side of the cry of the righteous man is the vested interest of oppressors in the absence of God. Atheism may not be the conscious choice of those who benefit from injustice, but they are at least anxious that the question of God should not become too explicit:

> For the wicked boasts of the desires of his heart,
> And the man greedy for gain curses and renounces the Lord.
> In the pride of his countenance the wicked does not seek him;
> All his thoughts are, 'There is no God' (Psalm 10.3f.).

Those who benefit from the injustices of the world know that they have much to lose by acknowledging God. Maybe this is not a conscious matter, but it is enough to make *us* run away from and avoid anything that threatens to bring *us* into direct contact with God. I deliberately say '*us*' here, because events are making it clear to *us* in the Western world that we have much to lose if anything like justice is to be realized for the poorer nations. I have already mentioned the pastor from Bolivia who pointed out that in his country Christians are pressing people to demand a fair price for their raw materials. This, he said, must inevitably reduce the standard of living in the Western world. The awakening of the Bolivian people to their own dignity and rights is being furthered by Christians who speak of a God who calls people to receive their humanity. This is not a comfortable matter for us, and it would not be surprising if we secretly hoped that it would not happen in our time.

It is the hardness of heart of the oppressor that makes the oppressed, as he experiences the injustice and lovelessness of the world, agree with the oppressor that: 'There is no God.'

In this country we are no more articulate about our unbelief than we are about our belief. Few people admit to atheism. After all, if to talk of God makes no difference, then neither will talking about there being no God make any difference. The cynicism that is part and parcel of the outlook of many people goes deeper than words. Talking about God on its own will not change it.

Only the glory of God shining in the world through all that denies God in the world can make it possible for men to believe in God.

> To cease to believe in God is to imagine the world as the oppressor wants it to be. To believe in God is to oppose even the most plausible and overwhelming of oppressors. Faith cannot admit their claim to dominance; 'You shall have no other God beside me' . . . Whatever force the oppressor may exert, it meets a significant limit in those who are really able to believe in God, for faith is the refusal to let the world be ultimately safe for oppressors.[7]

Wherever the cruelty of the world hides the light of God, we must work to uncover that light, and we must work with all those who are attacking the evils of the world under whatever banner they may be doing this. Christians whose faith in a loving God has driven them to an involvement in life, find themselves in company with people whose involvement in life has driven them to unbelief. The suffering they encounter in their involvement has led them to the conviction that the universe cannot possibly be on the side of humanity.

The pressure of unbelief upon Christians is in this way intensified. Christians ought to support and work with those who cannot go beyond humanism to faith in God, but they do not wish to share their unbelief. If they are not to be forced into unbelief themselves they must face the question: '*What* God do you believe in?' It may be that the answer to this question can only be known from within this kind of involvement.

> Maybe we can only speak of God from within a precarious and practical but uncompromising compassion, suffering with those who suffer. There we can speak of a suffering God and do some justice to the mysterious centre of the revelation and action of God in Jesus Christ.

The world remains ambiguous. It does not truly reflect the glory of God. But faith cannot wait until all that denies God is done away. It is within an ambiguous world that faith must be faith. It is from within an ambiguous experience of the world that faith must speak of God. Throughout this book I have spoken of my concern for people who are trapped and oppressed in a world in which they feel unable to realize their full humanity. I do not believe that we can by ourselves overcome this situation. We need a saviour, and it is because I believe that it is God who saves that I want to speak of God.

I do not feel, however, that I can start from the things that are actually being said about God. It is not that the things that are being said are untrue, but that they do not connect with any identifiable experience in life. Even people who speak about God seem unable to connect what they say to any concrete reality. The words do not point to any changes that have been made, nor do they effect any new changes. The traditional words about God have lost their power. It was this that led Bonhoeffer to say that we may be in a period of history when it is not possible to speak of God at all:

Reconciliation and redemption, regeneration and the Holy Spirit, love of our enemies, cross and resurrection, life in Christ and Christian discipleship – all these things are so difficult and so remote that we hardly venture any more to speak of them. In the traditional words and acts we suspect that there may be something quite new and revolutionary, though we cannot as yet grasp or express it. That is our own fault. Our church, which has been fighting in these years only for its self-preservation, as though that were an end in itself, is incapable of taking the word of reconciliation and redemption to mankind and the world. Our earlier words are therefore bound to lose their force and cease, and our being Christians today will be limited to two things: prayer and righteous action among men. All Christian thinking, speaking, and organizing must be born anew out of this prayer and action . . .

We are not yet out of the melting pot, and any attempt to help the church prematurely to a new expansion of its organization will merely delay its conversion and purification. It is not for us to prophesy the day (though the day will come) when men will once more be called so to utter the word of God that the world will be changed and renewed by it.[9]

I do not want to show the kind of impatience that will only delay the church's purgation. I do, however, feel constrained to say something about God and this is why I have written this book.

What, then, is it that I can say about God?

I have no simple message that can be spoken in every situation. The integrity of word and action is what constitutes an effective word. That word we have to struggle to discover, 'hear' and produce. I do not feel that the things that are being said about God reckon sufficiently with the tensions of life. I start with the tensions of life, the despair, resignation and cynicism, of people who have given up hoping that life can be different. Simply to say, 'God loves you', changes nothing. To be with people where they are and to enter into their experience brings something new into a situation. From within this kind of solidarity it becomes possible to speak of a suffering God. To speak of a suffering God does not explain suffering, but it shows a God who takes responsibility for suffering by sharing in the world's suffering. This is not abstract speculation about God, for it comes from a knowledge of Jesus Christ as the Word of God. In the life of Jesus Christ there is a reality that we can recognize because we know it to be true of our own experience. We, too, see pride poisoning good works, possessors of power silencing claims to justice, love being betrayed, ideals turning to fanaticism. Jesus' life and death do away with any easy expectations and confront us with the fact that these things cannot be dealt with without suffering.

> At the same time suffering is not glorified; it is seen in the light of the cross as injustice, cruelty and wanton destruction. It is not approved and no Christian cult of suffering can be derived from it. In Jesus there was a realistic facing of suffering and sin in the world, and a voluntary acceptance and shaping of suffering so that it is turned into the way of overcoming evil. Into that way he calls disciples . . .[10]

Every speaking about God is also a speaking about the world and how we understand the world. Christian speaking cuts no ice with many people, for it does not seem to refer to the world they know. Those who speak of a 'God of the gaps', who is brought in when everything else fails, have a vested interest in keeping man in a state of weakness and dependence. I see the development of science and technology as a positive step towards man's adulthood, in which man takes responsibility for the world.

> The Christian faith, so far from seeking to keep men in strings, calls them to maturity, not to the maturity of the adolescent revolting *against* a father, but of the 'full-grown man' entering into the responsible freedom of the son and heir.[11]

Of course if we insist on maintaining an understanding of the world as a mechanistic closed system, there is no room for God:

> As a factor introduced to make the system work he is redundant. In that sense it is possible to answer every question without God – even the ones that before we thought to admit only of a religious solution. And at the level of control things get along, for good or for ill, just as well without him. It is not necessary to bring him in.
>
> But in another sense it is not possible to leave him out – any more than it is possible to run an economy or cope with the population explosion without in the last analysis treating persons as persons, without reckoning with the dimension of the 'Thou'. God is a reality of life whom one cannot ultimately evade.[12]

If we try to take the world to pieces and say just where God comes in, we shall fail, just as we would if we tried to cut up a person in order to discover what makes him tick. The nature of persons and what gives significance to human life cannot be analysed in this way. I do not want to talk about what is happening in the world as if it were a matter of some sort of automatic progress. The world is not a machine but a personal creation. Moreover, it is a personal creation in which man has some responsibility. The development of technology has come about not only because God is personally involved in the world and in what happens in it, but because mankind is also personally involved in it. Mankind, that is, men and women and groups of men and women, have had visions and dreams as well as nightmares about how it should develop, and they have *chosen* that it should develop in certain ways. They have made their choices on the basis of the particular values they hold. As well as leading to much that is good, their choices have led to untold human suffering that could have been avoided had other choices been made. We cannot talk about technology as if it were all gain when we see the suffering of people in the tin mines of Bolivia or in the city of Hiroshima.

The whole of life is a dialogue with God. It is in the personal give and take of this dialogue that the reality of God is known: 'The one who is superfluous as a hypothesis becomes all too present as a subject of encounter.'[13]

God gives us the raw material of a world and of life. Within this world and all that happens in it he addresses us, inviting us to share with him in the creation of a truly human world. But we are so entangled in a world that is off-course, and so alienated from our true selves, that we have lost the freedom to respond. We need saving. It is the recognition of the need for saving that presses me to try to find a way of speaking of God as saviour.

To speak of extraordinary and supernatural interventions would not get to the heart of the matter, which is a *personal* encounter with God. In personal meetings we meet with persons who are different from ourselves and who behave in different and unexpected ways. In our meetings with God we meet in the midst of our strugglings, our partial successes and partial failures, the unexpected differences that make all the difference in the world.

This encounter is first and foremost something that happens. To recognize and accept it as an encounter with God depends on our receptivity. There can be no proof that this is the case. There is, moreover, no adequate way of expressing its meaning.

The Bible tells how God makes himself known in his saving activity. The first Christians believed that they experienced the same saving activity in Jesus Christ. It was the meaning of this experience that they tried to express in the New Testament. They do not give a simple unified answer, and no such answer can be given until all is completed. In the meantime we have a variety of pictures and metaphors which give different ways into an understanding of salvation.

Here, for instance, are some of the biblical pictures which seem to me to have resonances with life as I know it and as I have described it in this book.

Jesus Christ is 'representative' of mankind and 'pioneer' of a new and saving way of life (Hebrews 5.9; 12.2). The idea of representation is familiar enough to us. In a society like ours with its large institutions, most people have some experience of acting in a representative capacity. A representative stands for others, acting not on his own but on their behalf. His purpose is not to take away but to enlarge other people's freedom. Those he represents are participants in, not objects of, his activity and, as every representative learns to his cost, the members can reject what has been done for them.

In the 'pioneer' the stress is on a break-through in which something new is achieved by one person and so becomes a possibility for others. The result is due partly to the fact that people now see that what has been done once can be done again, and partly to the fact that obstacles in the way of achievement have been dealt with. Obvious examples are the four-minute mile or the navigation of the Amazon, but the setting up of the first co-operative venture or the creation of a democratic state are more apt. In Jesus' life there was a break-through into a new pattern of living, so that something new entered the whole stream of human history. It is this fact that Paul struggles to express when, in the Epistle to the Romans, he claims that in Jesus the whole process of man's alienation has been reversed: 'So one man's act of righteousness leads to acquittal and life for all men' (Romans 5.18).

The solidarity of mankind appears again in the picture of 'the one new man' (Ephesians 2.15). Jesus Christ stands for all men, and in him reconciliation between men, groups and nations becomes possible. The solidarity of man becomes a reality. Reconciliation, however, does not come about automatically, but must take place by men and nations

actually being reconciled. In this, the saving act of God in the forgiveness of sins is fundamental.

In our own experience of life, one of the greatest causes of distress
is the feeling that things do not hang together. There is no meaning,
no integrating factor, no centre to life. The conviction that all things
come together in Christ is fundamental to the experience of the New
Testament and is expressed in different ways. A picture that I find
evocative is that of the stone that was rejected and which 'has become
the head of the corner' (Mark 12.10). It is significant that this saying
comes at the beginning of the passion story, for the fact is that Jesus
Christ was not and is not accepted as the one who gives shape and
meaning to the whole of life. For him to become the centre demands
a reversal of our whole evaluation of life.

We rightly resist any attempt to take away the freedoms we have,
but at the same time we know that many freedoms have already been
lost. 'Bondage' and 'liberation' are constant themes in the Bible.[14]
Salvation is pictured as release from all that enslaves man. Freedom
does not mean that everything is possible, but it does mean that we
need not accept the inevitability of life as it is. We believe that there
are choices, and sometimes venture to make the harder choice in the
belief that some things that look impossible may in fact be possible.

'Freedom' is a feature of the relationship between God and man.
God does not bludgeon man into submission. Jesus Christ's resurrection means his sovereignty. Jesus is Lord, but he differs from those
who lord it over us. They demand obedience. Christ effects freedom.

> He does not just call us to it; . . . Jesus gives freedom. That is what
> makes him unmistakably Lord and inseparably unites the earthly
> with the exalted Lord. He was free in that he came to serve, and he
> remains Lord by serving us.[15]

God seeks to win man's free response and is prepared to go on
doing this whatever the cost to himself. (Love is about this kind of
persistence, not about how we feel.) However resistant men may be,
God will not let them go. The message of salvation is the invitation to
share in Jesus' way of loving service. The gift of salvation is the freedom
that enables us to accept. Acceptance means taking up a cross, with
no assurance beyond the knowledge that nothing can separate us from
the love of God and that in every situation there is a creative and
saving possibility:

> The man who believes in providence does not believe that a special
> divine activity will alter the conditions of finitude and estrangement.
> He believes and asserts with the courage of faith, that no situation
> whatsoever can frustrate the fulfilment of his ultimate destiny, that
> nothing can separate him from the love of God which is in Jesus
> Christ.[16]

And again:

> Providence means that there is a creative and saving possibility implied in every situation, which cannot be destroyed by any event.[17]

The themes I have mentioned are only a few of the ways of glimpsing the mystery of God's saving activity. The fact of salvation is primary. Understanding it can only be known in our responding: 'If any man will do his will, he shall know of the doctrine' (John 7.17AV).

There is good reason why we should not expect to be able to speak directly and clearly about salvation. Salvation cannot be known as a personal possession. Only when the whole world has come to salvation shall we know the truth about salvation. That will be when God's purpose of reconciling all things in Christ is fulfilled (Ephesians 1.10; Colossians 1.20). Until then, we must share in the tension of incompleteness. Our attempts to find some way of speaking about God come out of this tension.

2 Finding the word

If it is to be effective, the word must be addressed to men and women in the whole of their lives. The gospel is not an unchanging word but is good news for people where they are. This fact is illustrated by the amazing response made to the preaching of John Wesley. Some people imagine that if they follow the same approach today, the same fire of revival will spread across the country. But today the situation is different.

John Wesley's ministry (1738–90) coincided with the early days of the Industrial Revolution. Society was in an upheaval. There was a great movement of population as labourers flooded into the north and west, to work in the mines and factories and to construct docks and roads. The traditional hierarchical society which had characterized Europe for many centuries was being eroded. A new society was taking its place.

> This was a time when the entire Atlantic world, moved by the desire for greater personal autonomy and roused by the slogan of liberty and equality, rose to overturn the privileged governing classes, bringing the long-suppressed, inarticulate lower classes on to the stage of events . . . The lower ranks in France and England were exposed to great social and economic dislocations, accompanied by a disorientation of the traditional family structure. Such changes produced widespread and profound anxiety . . . It was to the anxious, the dislocated, the rootless, the disturbed – that the Methodist preachers came with their doctrine of reassurance.[18]

It was with people who, *because* they were marginal, were neglected by the established church, that Wesley had the greatest success.

Wesley spoke to their condition not only by his message of assurance, but by giving them a sense of their own dignity and destiny, and giving them 'the language and art to express their antagonism to grim conditions and injustice'.[19]

Wesley did not simply repeat a word from the past, but searched for the word of God for these uprooted people. What he said sounded strange, dangerous and even blasphemous to many of the religious people of his time. In Liskeard a Mr Ough, who was churchwarden of the parish church, was thrown out of a service for his enthusiastic 'Alleluias'. Wesley, like many other great missionaries, was considered by some to be an atheist:

> I was informed that the commanding officer had given strict orders, neither Mr Wesley, nor any of his people, should be admitted (to Bridewell prison) for they were all atheists.[20]

Wesley and his followers brought their own gifts and dispositions which gave the movement its particular direction, and no historian has yet made a satisfactory assessment of just what the Methodist contribution to the history of this country has been. All I want to point to here is the fact that the word of the gospel is never spoken *in vacuo* but is always a response to a specific historical situation. Today we cannot simply repeat a word that was addressed to people in different conditions. We must struggle to discover what the word is for our time and place. The point is re-enforced by two illustrations from the fundamentally different circumstances of the twentieth century.

Leslie Hunter, who was Bishop of Sheffield from 1939–62, had this to say about the situation:

> In industrial society a new phenomenon as far as we know has arisen – namely, multitudes who are neither bad nor worldly, in the middle-class sense of the word, but are apparently without any feeling of spiritual need. They are mass-producing and mass-produced. Day after day they follow a limited and limiting routine – out to work, back home, out to club or pub, cinema or dog-track and then home to bed . . . These immense populations are the unresisting product of a machine age, and it is going to be uncommonly hard to get through to any thought or aspiration which might become a hunger for God.
>
> Nevertheless, that is not the whole story. Very many of those who have some spiritual and cultural hunger have no taste for the food we offer . . . The intellectual class which has the ear of the more thoughtful technician is that which is confident that greater advances are more likely to come through scientific knowledge coupled with social idealism than through the influence of religious faith. The majority of people in industrial society are being both

consciously and unconsciously, influenced by the scientific outlook on life. Spiritual values and the life of prayer are strange to them . . . The evangelistic task of the church in industrial society is formidable, and it will be a long-term policy which will not be short-circuited just by playing the old records with louder needles and more amplifiers, or by tip and run commando raids.[21]

The bishop recognized that the church was in a particular kind of mission situation. In his response there were two main thrusts: an intensive engagement with people in some of the main areas of life and a robust theology. As regards the first, he recognized that industry is fundamental to the whole shape and ethos of society, and appointed the Rev. E. R. Wickham as industrial chaplain.[22] This was only one of a number of special arpointments which aimed to engage specific groups in society and to strengthen the life of the parishes.

As regards the second main thrust the bishop had this to say:

All the missions and revivals which have had staying power and have borne fruit have had a core of belief – an intellectual backbone – yes, theology. 'The Sword of the Spirit is the word of God.' In recent times, a lack of intellectual robustness and an excess of sentimentality – which I would distinguish from emotion and fine passion – together with the fact that the great words of the faith have lost the freshness of their minting and become somewhat conventionalized in our speaking, have contributed to the loss of a virile faith amongst the people in the living God of Christ's revealing.[23]

The results of Bishop Hunter's ministry differ from those of John Wesley's mission. One result is that in a number of places throughout the world the church's style of mission is changing. Mission in the past often consisted of a comprehensive presentation of Christian belief. Mission today is a matter of finding ways into the minds and imaginations of people whose thinking moves in a framework in which there is no place for God. There are all sorts of different ways of opening people up to the larger world. Curiosity and interest is a good starter – and for many people this is not aroused by 'religious' topics. I remember making some forge-men very irritated by speaking about cybernation, but it certainly got them thinking outside their normal range of subjects. More effectively I heard someone talking to a similar group of men about young people in industry. When they had got beyond the stock remarks about long-haired layabouts, the men started talking about their own children. Concern for other people is another way of opening people's minds to a world in which there is mystery and in which there is therefore room for God. What is needed is not primarily information and exhortation, but a breakthrough into this closed world. The cultural situation has changed and the old approach, which speaks from a different framework, simply bounces off people.

If the church is to present a gospel that is good news in today's world, she must help the world to understand itself. This means entering into a serious discussion about the world, and it produces a style of mission in which the first step is involvement with people and a concern with their experience of life.

It is lay people who know from the inside the strains and possibilities of living and believing in today's world. It is therefore lay people who can know and must speak the word to our world. This challenges a style of ministry and mission in which only the clergy know and speak the gospel. Today we are being forced back to an authentic form of the church as the whole people of God. This is a lesson we are finding hard to learn.

Bishop Hunter stressed the fact that mission in an industrial society is a long-term matter. It should therefore be enough to say that his ministry has demonstrated a style of mission that is concerned with the world and that recognizes the role of lay people as well as clergy. It has led to a complete change in the relation of the church to a particular part of industrial society. It has opened up the expectations of many people about life, about the church and about Christian faith; and in a whole section of society a door that was closing has been kept open to the gospel.

A more recent example of ministry picks up the theme of social and cultural change and relates directly to life in North East England. Ian Ramsey, Bishop of Durham from 1966–1972, made clear that he saw the church's task as that of helping to create a new society. The theological struggle to find the word of God for today could not be achieved without the help of other disciplines. Nor should academic theologians attempt to work without the experience of people in the 'front line'. Theology must be a co-operative task. Something of what this implied was conveyed in his enthronement sermon:

> There has just been published . . . a study entitled *Challenge to the Changing North* which sets out the main problems which face this and neighbouring counties, and makes a number of recommendations for a prosperous future. As we would expect, it is an expert, thorough, and quite first-rate piece of work . . .
>
> But if our end is the true welfare of those who live in village and town, true prosperity for the region, a master-plan can never finally be successful unless it can win the spontaneous devotion of those it concerns . . . No plan will be successful if it does not convince, if it does not appeal to man's spirit. To make plans for the prosperity of our region succeed we must discover that which wins man's true allegiance.
>
> But not only social blue-prints – theology as well, can be authoritarian and disastrously oppressive. Both need to be redeemed so that they can be expressive of a vision when each will then possess the kind of authority which all of us need to acknowledge if we are

to find our fulfilment and our life. So I see us reaching a revitalized theology, as well as a transformed society, when we grapple together as men of faith with the intellectual and social problems of our time. The alternative is not only social calamity; it is the loss of our very souls as well.[24]

Bishop Ramsey continued throughout his episcopate to work with all sorts of people in the North East and far beyond, in order to grapple with the issues they faced; with the miners at their annual gala,[25] with industrialists and planners, scientists,[26] hospital authorities, young people, educationalists and a host of others.

The enthusiastic acceptance by the miners of Ian Ramsey as 'their bishop' contrasted with the cold reception I witnessed from a group of academic theologians. Their response to his call for a mutual learning process between a selected group of clergy and lay people and some academic theologians was to say: 'We are very busy people. We have our own job to do. But of course we are glad to *help* you in any possible way.'

The question of *how* all these co-operations could be developed into a workable strategy continued to occupy the bishop's mind until the end of his life. His death after such a short episcopate left such a working-out unfinished. One outstanding result of his ministry that is evident to those of us who continue to work in the North East is that many people were roused by him from discouragement and boredom to catch something of the excitement and possibilities of life and the relevance of Christian faith to their situation.

I have spent some time on these three examples because in different ways all are responses to the peculiar needs and opportunities of their own time. In contrast, much of what is now being said about mission fails to get to grips with the peculiar nature of today's society and has no word that speaks directly to our condition.

There is good reason for anxiety about the state of Christian faith in our country. According to at least one set of statistics the United Kingdom is the only major country in the world in which there is an absolute decline in church membership.[27] These dismal figures must have something to say about the demands of mission in our society, but I am not sure that we have yet drawn the right conclusions.

There is a great deal of talk about mission and evangelism in which three emphases demand comment:

First, the difference between mission and evangelism is stressed:

Mission . . . speaks of the whole context of Christian ministry. Evangelism in contrast is a narrow and specific element within mission; that is the task of proclaiming Jesus as Saviour and Lord, seeking to lead men and women into a personal relationship with him . . . The church tends to find 'mission' easier to engage in than evangelism . . . The church must awaken to its evangelistic task.[28]

This sharp distinction between mission and evangelism misses the point that one of the main theological questions we have to tackle is how God's *personal* invitation in Jesus Christ can be known and responded to in our *total* experience of life.

Secondly, some proposals for evangelism advocate the setting of specific targets for growth in church membership.[29] There is an incidental gain in that the studies that back up these proposals draw attention to deep-seated authority problems in the church. They demonstrate, for instance, that any significant increase in numbers in a congregation can only occur if there is a corresponding increase in lay leadership and a break with traditional clerical domination.[30] But the weaknesses outweigh the gains. Though the proposals are strong on the mechanics of growth, they are weak theologically in that their main concern is with the church, not the kingdom. Jesus brings into effect God's rule in the world. The church's *raison d'être* is as agent of that purpose – that is, of the kingdom. As with individuals, the church only finds its life as it loses it in the service of others. When the church's main concern is with itself, the actual world it is called to serve and for which it should be prepared to lay down its life is lost sight of.

The third emphasis is on a clear articulation of the gospel. A criticism of Christians in the North East for lacking confidence in speaking about their faith, was, for instance, made by the ecumenical team already mentioned. Two comments sum up their complaint:

> Relatively few Christians that we talked with were able to state clearly what they believed. Many were embarrassed when asked; some could offer only vague moralisms, others (usually clergy) propounded wonderful abstractions, and others simply dodged the question altogether.
>
> Some of us wondered what was the difference between a chaplain and an industrial psychologist, if the chaplain never clearly expresses the faith by which he operates. (Not that many Christians are in a position to criticize chaplains on this score.)[31]

There is substance in this criticism, but it is not lack of confidence, nor a desire to be acceptable to others, that makes us tongue-tied. It is a genuine problem about *what* word should be spoken and indeed whether *any* word can be spoken. I believe that, in spite of real difficulties, and in spite of our limited vision, we must continue to struggle to find helpful and truthful ways of speaking about God.

My aim is not to criticize particular approaches to mission and evangelism, but to focus on how we can help each other to discover God's word for our own time.

A first need is to give serious attention to what is happening in the world and to make this the subject of our praying, doing and thinking.

It is not a purely intellectual search, for the material of our reflection is what comes out of our praying and doing. But reflection there must be, and this requires not a monologue, but a wide-ranging conversation in which everyone has something to learn and to contribute. It is essential that opportunities for this kind of conversation are opened up.

This is happening in all sorts of ways. It happens, for instance, quite informally when someone listens to the problems of a young family where the husband is employed on a North Sea oil rig, or when people share the problems of aging or of their children's schooling. More formally it happens when a cross-section of people are drawn together to discuss the implications of micro-processors for the life of the region. But it is not happening enough, and often it is not happening at all in the very place where it should be happening – in the life of church congregations.

If we are to get a true picture of the world, our own biased perceptions need to be challenged. This is one reason why theological reflection should be a joint effort and why people from outside as well as those inside the church should be involved. Moreover, we must go beyond impressions and prejudices to hard analysis. This requires the help of people with specialist knowledge and experience:

> It is by all disciplines uniting in a common concern with the social and moral problems and possibilities which science brings to contemporary society, that we may discover a new culture, and indeed a new civilisation.[32]

A second need is just as important as the first, but for most people it is not the best starting point. It is the need to come to terms with the significance of Christian tradition for our situation. We have to struggle with two histories: the biblical history in which God has been named and our own history in which God calls us to a specific obedience. Neither can be understood without the other, and we need to discover the resonances and connections between them. This means that we must study the Bible and Christian tradition not as a way of finding ready-made answers to our questions, but in their own right and in order to hear the questions that they put to us. To do this adequately we need the help of academic theologians. Whatever flair, inspiration, godliness or human sympathy we may have, should be supported by a respect for truth. Our insights and hunches need to be located in the context of the whole Christian tradition. We need tutoring in ways of disciplined thought so that we give proper attention to the detailed evidence upon which mature and considered views can be based. This is the kind of groundwork that must be done if we are to make any useful contribution of our own.

An example of how this is being done is afforded by the co-operation that is being developed between industrial chaplains and some academic theologians. A number of industrial chaplains from all over Britain meet with a few academic theologians for twenty-four hours every six months. Their aim is to work through some of the theological questions that emerge in their work. Key topics that have been identified in the meetings – theology and politics, work, the nature of the theological process, the place of lay people in the mission of the church and so on – are followed up by individuals and groups between meetings. The academic theologians contribute by challenging the assumptions that a group of people working in the same field may take for granted, by demanding that loose statements are clarified, by showing how the resources of Christian tradition are relevant to particular questions, and by contributing from their own particular expertise. A further 'spin-off' from this co-operation is that individual chaplains have undertaken to develop a theological issue arising in their own work by undertaking a university diploma or degree by thesis. The academic theologians also gain by earthing their theology in a particular important area of experience.

This example has led us into a consideration of the third factor we must take into account if we are to discover God's word for our time. We must not only give attention to what is happening in our world today and to the Christian tradition, but we must discover the connections between these two histories:

> To use William Temple's metaphor, we have to find the 'eyes' and discover 'hooks' that fit them, demanding on our part both a sensitive and informed understanding of the real problems of our time and place, and also the bearing of Christianity upon the secular problem and the human predicament in terms of judgment, promise and practical implication.[33]

We cannot draw answers to our questions directly out of the Bible, but we can recognize that at a fundamental level the human and the godly are inseparable.

Leslie Hunter pointed out that people have no taste for the fare the church offers. It is out of a sharing in the things that most nearly concern people and out of a sharing in their tensions that speaking about God becomes a possibility. The struggle to find God's word for today is spear-headed by those Christians who are most deeply involved in today's life. They are engaged for the most part with people who are outside the churches, and the conversation, which is about everyday things, is in everyday language. In these circumstances the Christian word is often a matter of drawing attention to the fundamental human questions involved. For example, here is one Christian's contribution to the discussion I have mentioned about microprocessors:

We are being forced to think out afresh what it really means to be human. What part does work play, and leisure, in human fulfilment? If the microelectronic revolution brings us back to such fundamentals, it could herald a major advance in human spiritual evolution as well as technical evolution. We need to give urgent and equal attention to both aspects.[34]

This is typical of an oblique and indirect word that can be effective in opening up the human and spiritual dimension of an issue – in this case technological change. Once people have been alerted to these dimensions, they may begin to see other implications, and some at least will want to go further. As one man put it, 'You get a niggle in your mind'.

To those, however, who are used to more traditional ways of Christian speaking, the fact that no more is said appears as timidity and a failure to make a clear Christian witness. This was in effect what the ecumenical visitors were saying. Two things need to be said in response to this criticism. First, we should look again at the way Jesus spoke in parables and questions. He captured people's imaginations by a story or a saying and left them to work out the implications for themselves. There are occasions when this is the right approach for us to take. Secondly, we would readily admit that if this were *all* that was happening it would certainly not be enough.

In fact a lot more is happening, and in a number of ways people are attempting to be more explicit about their faith. One example concerns a few men who besides being managers or trade unionists are church members. These men met with me for some months to examine how their faith could help them to face the questions they encountered at work. After they had described their work situations in some detail, we looked at what Christian faith has to say about – being a representative, change, conflict, compromise and the use of power. Perhaps our most telling discovery was the realization that the risks that managers and trade unionists take in attempting to change the climate and practice of industrial relations are matched by the risks entailed in the life of faith as these are portrayed in the Bible and in the lives of Christians since then. This kind of exploration would not be helpful to everyone, for it presupposes a willingness to give serious attention to Christian tradition. It is, however, the kind of thing that would help many congregations. Yet the men told me that none of these subjects had been touched on in their churches.

I hope I have said enough to underline how seriously the struggle with both sides of the equation – Christian faith and contemporary life – is being taken and must be taken by those whose starting point is involvement in life, Acting faithfully and speaking even indirectly about Christian faith is possible only on the basis of some overall grasp of the scope and nature of Christianity. One cannot venture far in new ways of mission unless one has thought through how one's own efforts fit into the larger context. It has rightly been said that 'there is no revolution without a theory'. If the insights that emerge out of involvement in life are not worked through, one's speaking of God is soon reduced to slogans and platitudes.

The process of discovering God's word for our time consists of a conversation in which many people are involved. In this conversation serious attention is given to what is happening in the world and to God's revelation in Jesus Christ. It should not be surprising that this process looks untidy and that what is said seems tentative and limited. We are still groping to discover what can be gospel for people today. Faithfulness demands that we do not retreat into the safety of conventional ways of speaking, but that we remain open to the questions that life puts against our faith; and that in faith we continue to search for the truth that makes men free.

3 *Responding to the word*

I come back to the place I started from: to Rosie's question 'What is it all about?', to the elderly man in the rolling mill, the women in the calculator factory, the engineering and shipyard workers, Carole, the thousands of unemployed people and their families, the whole mass of people who are outside the churches and to those of us inside the churches who also ask: 'What is life about?' 'Who is this God who expresses himself in our world?' 'What does he offer?' 'What does he want of us?' 'What is salvation and what could it be?'

In all this searching, certain things have become clear. If salvation is to mean anything to any of us, it must mean something to all of us. In the collectivization of our industrial society we are forced to think in terms of shared realities and shared hopes: 'The whole creation has been groaning in travail together' (Romans 8.22). If the world is in process of becoming one in Christ, we are bound to be in tension until this is completed. Participation in Christ will mean not only sharing in joy, but in the agony of alienation, which is the condition of whole groups of people and whole areas of life in which reconciliation has not yet taken place.

The fact that so many of the people I have mentioned are not Christians is not simply a personal matter but concerns their whole milieu. So long as the church insists on thinking only in terms of saving individuals and does not take account of the different groups and cultures to which people belong, it will fail in its mission to industrial society.

A graphic illustration of the influence of the whole setting of life on religious faith is given in *An Introduction to Religious Sociology* by Canon Boulard:

Boulard has drawn up a map of France showing the different dioceses shaded according to the degree of faithfulness in religious practice. The north-west of France, a large rural area including Normandy and Brittany is shown as an area of very high fidelity to the church. But running almost from seaboard to seaboard right across the peninsula to Brittany, is a long corridor of parishes with minority religious practice. Why should this be? The reason is basically geological! There is a geological fault making granite-quarrying a major industry in the parishes falling along this fault. It is a fact, apparently, that when men are subjected to the processes and conditions of the quarry industry of this area, they become secularized, rejecting, seemingly, belief in God, in the church or in Christian assumptions. In other words, the quarry industry seems to make men 'bloody-minded', it gives them 'a chip on the shoulder', to use phrases we would use in similar English circumstances. As Boulard says, 'Granite quarries and dechristianization go together' . . .

If the church really wishes to increase fidelity in that corridor of industry, then somehow she has to influence the granite quarrying industry, though of course that is a proper Christian end in itself.

The contemporary church has hardly begun to conceive of mission and ministry in this sense.[35]

Salvation means struggling for a more human world. In such a world it becomes possible for people to know life as a dialogue with God as one who offers them their humanity. This means wrestling with all that is wrong in industrial society: with a technological economic system that treats people and communities as expendable, with a political and bureaucratic system whose assumptions go unquestioned by people who feel they have no stake in it, with the deadening of human creativity in a society whose aim is expressed only in terms of GNP, with indifference to the environment and with all forms of discrimination. Salvation is the transformation of the whole of life. It becomes a reality and a possibility wherever people work for more human conditions. It is in the service of others and of our world that we may come to know God who is there before us, and that others may come to know God through us.

Response to God's offer is the response of a community and of individuals within a community. This points to the need for a Christian community. We might conclude from what I have been saying that the decline of Christian faith is entirely due to industrialization. The church is also at fault. People cannot wait to receive their humanity until industrialization has been changed. Their present exclusion from Christian faith is not only due to industry, but to the church.

The church presents a culturally biassed faith as though it were the only possible expression of Christianity. Yet Christian faith can be expressed in many different ways. People in Asia, Africa and Latin America are rejecting the Western form in which Christianity has come to them and are discovering a faith that comes out of and speaks to their own culture and conditions. We must recognize the deep cultural divisions in our own country, and the meaninglessness to the majority of people of the 'middle-class' Jesus of the churches.

An example brings this point home. Keith is a full-time worker responsible for a project, the Eastern Ravens Trust, in Stockton which aims to help emotionally deprived young people. There are many young people who do not fit the institutional arrangements of education and leisure and who get little support from their homes. They appear disruptive and anti-social, and it is only a matter of time before they are in trouble with the police. In this project a number of trained voluntary workers invite young people, who are potentially in this class, to join a group that meets weekly for informal activities. Each group consists of not more than eight young people with two or three young adults. The young person can continue in the same group from the age of eight until leaving school. Within stable relationships with adults and people of his/her own age, the young person explores all sorts of occupations, thus learning a lot about himself, and his relationships with others and discovering new interests and skills.

The crux of the story is that Keith is a church member and wants to share what his faith gives him with these young people and their parents. But, though some have attended church at his invitation, they were ill at ease and did not continue. The church expressed a culture that was foreign to them.

The church as it is, and this includes all denominations, excludes whole groups and classes of people to whose condition and culture it does not speak. Here is what a young Roman Catholic woman said of the church:

> Christianity should contain all vocations without exception since it is catholic. In consequence the church should, also. But in my eyes Christianity is catholic by right but not in fact. So many things are outside it . . .
>
> But everything is so closely bound up together that Christianity cannot be really incarnated unless it is catholic in the sense that I have defined[36]

Simone Weil, who wrote these words, refused to identify herself with the church over against all the people and things that stood outside the church. She gave this as her reason for not being baptized:

> Having so intense and so painful a sense of this urgency (of the essential unity of all things in Christ), I should betray the truth, that is to say the aspect of truth that I see, if I left the point where I have been since my birth, at the intersection of Christianity and everything that is not Christianity.[37]

The Church in its present form cannot do all that is needed. Yet people need some form of Christian community. We must ask 'In what kind of Christian communities can faith arise and be sustained?' Some form of Christian community is needed within each culture in which the tensions and joys of that community can be offered and transformed.

Some people believe that new indigenous churches will emerge. There are, for instance, negro churches, underground churches in countries where the state is hostile to religion, and in our own country there was the short-lived experiment of labour churches. Such churches emerged in critical situations. I do not believe our own country is in a revolutionary state, and I therefore look for a less extreme answer to our need. I want to see an increase in the number of more or less provisional and temporary groupings emerging at the intersections between 'Christianity and everything that is not Christianity'.

In principle such groupings include any association in which Christians participate with non-Christians. People come together around many different aims, and for Christians it is enough to be sharing in making a more human world. By his commitment to specific human objectives alongside those who may be motivated by quite different considerations, Christians are saying, 'We are with you. We want the same things that you want. We are one in our humanity.' It is in active commitment to specific objectives that Christianity becomes incarnated, embodied, and people are able to see (as distinct from hearing) what kind of God and what kind of kingdom Christians hope in.

The Christian brings from his faith a specific perspective on what it is to be human and on what would constitute a human world. This becomes apparent in what he stands for and in what he will not stand. In all this his personal faith is implicit.

His own motivation comes from his personal and conscious response to God, and he wants to share this faith with others. His reason for wanting to do this is that the more he is active in the world the more he is conscious of the world's need for a saviour. It is within his active involvement that this kind of sharing has point. This sharing may take an indirect, oblique form, or it may be of a more direct kind. Both have a necessary place on the frontiers between the church and the world. The following is an example of a grouping in which the approach to Christian faith varies.

A group that had been recruited from the day-to-day work of an industrial chaplain over a number of years, meets at his house one Sunday each month. This is primarily a discussion group that aims to make explicit links between life and Christian faith, and its subjects range from stress in industry to creation and redemption. Some members attend their own churches, while for others this is the only church link. All get different things out of the group: an opportunity for serious discussion of the issues of life, a place of personal acceptance, a chance to work through doubts and hopes both 'secular' and 'religious', an honest recognition of the tensions between life as it is experienced and traditional expressions of Christian faith. To say that 'no holds are barred' sums up the feelings of members for whom in one way or another the lid is taken off what is felt to be oppressive in life and in the church. It is an open space of meeting between what is Christian and what is not Christian.

This is not a church, but a place of refreshment *en route*. If the present Christian communities cannot help people, this kind of provisional association must sustain them in their search. I could multiply examples of this kind, for many Christians are working on the 'frontier'. Rather than doing that, however, I want to point to further possibilities in this kind of 'open' association.

It is possible and necessary at times to be quite explicit in speaking about God. The need is twofold. First, there is a need to clear away a mass of misconceptions and to make some basic information about Christianity available. Secondly, there is need to convey the nature of God's personal invitation. Misconceptions arise from the 'public' face of Christianity. These misconceptions may be challenged simply by the fact that Christians in their involvement in life present a reality that is different from what people have previously observed and from the fantasies they have built up. The fact is that the majority of people have very little knowledge of the most elementary matters of Christian faith. Without some background information, people can hardly be expected to respond to God as he has revealed himself in Jesus Christ.

Secondly, there is a need to receive God's word as a personal invitation. It is possible in general discussions about the world to distance ourselves from the matter. We need to discover that we ourselves are communally and individually part of the world's problem and can personally be part of its salvation. It is not only people in general but we ourselves who need salvation. At some point each of us needs to know God in Jesus Christ in a personal way. It is possible to put people in the way of making this personal discovery. There is no right way and no right time for doing this, and if we wait for the right time and the right words we shall do nothing. We do, however, need to be sensitive to the effect of our words. There is no sense in going on speaking when people's eyes have glazed over, and when all they hear is what one man described as 'buzz words'. On the other hand, when there is response we should be quite concrete about discipleship, forgiveness and the way of grace in the community of faith. Whatever word we may speak is, however, only a means of opening another person to God's own word to them.

It may come as a surprise to some to know how much prayer is a possibility in these provisional associations. Life is so busy and noisy that many people long for some stillness and silence. An example that comes to mind is of an extra-mural study group that I was associated with for some years. At the beginning of each year we planned our programme together, often beginning with a residential weekend. On one occasion several members who had been experimenting with trans-cendental meditation suggested that our residential weekend should consist of the practice of contemplation. In order to give some shape to our programme they suggested that we used the book *Contemplating Now* by Monica Furlong. Different members introduced each chapter by saying what he or she had found helpful in it, and after each short introduction there was one hour's silence which members could use as they wished.

For many people prayer is associated with all sorts of constraints or with pre-Christian ideas about placating the gods. When it is linked to discipleship, prayer becomes part of a way of life.

Rather than speaking of prayer Monica Furlong speaks of contem-plation, 'the word men have used, in the West, to describe man's struggle to become still enough to reflect the face of God, or, in the East, the effort (or non-effort) to live fully in the present moment.'[38] This waiting attention given to the present moment is a quality that is present in many people, though its association with Christian prayer often goes unrecognized.

I have been speaking about what is happening in all sorts of ways on the 'frontiers' to help people to hear and respond to God's word. There are many people who look for something that they do not feel they can receive in the regular life of our congregations. There are also things that must happen in the church congregations. I will return to the example of Keith and the young people he works with. Keith pointed out that he, too, wants something from the Christian com-munity. He has only been in the area for a few years. In his previous church a group that was actively involved in issues of social justice met regularly to study what the Bible had to say about these matters in its teaching on wealth, the poor and hypocrisy. He feels the need to link all his activities to this kind of reflection. Another need for him and, he believes, for many other church members, is for help in the basic disciplines of prayer. It is in his membership of a regular congregation that he looks for sustenance for his involvement outside the church.

Many different things must go on at the same time. What is hopeful about our situation is its fluidity. We are in a process of change and 'any attempt to help the church prematurely will merely delay its conversion and purgation.'[39] We must learn to live with this untidiness and recognize how creative it can be.

We are all in an 'in-between' state. We are only part-way in both believing and obeying. Some do the work of God but say they do not believe. Others say they believe but do not obey. Those who now obey may become believers and cease to obey. Those who now believe may try to obey and in the process cease to believe. How can we believe *and* obey?

Where Bonhoeffer speaks of the need for 'prayer and righteous action among men',[40] others speak of the need for struggle and contemplation. The following summary of the aims of the Taize Community's world-wide youth project sums up much of what I have been saying:

> Two attitudes that seemed to contradict or oppose each other,
> and finally one is found to lie at the heart of the other,
> one begetting the other
> in a ceaseless exchange.
> STRUGGLE, within ourselves,
> to be freed from interior prisons
> and from the desire to imprison others;
> to throw aside all that breaks our communion,
> And struggle in company with the man who is poor,
> so that his voice may be heard,
> oppressions smashed
> so that together we can be reborn
> to new relationships in communion.
> CONTEMPLATION
> setting out in quest
> of a communion with the Risen Christ,
> so that the gift of our lives can be rooted there,
> and so that little by little
> our way of seeing can be transformed
> until we consider man and the universe
> with the eyes of Christ himself.
> Still situated in the underground movement of the church,
> more and more aware that we are not alone in our struggle,
> each one borne forward by the other,
> STRUGGLE AND CONTEMPLATION
> TO BECOME MEN AND WOMEN OF COMMUNION.[41]

The struggle for faith is part of the struggle to be human. The possibility of Rosie and the others discovering their humanity and discovering faith is part of the discovery of humanity and the discovery of faith for us all. There is only one humanity, and it is the humanity that is offered to God in and through Jesus Christ. Moments when we anticipate the perfection of our humanity may be celebrated now, but for final perfection we must wait.

I have spoken tentatively. I offer no ready answers to the questions I have raised. We are just touching the fringes of so much more. What we must do is to be open, to help people to be open and to give them points of entry to the riches of Christian faith and living and more fundamentally to God's word to them. We must set fires alight in terms of hope and expectancy. What happens then we cannot control, for in the end it is not we who find God but he who finds us.

Notes

Chapter I

1. According to a survey carried out by National Opinion Polls in 1976, 36.4% of adults reported what they call religious experience . . . 'Almost a quarter of self-confessed atheists felt at times moved by a power outside themselves', Hugh Montefiore, *Taking our Past into our Future*, Fount Books 1978, p. 41.
2. David E. Jenkins, *The Glory of Man*, SCM Press 1967, pp. 3f.
3. John A. T. Robinson, *Exploration into God*, SCM Press 1967, pp. 21f.
4. Dietrich Bonhoeffer, *Ethics*, SCM Press 1971, p. 53.
5. Hans Küng, *On Being a Christian*, Fount Books 1978, p. 249.
6. Ibid., p. 257.
7. David E. Jenkins, *The Glory of Man*, p. 58.
8. Ripyard Cuddling, 'Elegy in a Tyneside Shipyard', first published in *Writing*, edited by the Federation of Worker Writers and Community Publishers; it appeared in *The Guardian*, 13 November 1978. The poet's real name is John Davitt and he has worked for many years as a welder and as a driller in a Tyneside shipyard.
9. Peter Berger, *The Social Reality of Religion*, Penguin Books 1973.
10. Jürgen Moltmann, *The Crucified God*, SCM Press 1974, p. 329.
11. Ulrich Simon, *A Theology of Auschwitz*, SPCK 1978, p. 30.
12. Ibid., p. 27.
13. E. R. Wickham, *Encounter with Modern Society*, Lutterworth Press 1964, p. 17.
14. Ibid., pp. 74f.
15. David E. Jenkins, *The Contradiction of Christianity*, SCM Press 1976, p. 71.
16. De Tocqueville, quoted by Richard Hoggart, *The Uses of Literacy*, Penguin Books 1958, p. 137.
17. Pierre Teilhard de Chardin, *Le Milieu Divin*, Fontana Books 1964, p. 68.
18. The idea of the two journeys is suggested by Elizabeth O'Connor, *Journey Inward, Journey Outward*, Harper and Row 1975.
19. That this is a constant tendency in the churches historically has been well documented, for instance in E. R. Wickham, *Church and People in an Industrial City*, Lutterworth Press 1957. The same tendency seems to be present in secular movements such as the Labour Party and the trade unions. Perhaps we have to look to some of the South American theologians for a more radical approach, e.g. Paulo Freire, *Pedagogy of the Oppressed*, Penguin Books 1972.

Chapter II

1. Dietrich Bonhoeffer, *Letters and Papers from Prison*. The Enlarged Edition, SCM Press 1971, p. 281.
2. David E. Jenkins, 'Introductory Notes towards Formulating an Investigation of Theological Method', unpublished, Leeds, May 1979.
3. Kenneth Warren, *North East England*, Oxford University Press 1973, p. 13.

4. Nationalization of the railways took place in 1947: nationalization of mining in 1946, of steel in 1967 and of shipbuilding in 1977.

5. 'In 1932, the worst year of the slump, the unemployment rate in County Durham reached 40 per cent of the insured population, while in January 1933 the shipbuilding town of Jarrow experienced 77.9 per cent unemployed', *Durham County and City with Teesside,* edited by John C. Dewdney, British Association for the Advancement of Science 1970, p. 272.

6. Lord Hailsham, *The Door Wherein I Went,* Fount Books 1978, p. 208.

7. Ibid. His recommendations appeared in the report, *The North East: A Programme for Regional Development and Growth,* HMSO 1963.

8. Ibid., p. 212.

9. Ibid., pp. 212f.

10. *Outline Strategy for the North,* Northern Economic Planning Council – HMSO 1969, p. 14.

11. *Challenge of the Changing North,* Northern Economic Planning Council – HMSO 1966, p. 72.

12. *Strategic Plan for the Northern Region,* Northern Region Strategy Team – HMSO 1977.

13. In the course of an informal conversation with the Director of the Northern Region Strategy Team.

14. David Welbourn, 'Worker Participation in Sunderland – its likely Pattern and Progress', Project for Diploma in Management Studies, Sunderland Polytechnic 1978.

15. The quotation and information on this page come from a talk given by Andrew Gillespie of the Centre for Urban and Regional Development Studies at Newcastle University, at a meeting of the Northumbrian Industrial Mission in May 1979.

16. *Strategic Plan for the Northern Region,* 2.80.

17. *Social Consequences and Implications of the Teesside Structure Plan,* North East Area Studies (Durham University) 1975. As local structure plans are influenced by regional policies, this report provides a critique of regional objectives in general.

18. *The Costs of Industrial Change,* Community Development Project Inter-Project Editorial Team, published January 1977, p. 5.

19. Op. cit., p. 96.

20. Herbert Marcuse, *One Dimensional Man,* Sphere Books 1968, p. 57

21. 'Burning Issues', *Anticipation* no. 25, January 1979, p. 75. *Anticipation* is published by the Division of Church and Society of the World Council of Churches. 'Burning Issues' contains some of the preparatory material for the World Council of Churches' world conference on 'Faith, Science and the Future' at MIT, near Boston, Mass., 12–24 July 1979.

22. Charles Elliott, 'Economics and Choice: The Crucial Battleground', paper presented to the Lambeth Conference 1978, p. 2. A shortened version appears in *Theology,* January 1979, pp. 10–16. Quotations are from the original typescript.

23. A. Maslow, *Motivation and Personality,* Harper and Row 1954.

24. Charles Elliott, op. cit., p. 3.

25. David E. Jenkins, 'A Spirituality for the Dark Night of our Institutions', unpublished paper.

26. Charles Elliott, op. cit., p. 12.

27. *Mining and Social Change,* edited by Martin Bulmer, Croom Helm 1978, p. 27.

28. Ibid., p. 27.

29. Ibid., p. 30, quoting Jack Lawson.

30. Ibid., p. 98.

31. R. Moore, *Pitmen, Preachers and Politics,* Cambridge University Press 1974,

      p. 23.
32. David Douglas, *Pit Talk Life in Co. Durham*, History Workshop Pamphlets, no. 6, ed., Raphael Samuel, tutor in social history, Ruskin College, Oxford 1972, pp. 68f.
33. R. Moore, op. cit., p. 225.
34. *Mining and Social Change*, p. 128.
35. Speech made at Shildon, quoted in Edward J. Milnc, *No Shining Armour*, John Calder 1976, p. 126.
36. *No Shining Armour*, p. 81.
37. Hailsham, op. cit., p. 201.
38. R. Moore, op. cit., p. 9
39. Haddon Willmer, 'Politics and a Sense for the Whole in Christian Judgment on the National Front', *Theology and Politics. Working Papers from Industrial Mission* 1, p. 41.
40. Ibid., p. 41.
41. David E. Jenkins, *The Contradiction of Christianity*, SCM Press, 1976, p. 32.
42. Haddon Willmer, 'Theology and Everyday Politics', *Theology and Politics*, p. 19.
43. John D. Davies, *Beginning Now*, Collins 1971, p. 89. This commentary on Genesis 1–3 is written from within the experience of political discrimination in South Africa.
44. Reinhold Niebuhr, *An Interpretation of Christian Ethics*, SCM Press 1936, pp. 151, 150.
45. W. R. Garside, *The Durham Miners 1919–1960*, Allen and Unwin 1971, p. 56.
46. E. F. Schumacher, *Small is Beautiful*, Abacus Books 1974.
47. The people who head the nationalized industries, chair government committees, and so on are drawn from a very small élite. For example: 'A leading industrialist (Rugby and Cambridge) is not only a Director of the Bank of England and a President of the Federation of British Industries. He also chairs an advisory Council and a Royal Commission, and no sooner has the work of the latter come to an end than he is invited to head another committee on the future of broadcasting.' The reference is to Sir Henry Pilkington, in *Power in Britain*, ed. John Urry and John Wakeford, Heinemann Education Books 1973, p. 207. See also the diagram of the Shell group of companies in Christopher Tugendhat, *The Multinationals*, Penguin Books 1973, p. 115.
48. Charles Elliott, op. cit., p. 11.
49. Charles Reich, *The Greening of America*, Allen Lane 1970, p. 12.
50. H. Marcuse, *One Dimensional Man*, p. 9.
51. Reinhold Niebuhr, *An Interpretation of Christian Ethics*. p. 26.
52. The motto of the AEUW, (Amalgamated Union of Engineering Workers).
53. A typical trade union motto is, 'United we stand, divided we fall'; see John Gorman, *Banner Bright*, Allen Lane 1973, p. 79.
54. Richard Brown and Peter Brannen, 'Social Relations and Social Perspectives among Shipyard Workers. A Preliminary Statement', University of Durham 1969, unpublished. A revised version was published in *Sociology*, vol. IV, nos 1 and 2, January, May 1970.
55. Vesting day is the day nationalization came into effect. The following verse, though intended to be humorous, nevertheless gives an indication of the hopes some workers placed on nationalization.

      It looks as though its on the cards
      They're going to nationalize the yards
      We'll all be Civil Servants then
      Under the wing of Tony Benn

The wages for each shipyard force
Will double every month of course
Large bonuses and other things
Will help us all to live like Kings.

(From Ripyard Cuddling, 'Benn's Men', *Evening Chronicle*, Newcastle, 27 March 1975)

56. *Shipbuilding News 7*, March 1978
57. In 1952, Britain produced 30% of the total world output, with Japan (12.2%) and Germany (11.6%) coming next. Today Japan leads with 50% followed by Korea with 30%; Britain and others share the remaining 20%.
58. Richard Hyman, *Strikes*, Fontana Books 1972, p. 108.
59. Ibid., p. 114.
60. Joe Roeber, *Social Change at Work, The ICI Weekly Staff Agreement*, Duckworth 1975.
61. *Lucas – An Alternative Plan*, published by IWS, Bertrand Russell House, Gamble Street, Nottingham.
62. Dennis Marsden and Evan Duff, *Workless*, Penguin Books 1975, pp. 204, 82.
63. *North East Development Council Statistical Memorandum*, January 1979.
64. *Strategic Plan for the Northern Region*, vol. i, Northern Region Strategy Team 1977, 2.27.
65. Ibid., 2.35, 2.39, 2.40.
66. Ibid., 2.26.
67. Ibid., 2.44.
68. Ken Coates and Richard Silburn, *Poverty: The Forgotten Englishmen*, Penguin Books 1970, p. 35. The figures are those of Abel-Smith/Townsend, 1960.
69. Ibid., p. 23, based on BMA, Report on neutritional needs, 1950.
70. Marsden and Duff, *Workless*, pp. 145f.
71. *Social Consequences and Implications of the Teesside Structure Plan*, p. 332.
72. William Hall, *Impasse*, 1978 privately printed. Quotation is from the inside cover. Impasse is a do-it-yourself workshop for unemployed people and is situated in Middlesborough.
73. Neruda of Chile, quoted by Sheila Cassidy, *Audacity to Believe*, Fount Books 1978, p. 35.
74. J. Atherton, 'Unemployment and the Young Unskilled Worker: What Future?', *The William Temple Foundation Bulletin 5*, November 1977.
75. David E. Jenkins, *The Contradiction of Christianity*, p. 49.
76. Ibid, pp. 47–9.
77. Dietrich Bonhoeffer, *Ethics*, p. 170.

Chapter III

1. 'Burning Issues', p. 22.
2. Schumacher, *Small is Beautiful*, p. 11.
3. Jack Owen, *Ironmen. A Short Story of the History of the Union*, National Union of Blastfurnacemen 1953, p. 23, quoted by P. Stubley, 'The Churches and the Iron and Steel Industry in Middlesborough 1890–1914', MA thesis, Durham University 1979.
4. Eduard Schweizer, *Jesus*, SCM Press 1971, p. 1.
5. Ibid., pp. 2f.
6. Trevor Beeson, *Britain Today and Tomorrow*, Fount Books 1978, p. 130, quoting the BCC report.
7. Ibid., p. 131.
8. Ibid., p. 134.

9. Paulo Freire, *Pedagogy of the Oppressed*, Penguin Books 1972.
10. T. Paul Verghese, *The Freedom of Man*, Westminster Press 1972, p. 57.
11. Ibid., pp. 79f.
12. Sebastian Moore, *The Crucified is No Stranger*, Darton, Longman and Todd 1977, p. 33. I am indebted to this book for the discussion of the two frameworks.
13. J. B. Metz, *Theology of the World*, Burns and Oates/Herder and Herder 1969, p. 95.
14. Reinhold Niebuhr, *An Interpretation of Christian Ethics*, pp. 236f.
15. Ibid., p. 240.
16. S. Moore, op. cit., p. 54.
17. Jürgen Moltmann, *The Church in the Power of the Spirit*, SCM Press 1977, pp. 166f.
18. Hans Küng, *On Being a Christian*, p. 572.
19. Hans Küng, op. cit., pp. 578f., quoting Dorothee Sölle.
20. Ibid., p. 478.
21. David E. Jenkins, 'Who is this Jesus Christ?', *Ecumenical Review*, XXVI, no. 4, 1974, pp. 399f.
22. Küng, op. cit., p. 477.
23. 'Theology of Hope', in *A Rahner Reader*, ed. G. A. McCool, Darton, Longman and Todd 1975, p. 224.
24. Victor de Waal, *What is the Church?*, SCM Press 1969, p. 48.
25. E. R. Wickham, *Encounter with Modern Society*, pp. 13, 15.
26. Jürgen Moltmann, *Theology of Hope*, SCM Press 1967, p. 18.
27. From *The Scotsman*, 22 December 1825, quoted in *Industrialization and Culture 1830–1914*, ed. Christopher Harvie, Graham Martin and Aaron Scharf, Open University Press 1970, p. 82.

Chapter IV

1. *Building a Chieftain Tank and the Alternative*, Vickers National Combine Committee of Shop Stewards, p. 12. Available from Vickers North East Working Group, c/o Benwell CDP, 87 Adelaide Terrace, Newcastle upon Tyne 4.
2. Ibid.
3. Ibid., p. 11.
4. Annual Report of SNAP, 1977–78.
5. Ibid.
6. Ibid.
7. Küng, *On Being a Christian*, p. 358.
8. Gerhard von Rad, *The Message of the Prophets*, SCM Press 1968, p. 100.
9. José Miguel Bonino, *Revolutionary Theology Come of Age*, SPCK 1975, p. 137, quoting Gustavo Gutierrez.
10. Ibid., pp. 138f.
11. Ibid., p. 142.
12. David Sheppard, when he was Bishop of Woolwich, noted (*a*) that the percentage of the population attending church declined from the outskirts to the inner city: Surrey 9%, Blackheath and Dulwich 4%, outer suburban 3.25%, inner suburban 1.8%, working class 0.9%; (*b*) that those who attended church were not representative of the area. 'It is not, I think, an exaggeration to suggest that, on average, half the congregation in a working-class parish either would not think of themselves as belonging to the main stream of working-class life, or travel to church from the suburbs.' (*c*) Though there was some difference in the Roman Catholic position, all denominations were similarly affected. 'Taking five missions or mission halls I know in East London, the number of church-going couples under

sixty-five who live within a mile or so of all five could be counted on the fingers of one hand.' See David Sheppard, *Built as a City*, Hodder and Stoughton 1975, pp. 46f.

13. See my *Theology in an Industrial Society*, SCM Press 1975, p. 32. I point here to the false polarization between Mission A and Mission B, but do not fully develop my own Mission C position.

14. Dietrich Bonhoeffer, *Letters and Papers from Prison*, The Enlarged Edition, SCM Press 1971, p. 382.

15. I am indebted to J. M. Bonino, *Revolutionary Theology Come of Age*, p. 156, for this classification. I have changed his 'revolutionary' category to 'socially-concerned' as being more descriptive of this 'family' as it exists in North East England.

16. Emmanuel Sullivan SA, 'Can the Pentecostal Movement renew the Churches?', *Study Encounter* VIII, 4, 1972.

17. W. J. Hollenweger, 'Creator Spiritus', *Theology*, January 1978, p. 39.

18. Reich, *The Greening of America*, p. 5.

19. Hollenweger, op. cit., p. 34.

20. Edward Norman, *Christianity and the World Order*, Oxford University Press 1979, p. 4.

21. See *Letters and Papers from Prison*, p. 383: 'Our own church will have to take the field against the vices of *hubris*, power-worship, envy, and humbug, as the roots of all evil.'

22. Bonino, op. cit., p. 158.

23. Ibid., p. 160.

24. Avery Dulles SJ, *Models of the Church*, Gill and Macmillan 1976, p. 39.

25. Bonhoeffer, *Letters and Papers from Prison*, p. 382.

26. John Macquarrie, *The Faith of the People of God*, SCM Press 1972, p. 35.

Chapter V

1. *Letters and Papers from Prison*, p. 300.

2. Ibid., p. 280.

3. Ibid., p. 281.

4. T. F. Torrance, *Karl Barth. An Introduction to his Early Theology, 1910–1931*, SCM Press 1962, p. 96.

5. *Letters and Papers from Prison*, pp. 281f.

6. Ibid., p. 282.

7. Haddon Willmer, *Christian Involvement in World Development and Theological Life*, unpublished.

8. Ibid.

9. *Letters and Papers from Prison*, pp. 299f.

10. Haddon Willmer, *Christian Involvement*.

11. John A. T. Robinson, *The New Reformation?*, SCM Press 1965, p. 120.

12. Ibid., p. 119.

13. Ibid., p. 119.

14. See, for instance, Exodus 13.14; Galatians 4.3.

15. Ernst Käsemann, *Jesus Means Freedom*, SCM Press 1969, p. 155.

16. Paul Tillich, *Systematic Theology*, vol. 1, Nisbet 1952, p. 296.

17. Paul Tillich, *The Shaking of the Foundations*, Penguin Books 1963, p. 106.

18. Bernard Semmel, *The Methodist Revolution*, Heinemann 1973, p. 7.

19. *Mining and Social Change*, edited by Martin Bulmer, p. 30.

20. John Wesley's *Journal*, as abridged by Nehemiah Curnock, Epworth Press 1967, p. 96: entry for Saturday, 29 March 1740.

21. *The Christian News-Letter*, Supplement to no. 249, 12 December 1945.

22. The Right Revd E. R. Wickham, who was senior chaplain of the Sheffield

Industrial Mission (1944–1960), is now Bishop of Middleton.
23. 'The Bishop's Letter', *Sheffield Diocesan Review*, 15 November 1941.
24. Enthronement sermon, 15 December 1966, *Bishoprick*, February 1967, pp. 25–7.
25. 17 July 1971. For the sermon preached on this occasion see *Bishoprick*, August 1971, p. 52.
26. Sermon preached to the British Association in Durham Cathedral, 6 September 1970, *Bishoprick*, November 1970, p. 2.
27. *New Horizons*, the annual report of the British and Foreign Bible Society, 1978. Projected figures for the growth of the church throughout the world between 1975 and 2000 are (figures in millions):

	1975	2000	increase
Third World	489	1118	+129%
USA and Europe	670	796	+ 19%
UK (extracted from above)	7.8	5.9	− 25%

28. 'Report of Evangelism Support Group', Durham Diocesan Mission committee minutes, 26 April 1978, para 6(c).
29. *Let my People Grow. Proposal for a concerted effort in evangelism*, Evangelical Alliance, October 1976.
30. *Divide and Conquer*, work paper no. 2 for the Urban Church Project, directed by David Wasdell, October 1975.
31. Report of international ecumenical team visit, 20 April – 20 May 1979, pp. 10f. Extracts from this report are included in *As Others See Us*, British Council of Churches 1979.
32. Ian T. Ramsey, sermon preached to the British Association, *Bishoprick*, November 1970.
33. E. R. Wickham, *Church and People in an Industrial City*, p. 236.
34. From a talk by the Rev. David Welbourn at a conference 'What Price the Chip?', organized by the Industrial Mission in Sunderland in February 1979.
35. E. R. Wickham, *Encounter with Modern Society*, p. 18.
36. Simone Weil, *Waiting on God*, Fontana Books 1959, pp. 41f.
37. Ibid., p. 42.
38. Monica Furlong, *Contemplating Now*, Hodder and Stoughton 1971, pp. 13f.
39. *Letters and Papers from Prison*, p. 300.
40. Ibid.
41. *Dare to Live*, SPCK 1973, p. 78. Taizé is an ecumenical religious community in France.

Index